In This Remote Country

In This Remote Country

*French Colonial Culture
in the Anglo-American
Imagination, 1780–1860*

EDWARD WATTS

Chapel Hill   The University *of* North Carolina Press

Designed by Kimberly Bryant
Set in Monticello by Keystone Typesetting, Inc.

The paper in this book meets the guidelines for
permanence and durability of the Committee on
Production Guidelines for Book Longevity of
the Council on Library Resources.

Library of Congress Cataloging-in-Publication Data
Watts, Edward.
In this remote country : French colonial culture in the
Anglo-American imagination, 1780–1860 / Edward
Watts.
p. cm.
Includes bibliographical references and index.
ISBN-13: 978-0-8078-3046-8 (cloth: alk. paper)
ISBN-10: 0-8078-3046-1 (cloth: alk. paper)
ISBN-13: 978-0-8078-5762-5 (pbk.: alk. paper)
ISBN-10: 0-8078-5762-9 (pbk.: alk. paper)
1. United States—Intellectual life—1783–1865. 2. New
France—Civilization—Foreign public opinion, American
—History. 3. Public opinion—United States—History.
4. United States—Civilization—French influences.
5. New France—Historiography. 6. New France—In
literature. 7. National characteristics, American. I. Title.
E164.W35   2006
973.3—dc22   2006005177

cloth   10 09 08 07 06   5 4 3 2 1
paper   10 09 08 07 06   5 4 3 2 1

To Stephanie Wengert Watts

Contents

Acknowledgments

Several debts were incurred during the composition of this book. Thanks to Douglass Noverr, chair of Writing, Rhetoric, and American Cultures at Michigan State University, I had a sabbatical in the Spring 2004 semester. Faculty members in that department, and in MSU's English Department, my new professional home since the summer of that year, were all very helpful as well. I want to thank in particular Stephen Carl Arch, Steve Rachman, Scott Michaelsen, Gary Hoppenstand, Pat LeBeau, and Pat O'Donnell for their support and encouragement. I also thank graduate students Paul Kucera and Michele Costello, who brought other texts to my attention.

Sections of this book were presented at American Literature Association, Society of Early Americanists, and Western Literature Association meetings. I thank my colleagues in those organizations for their helpful responses. I had the honor of delivering a version of Chapter 1 as the 2004 Zucker Lecture at the John Carter Brown Library, and I thank the graduate students of Brown University's English Department for that opportunity.

At the University of North Carolina Press, I want to thank Sian Hunter for continuing to ask, "So what are you working on?" and then for responding so energetically when I finally told her about this project. The anonymous readers both forced me to think harder about the project through a cycle of revision, for which I am grateful. Thanks as well to Paula Wald and Grace Carino for making my writing better than I deserve.

Finally, I thank my family for their unflagging support. This time, though, I give my greatest thanks for and to my wife, Stephanie, for twenty years of everything.

In This Remote Country

The Word *Paisible*

If these countries had continued to belong to the
French, the population would certainly have been
more gay than the present American race; it would
have enjoyed more highly, whatever it should have
possessed, but it would have had less of comfort and
wealth, and ages would have passed away, before man
had become master of those regions, which have been
reclaimed in less than fifty years by the Americans.

Michael Chevalier, *Society, Manners,*
and Politics in the United States (1839)

When Michael Chevalier, a French nobleman and economist, traveled in the United
States in the 1830s and wrote about his experience in his *Society, Manners, and Politics in
the United States* (1839), almost eighty years had
passed since the French had lost their colonies in
North America—Acadia, Upper and Lower Canada, and Upper and Lower Louisiana—an expanse
stretching up the St. Lawrence River, through the
Great Lakes, and down the Ohio and Mississippi
rivers to their mouth. Although the Canadas were
still British colonies, and although fewer and fewer
actual descendants of the French colonials lived in
the organized areas of the United States, the memory of the French era in the middle of the continent retained a powerful imaginative and symbolic presence in the decades before the Civil War.
In pondering the differences between "the present

American race" and the patterns of the settlement that characterized French colonialism before 1763 in what would become the United States, Chevalier conceded that a French nation in those regions would have "had less of comfort and wealth" but would have "enjoyed more highly, whatever it should have possessed."[1] The distinction he drew—between the ambitious, Protestant Anglos and the complacent, Catholic French—in 1839 was meant to illustrate how the rising American empire was not somehow predestined but rather was the result of patterns established well before 1776. As Anglo-Americans occupied and colonized the French frontier, how they would treat the French, their lands, and their Indian allies —rhetorically as well as legally and economically—would reflect greatly upon the kind of country they meant to become: an ambitious empire based on the British model, or a more loosely imagined and structured French-style confederation?

This book is about how Anglo-Americans in the decades leading up to the Civil War looked around at their country and asked themselves the same question, slightly rephrased: What if we behaved more like the French and were nicer to the Indians, less intent on wealth and land, and more tolerant of our neighbors? Large-scale Anglo immigration into the French frontier started in earnest after 1815 with the end of the War of 1812 and the end of British and Indian military threats and the coming of steam-driven navigation to the western rivers. From the start, virtually everyone who wrote about the French and the Anglo-Americans noted a stark contrast between them. As the French and the Anglos collided, in fact, two contrasting worldviews collided, and the observers of this collision were fully aware of its implications for the identity, role, and identity of the new American nation.

Again, Chevalier made the crucial distinctions. Of the Anglo, he wrote:

Behold how he makes his way over the rocks and the precipices; see how he struggles in close fight with the rivers, with the swamps, with the primeval forests; see how he slaughters the wolf and the bear, how he exterminates the Indian, who in his eyes is only another wild beast! In this conflict with the external world, with the land and the waters, with mountains and with pestilential marshes, he appears full of the impetuosity with which Greece flung itself into Asia at the voice of Alexander; of that fanatical daring with which Mahomet inspired his Arabs for the conquest of eastern Europe; of that delirious courage which animated our fathers forty years ago, when they threw themselves upon Europe.[2]

Chevalier—like his fellow French travelers and writers Alexis de Tocqueville, René de Chateaubriand, and Hector St. John de Crèvecoeur—ultimately valued Anglo ambition over French complacency, a value reflected in the fact that Tocqueville, Chevalier, and Chateaubriand all advocated the French colonization of North Africa in 1828 and Mexico in 1831. Thus, each reflects the cosmopolitan French imperialist agenda of the nineteenth century and is not to be mistaken as a spokesman for the pre-1763 French frontier itself or its nineteenth-century leftovers. In fact, these French travelers observed their erstwhile compatriots as just one more group of Americans whose presence complicated the new nation they had come to observe and record.

For purposes of this book, however, what matters is that all four cosmopolitan Frenchmen saw the Anglo-Americans as fellow travelers in the European effort to colonize as many lands as possible. Just as important, they saw the old French colonies in North America, especially Upper Louisiana and Upper Canada, as failures in that regard for not embracing the world-conquering attitude and ideology of the "white" man's ability and responsibility to govern all peoples and places. The French colonies failed, from the cosmopolitan perspective, because they did not subjugate the nonwhite indigenes, did not exploit natural resources, and did not constantly pursue growth and expansion. On the other hand, the Anglos removed the Indians, commercialized their fertile soil, and always sought open lands to own and call their own. In fact, all four saw in the post-Revolutionary Anglo-American nation the potential to supersede European imperial aspiration through its inspired mixture of democratic energy, capitalist ambition, and sense of its own mission: that's why each studied it so closely.

So why did the old French frontier still evoke so much of their attention? Why did so many writers—French, Anglo, and otherwise—contemplate what might had happened if the French had kept their North American colonies? While one can see why these French writers would ponder this question, even if only to dismiss it, Anglo-Americans themselves also kept returning to the French colonials in hundreds of texts—histories, travel books, judges' opinions, novels, short stories, poems, and pamphlets. Many of these texts maintain the distinction between French and Anglo attitudes and ideologies toward land, race, economics, gender, and progress and favor the Anglo triumph. However, in many others, the nostalgia implied by Chevalier for what might have been is put to far greater and more direct rhetorical purposes. That is, the memory of the French was used to imagine a nation more like the one Chevalier imagined: less greedy, less racist, less aggressive. This book is about how competing ways of imagining the nation were contested and entangled in epitome through contrasting narratives and representations of the French frontier and the question of its relevance for antebellum America.

By calling forth an American past defined by happiness, peacefulness, and deliberation, dissident Anglo writers challenged the imperialist characteristics of so much Anglo-American discourse in the antebellum decades. The archive is teeming with positive references to the French; I have endeavored only to cull the most meaningful. Moreover, this book is not meant to be comprehensive. *In This Remote Country* explores how the antebellum nation thought about what kind of nation it wanted to become. Did it want to continue and complete the mission of western Europe, to become an empire, at the expense of all the other peoples and resources that might get in its way, not to mention the republican values enunciated at its dedication? Or could it learn to live in peace with itself, its neighbors, and the rest of the world, happy on the margins of world power rather than at its center? Hundreds of writers in the new nation asked this question, and they used the symbol of the French frontier as a path not taken.

Obviously, the Anglo empire builders won the battle for the right to define America's past and, hence, its future: the French history on the western Great Lakes, and in the Ohio and Mississippi basins, has been nearly forgotten in the nation's popular imagination. When it has been recalled, it was as a mere footnote in a master narrative of conquest, or a false step, a sidebar in the larger story of Anglo ascent.[3] Yet Frederick Jackson Turner's myth of the lone Anglo male Protestant farmer learning democratic values through contact with the virgin soil of the American frontier has been consistently shadowed by the knowledge that, for a hundred years, French and mixed-race peoples had been farming, fighting, fishing, and trapping on that same soil.[4] However, as the memory of the French frontier faded, we find fewer and fewer literary references and rhetorical deployments. By the Civil War, the French themselves had moved into the distant West, interbred into Indian tribes, or assimilated into Anglo-America as just one more ethnic population. Their actual potential to displace the Anglo at the center of the national identity was by then minuscule.

Nonetheless, even as they faded in fact, up until 1860, their rhetorical presence—their power to represent an alternative, wiser whiteness—was mobilized again and again. In these texts, the French are used to tell a different American story, not in the hope of re-creating the French frontier in itself—that was a lost cause—but rather to remind American readers of a set of values the French had embodied and the Anglos had displaced, values that were more enlightened on subjects such as land, race, gender, religion, and nation. Along the same revisionist lines, contemporary social and cultural historians such as Eric Hinderaker, Richard White, Michael N. McConnell, Andrew R. L. Cayton, Colin Calloway, Wilma Dunaway, James Merrill, and others have reexamined the French presence in North America before 1763 as part of the larger profession-wide effort to rewrite American racial history.[5] Specifically, Leslie Choquette, Gordon Sayre, Elizabeth Perkins, and Lucy Eldersveld Murphy have engaged texts produced in New France in new and sophisticated ways.[6]

The most important of these, Sayre's *Les Sauvages Américains* (1997), revives the ethnographic writings of New France itself in a comparative study of French and English descriptions of indigenous Americans. Sayre occasionally touches on the appropriation of the history of the French frontier in the post-Revolutionary United States, concluding that "the image of New France was formed by nineteenth-century readers in the United States, not by Thoreau, who did so much research but never wrote a history, but by Francis Parkman." Parkman, writing mostly after the period addressed here, published his major books after the Civil War and the resulting need to police alternative American whitenesses—such as the myth of the southern cavalier. Sayre thus summarizes, paraphrasing Parkman: "The French sympathy for the Indian entangles them in a common destiny with the stereotype of the Vanishing Indian."[7] Sayre's view, however, inoculates the image of the French from larger debates concerning the shape and foundation of American racial nationalism and national identity throughout the earlier nineteenth century.

In the decades before the war, the frontier French saturated nearly every American text concerned with the West. Think of the many Frenchmen Lewis and Clark meet descending the Missouri during their westward ascent. Well before Parkman terminated their utility as a symbol for dissent by completing their deracination—a crucial distinction in the postbellum era of the melting pot for whites and Jim Crow and the Dawes Act for nonwhites—images of the frontier French played important roles in debates concerning American identity formation and legislative policy from the Revolution forward. Much of this debate occurred on the levels of symbol, metaphor, or image as Anglo-Americans considered the variety of usable pasts available to them. Long before Parkman ossified the image of the vanishing voyageur, there were hundreds of such textual references and representations, and each might be read in regard to the larger issues that surrounded the potential of the French model to challenge and critique Anglo dominance.

In This Remote Country addresses the most significant of these representations to study their role in larger conversations about race, identity, gender, and land in the decades they were published. In these texts, identifiably French, Métis, and French-identified personalities, lifeways, and histories were juxtaposed against their Anglo-American parallels. The contrast reveals important fissures in the nation's evolving ideas about moral rectitude and race-based slavery, greed and pleasure, self and community. Almost always, the narratives contrast the frontier before 1763—when Anglos' victory in the French and Indian War ended the French administration of what White has called a "middle ground" of interracial cohabitation —with the racially polarized Anglo frontier after the War of 1812. The period between 1763 and 1815 is often depicted as a moment when things might have gone another way, when the middle ground lingered beyond the withdrawal of French administration. After that, it was up to dissident writers and historians to preserve it, cherishing its controversial and counterdiscursive properties.

The French alternative almost actualized during those years was textually imagined as anodyne to the hypermasculine materialism and violence of Anglo-American patterns of settlement and dominion. For many writers, the Anglo model's sheer force of will and the resulting dominance it achieved proved the degeneracy of the French—their unsuitability to civilize the "savages" and occupy the "terra nullius," despite their whiteness. Among these writers, representations of the French acquire the shadings of "colonial discourse"—in which the Other is defined in oppositional terms:

whatever the Frenchman is, the Anglo is *not*. In response, defenders of the values symbolized by the French often responded in kind: wherever their Frenchmen are good, their Anglos are bad. For example, even Tocqueville used such oppositional imagery to describe the Michigan frontier in 1831: "The men who inhabit this small, cultivated plain belong to two races who, for almost a century, have existed on American soil, obeying the same laws. But they have nothing in common. They are English and French just as they appear on the banks of the Seine and the Thames."[8] Tocqueville's point here is to use the French as a model of indolence and sensuality to sharpen his appreciation of American materialism and determination, a mutually constitutive dyad. In fact, many of the texts described here struggle to impose their unilateral agendas—imperial or critical—on actual history or personal experience, resulting in the use of oversimplified binaries on both sides. Nonetheless, their imposition often embodies this book's most interesting subject: how history was forced into prefabricated narrative frames to serve more immediate authorial purposes. My organization of the chapters into somewhat oppositional dialogues is meant to re-create that exchange, not to continue it.

As Tocqueville reflects, in most Anglo or imperially minded texts the French were denigrated as slovenly and degraded, the authenticity of their whiteness challenged to invalidate their place in the nation's history, along with the values they represented. Important Anglo writers depicting the region—both British and American—used this imagery effectively to erase the pre-Anglo French presence in Illinois, Missouri, Indiana, Michigan, and Ohio: among others, George Rogers Clark, Gilbert Imlay, James Fenimore Cooper, Lyman Beecher, Timothy Flint, George Bancroft, and Henry Rowe Schoolcraft used the same imagery for both Indians and French, "savage" or "vanishing" (or both).[9] Most, moreover, obsessed over the French interbreeding with Indians as a sign of their degeneracy. For example, while Schoolcraft championed (and partook in) race mixing, he saw the French doing it in the wrong way, as I discuss in chapter 4. Rather than mitigating Indian traits by assimilating mixed-race children, the French usually raised their children in their mothers' tribes. For Schoolcraft, then, the French fathers of the Métis failed in the civilizing mission incumbent upon them as whites on the frontier. Schoolcraft sadly noted that their children grew up in "bastardized" tribal cultures and often selected "savage" lifeways over "civilized" ways of life, as did his one-quarter Ojibwa children.

For Schoolcraft and like-minded Anglo-American imperialists, the French had simply not protected their culture from degenerating in the New World. In the entangled, transcultural French and Indian communities they described, "white" cultural markers were present but not dominant—a development deplored as a step away from what had been imagined as white cultural and genetic dominion. On the level of rhetorical historiography, Anglo writers simply depicted the frontier French as somehow less than white, as part of the continent's prehistory, and so interesting only as a curiosity, as setting the stage, at best, for the coming purity, virtue, and power of the Anglo-Saxon empire. William Henry Harrison's anachronizing comment is typical: "The happiness the Indians enjoyed from their intercourse with the French is their perpetual theme—it is their golden age. Those who are old enough to remember it, speak of it with rapture, and the young ones are taught to venerate it as the ancients did the reign of Saturn."[10] Further taking away the whiteness of the French by referring to them as "Gallic" or "Celtic," Anglo-Saxonist writers linked genetic destiny to evidence of behavioral degeneracy in at least two ways: economic and cultural-racial. Economically, the French had never practiced the type of large-scale land speculation or commercial farming associated with Anglo ideas of the proper uses of "empty" lands. Moreover, their participation in a land-ownership system based in the French aristocracy (seigneurship) delegitimized French land rights after 1763, a step closer to the degeneracy of Norman elitism and away from Saxonism's vaunted republican egalitarianism.

Second, because the French openly intermarried (or at least interbred) with Indians, Anglo writers both implied and explicitly stated that they had indulged in the subhuman behaviors of the nonwhite races—that they had "gone bush"—while the Anglos had not, historical evidence notwithstanding. Along the same lines, the Anglos' representation of Catholicism as a creed disqualifying its followers from the responsibilities of citizenship in a republic was also part of their rhetorical deracination of the French: their supposedly uncritical loyalty to papal dogma precluded them from the free critical thought essential to the burden of the franchise—always subjects rather than citizens, peasants rather than proprietors. In 1835, in reference to the French and to more recently arrived Catholics, Calvinist preacher Lyman Beecher articulated bigoted nativist opinions that would engender "Know-Nothingist" discrimination against the Irish. If Catholicism in Ohio is not checked, he wrote, "our intelligence and virtue will falter and fall back into a dark minded vicious populace—a poor, uneducated, reckless mass of infuriated animalism, to push on resistless as the tornado, or to burn as if set on fire in Hell."[11] Beecher's diction—"dark," "vicious," and "animalism" —is the taxonomy of a European explorer describing a newly found tribe of nonwhites in an exotic location, not the even-handed language of a white writer describing a group of fellow citizens. This study shows that Anglo-Saxon racial nationalism was built on, among other things, intraracial exclusions earlier in the nineteenth century of peoples less willing to use their whiteness for personal and collective advantage, such as the French.

Anglo-Saxon whiteness, the darling of the emerging field of scientific racism at the time, was the highly contested result of debates concerning the concept of white citizenship earlier in the century. Scientific racism synthesized physiological and cultural definitions of difference and called the by-product conclusively biological.[12] One could be nonwhite, that is, based on behavior contrary to the values of "Anglo-Saxon" ascendance *almost* as much as by skin color. In fact, the increasing use of "Anglo-Saxon" in the antebellum decades reflects the narrowing of the range of behaviors deemed "white." In turn, the racial reassignment of the frontier French is emblematic of larger processes in the redefinition of notions of race, gender, and land use along more imperialist lines as the nineteenth century progressed.[13] First, Anglo-Saxonist writers identified the frontier French as distinctly "Other" in relation to the Anglo pioneers who came into the erstwhile French settlements slowly at first but then in great torrents after 1815. Second, with that potential threat to a linear narrative of Anglo expansion contained, writers promoting an exclusionary, monocultural blueprint for American identity simply identified the French as by choice and by genetics a less pure strain of white. In this way, they conveniently erased them, as they did all other challenges to their narrative of the ascent of a pure American strain of Anglo-Saxons.

At the macropolitical level, when pondering what type of nation the United States would become, Anglo-American writers asked their readers to choose between British and French colonial models for dealing with the divergent peoples and places they encountered and conquered as they engaged an aggressive agenda of expansionist empire building, even though the choice had already been made and the British model was in effect. The British model of conquest and colonization was inherited and intensified by Anglo-Americans as they occupied the region following the conclusion of the Indian Wars in 1794 at Fallen Timbers and after the British finally withdrew their occupation after the War of 1812. The irony, of course, is that the British had realized the failure of their own model and, after 1776, worked toward re-creating the more profitable interculturalism of the French management of the fur trade. The first post-Revolutionary Anglo-Americans west of the Appalachians likewise carried on the French model and settled without colonizing, inhabited without dominating.[14]

However, with large land speculators and others of a like mind coming in accelerating numbers, this model was discarded in favor of commercial agriculture, raced citizenship, and centralized forms of military, moral, and political authority. The last of these mattered most when it came to seizing the land from those who dared to be without land patents and deeds issued by the U.S. government: the French, the subsistence-level squatters, and the Indians. These were the intercultural leftovers, doomed to be displaced by the homogenizing nation builders and their mission of ethnic cleansing. As such, this episode might inform our understanding of larger changes in the nation's transition to empire that saw the Mexican War and the "opening" of the Pacific and Japan. In response, at home, the rapid rigidification of categories of identity devalued inclusive republican emphases on self-restraint, public interest, and reasonable rationalism in favor of more aggressive and exclusive concepts of race, class, gender, region, and religion. Each became a means of sorting Americans into slots on a hierarchy with the "WASP" male, preferably from New England, ascendant.

———————————————— Most French settlers simply defied such categorization: they were farmers and traders who did not care about wealth; Catholics who did not proselytize and were happy with Protestant and pagan neighbors; white people who refused to rule the "lower" races; and "ancient" people who refused to become modern. As these qualities were held up in opposition to Anglo values, the French became a useful source for writers who imagined the United States as something other than the manifestly destined, Anglo-Saxon empire of George Bancroft or Francis Parkman. The counterdiscursive potentials the French came to represent in their narratives must be read in a larger context: as critiques of the nation's imperial aspirations and transformations.

In each of the chapters that follow, the struggle over the representation of one aspect or demographic of the frontier French is addressed to show how differing images of the French reflected contending ideas of the nation both in the immediacy of the antebellum moment and on the larger stage of how Enlightenment values were challenged more generally by romanticism's excesses concerning race, self, and nation. Each shows how the French were used by writers to ask their readers to imagine that the nation had options—imperial nation or peripheral commonwealth—and that their destiny, like that of the French, might be in peace and pleasure rather than in conquest and confrontation. For example, when discussing Catholicism, I discuss Beecher's sermon *A Plea for the West*, written while he was on a tour of New England raising funds for his Lane Seminary in Cincinnati. The sermon itself, as mentioned above, trots out every shopworn stereotype of Catholics as obedient peasants incapable of critical thought. James Hall's literate and measured series of defenses of Catholicism and, implicitly, pluralism used the French to measure Beecher's distance from the values of the Revolution. But texts like Hall's, like the French themselves, were often erased from the American imperial archive: until very recently Hall's "The Catholic Question" was available only as a tattered pamphlet in special collections.[15] In contrast, Beecher's sermon remained in print for decades after its delivery.

In This Remote Country studies how, for almost every Beecher or Bancroft, there was a Hall or a Margaret Fuller to identify the antirepublican and groundless nature of excluding the French, Catholics, Métis, and Indians from full participation in a more inclusive American nation. Their ideal of inclusivity is reflected and established in narratives and stories about the West in which the French played important and positive roles. From independence to the Civil War, the inland French habitants and voyageurs were used to offer an alternative whiteness and an alternative American identity. Such writers held up the French settlements as less materialistic, less racialized, more democratic, more exciting, and ultimately freer than the Anglo-American civilization. One of my main points is that even as the French *themselves* were erased and largely forgotten, their memory retained a powerful presence in conversations the nation had about itself. More precisely, the French came to be an effective rhetorical weapon to combat exclusionary and discriminatory narratives of the nation as it became an empire.

Studying this use of their legacy might then be used to examine some of the most crucial fissures developing in the antebellum period in regard to race, gender, and economics.[16] Here, the relative youthfulness and isolation of the United States in the early nineteenth century must be taken into account. Australian Simon During's paired notions that "one can be nationalist without being imperialist" and "nationalism has different effects and meanings in a peripheral nation than in a world power" remind us of the unstable postcoloniality of the United States in the early nineteenth century. As a set of former colonies whose unity was far from achieved, the new nation betrayed defining anxieties about both its relationship to its former colonial parent and its own potential to become an imperial power in its own right.[17] Within this context, defenders of the French could be nationalist in the pre–"world power" United States without advocating the proto-imperialism of Jacksonian expansionism and racism.

American writers who used the French frontier to express their discontent with and dissidence from the emergent "Roman imperialism" of the United States (in the terms of J. G. A. Pocock) called upon nonimperialist forms of nationhood with a horizontal, rather than vertical, paradigm in mind, based, in turn, on the French model itself.[18] The Anglo model was constructed as a vertical stratification of races, regions, and religions—difference as either above or below, ahead or behind. The French model—at least as a rhetorical construct—was based on difference in nonhierarchized contexts and so denied social or ethnic stratification as a means of community building. Writers who invoked the French in positive ways were likely to be more generally dissident in their cultural politics: abolitionist, feminist, and upset about Indian removal and its aftereffects. Thus they demonstrate a more horizontal notion of difference, one that tolerated and even championed interculturalism and other forms of cultural plurality. *In This Remote Country* throughout combines close textual readings of such exchanges with an awareness of the complexities of their cultural politics to track an important simultaneity: at the same moment Anglo-Americans were debating about whether the frontier French mattered, they were debating whether to become an empire.

———————————— This book is not directly concerned with the details of the French presence on the western frontier or with the struggles between the British and the French in the French and Indian War. Therefore, I have not focused on rereadings of, for instance, Hennepin, Marquette, the Jesuit Relations, or La Salle or on their ties to the Indians. Sayre's work on that subject is exhaustive. Moreover, this study is not concerned with the difficult tensions surrounding the French Revolution of 1789 and its aftereffects, up through the War of 1812 and the end of the Napoleonic era. Roger Kennedy and others have studied the cultural and political effects on the United States catalyzed by the Revolution.[19] Anglo-Americans seemed to have viewed the leftover colonial French communities and populations and continental France itself as entirely separate entities. Along the same lines, the nineteenth-century cosmopolitan French travelers mentioned above had no direct link to the French colonies lost in 1763, well before the Revolution of 1789, and their texts much more often articulate the same transatlantic assumptions of the imperial Anglos, rather than embracing the localist pluralism of French colonials or the Anglo dissidents. Last, texts relating to New Orleans have been excluded: most of the representations of "Lower Louisiana" from the antebellum period imagine the region as equally Spanish and French, given the Spanish occupation between 1763 and 1803, and so it was rarely invoked in the same manner as more directly French regions and populations farther north.

This study addresses the history of the national imagination as it reconstructed the French, and so it only indirectly contributes to our understanding of the historical French themselves. My concern is with how the French—even in their Métis and female varieties—were appropriated by both imperial and dissident Anglo writers for their own purposes and interjected into nineteenth-century American conversations about masculinity, race, class, and capitalism. As the object of rhetorical reconstruction, then, the voyageur (and his Indian squaw and mixed-blood children), for example, takes on a significance separate from that of the real-life figure. This book examines the literary and historiographic reimagining of the frontier French to distinguish those who saw the United States as a manifestly destined empire from those who saw it as a set of communities bound together by ideals of liberty and local self-determination, as happily "peripheral."

One of the ideas the pro-French texts demonstrate is that not all white Anglo-Americans were greedy, racist imperialists and that those who were not found (or wanted their readers to find) in the stories of the French an alternative to the white man's burden of millennial ascendance and racial dominion. By exhuming a national past less based in greed and conquest—whether this view of the French is accurate or not—these writers articulated versions of nation, gender, and race distinctly at odds with the more dominant voices dictating the national identity. For example, both sides conceded that the French refused to "use" the land the way the Anglos did, and so their removal, actual or rhetorical, restages an argument going back to the seventeenth century.

The old, intra-Anglo conflict between the Puritan patriarchy's confrontationalism and Roger Williams's accommodationism foreshadows generations of conflict that ultimately has more at stake than just the whites' treatment of the natives.[20] At its core, it reflects contrasting conceptualizations of the kind of community Anglophone people would create in the New World. On the one hand is the highly racialized and hierarchized view that stakes its claim in the Puritan past. On the other, the intellectual descendants of Roger Williams (ironically) found in the Catholic French a past usable for countering the national legacy supposedly inherited from the Puritans, a past that demonstrated the openness, democracy, and moderation lacking in the Puritan legacy. In their reclamation of the French, they imagined their own nation as less obsessed with the purity of its whiteness, less commercial and profit-minded in its relation to natural resources, and more willing to share its communities with other peoples, genders, and races. In literary as well as nonliterary writing, they based that image on the legacy of the frontier French in the middle of the country. In the French, dissident writers found, or just as often imagined, an alternative founding myth through which to speak out against racial and ethnic discrimination, the industrialization of natural resources, and the enclosure of women. They saw these patterns as at odds with the values of inclusion and plurality they perceived as central to the nation's founding. Alternative representations offered by Henry Wadsworth Longfellow, Henry Marie Brackenridge, James Hall, Judith Kinzie, Margaret Fuller, John Richardson, and many others challenge the equations of "Americanness" with Anglo-Saxon racial identity, refuting the dominant version of imperial nationalism that accompanied such hegemonic events as Indian removal, land speculation, and the enforced separation of the genders and the races.

The dissident, pro-French Americans used the French not to rebuild Kaskaskia, as it were, but to redirect the empire that had already destroyed it. The "cultural work" they had in mind for their writing, then, might be viewed in the terms of postcolonial theorist Bill Ashcroft as "transformative": "Resistance which ossifies into simple opposition often becomes trapped in the very binary which imperial discourse uses to keep the colonized in colonial subjection. . . . But a difference which resists domination through the transformative capacity of the imagination is one which, ultimately, moves beyond these structures."[21] By invoking a French *and* Anglo based national history, the dissident writers did not mean to move the clock back to 1754. In fact, they conceded the fact of Anglo-American dominion. However, they also imagined that dominion need not be domination, that a nation need not become an empire.

————————— To organize this analysis, I break down French demographics and discuss how each subgroup was used and abused by Anglo-Americans to debate issues in their own time and nation.

Because my primary interest is in the role of the French frontier in public debates, I do not focus on unpublished journals and letters, except when they complement the public texts. Quite a few authors appear in a number of chapters—James Hall, Timothy Flint, Washington Irving, Henry Rowe Schoolcraft, George Bancroft, or William Warren, for example. Throughout, "national" histories—from Richard Hildreth, George Bancroft, and Samuel Eliot (as well as Parkman)—are used to create a backdrop for the changing place of the French frontier in nationalist historiography. However, for all the states in question, between 1830 and 1850 a remarkable string of history books were commissioned that employ very different methods and perspectives than those emanating from Boston and New York.

The writers of these state history books are the destination of chapter 1. National (and usually racially nationalist) Anglo historians could not ignore the fact that the French were the first "white" people in the much of the nation, and so they included them in the early sections of their usually multivolume national histories. Yet the French are unflaggingly depicted as representing episodes in failure. Claims of a meaningful, pre-Anglo French role in the nation's history are thus delegitimized and so cannot serve as a basis for legitimate claims to occupy the land by "right of conquest," as the Anglos argued for themselves. John Marshall's reiteration of American history as always already racialized foreshadowed the Anglocentric view. However, in the state histories of Illinois, Indiana, Michigan, and Wisconsin, where the French could not be so ignored, their achievements are noted as successful moments of interracial contact and cohabitation. For the state historians, the French represented, in a way, just one more tribe, rather than the dominant, race-appropriate history-shifting presence Anglo-Saxonist writers constructed as their heroes.

In chapter 2, Henry Wadsworth Longfellow, George Rogers Clark, Zadok Cramer, Henry Marie Brackenridge, Margaret Fuller, Henry Rowe Schoolcraft, Gilbert Imlay, and James Hall are among those writers who discussed the French villages and towns and their inhabitants. Whereas Anglo farmers owned their own land and sought to control it through radical ecological reengineering, the habitants rarely owned their own land and aspired to little of the ambitious social mobility, environmental transformation, or material avarice that characterized their incoming Yankee neighbors. Issues of class and individuality were at stake as the habitants' assimilability tested the limits of the ossifying American economic identity and its emphasis on aggressive acquisitiveness. Empire-building Anglo writers practiced a simultaneous rhetorical removal of the habitants, and, in turn, Anglo dissidents saw these removals as the acts of an empire, not a republic, especially Brackenridge.

Chapter 3 discusses class and masculinity on the frontier as the figure of the voyageur or coureur de bois was contrasted with the Anglo-American male, especially as these dichotomies are played out in Parkman's *The Oregon Trail*. This discussion pits radically different French and Anglo systems for reckoning the relation of the colony to its empire and the role of the white male in that process. In addition, while the French figure altered local Indian economies, he never terminated them, as did commercial farmers. William Warren, Washington Irving, and Lewis and Clark figure prominently in this section. In their texts, as they engage the debate over the "feminization" of the industrial-era male, deep insecurities are revealed about the bourgeois white man's ability to dominate others. Such laborers followed more traditional, bestialized ways of life as opposed to the physical inferiority and insecurity of the culturally and economically elite, and Parkman exposed the resulting paradoxes.

In chapter 4, the issue is family. From the late eighteenth century forward, the family in Anglo-America underwent tremendous transformations, moving toward the model of nuclear family with power resting in the hands of the property-owning white patriarch whose eminence and professional status often made him distant emotionally or physically from his children. Because there were very few French women on the French frontier, Frenchmen usually intermarried and such with Indian women, often to mutually beneficial ends. The result was Métis children. This chapter has three sections: the first addresses Henry Rowe Schoolcraft, his Métis wife, Jane Johnston Schoolcraft (Bame-Wa-Wa-Ge-Zhik-A-Quay), and his attempts to impose patriarchy on the upper Great Lakes; the second focuses on Juliette Kinzie's *Wau-Bun: The "Early Day" in the North-West* as it used the instability of gender and racial identities in the Great Lakes fur trade culture to reject the removal of woman and nonwhites from public life in antebellum America; and the third addresses the space between the Anglo concept of "half-blood" and the French concept of "Métis" and the subsequent ramifications for the evolving definition of race.

In the 1830s and 1840s, the debate over the lingering ethnic diversity of the frontier became combined with the threat to Anglo-American identity posed by Catholic immigration from central and southern Europe. Chapter 5 addresses the exchange between James Hall and Lyman Beecher as the two staged a critical struggle over which past should serve a model for dealing with the inevitability of a multiethnic nation: the French or the Anglo model. Catholicism was viewed suspiciously in the Republic, yet the legacy of the French missionaries and the schools they built on the French frontier was formidable. In texts by George Bancroft, Timothy Flint, Beecher, and Hall, the role of the frontier French in this controversy in the mid-nineteenth century epitomizes how a set of historical images and stories could be used in the service of or resistance to powerful and far-reaching ideas and, ultimately, policies in the nation.

Close textual readings of both literary and nonliterary texts compose the most central part of my method. However, the fields of book and publishing history, histories of readership and literacy, and theories from the arenas of nationalist and postcolonial studies must also be brought to bear to encompass the broad range of rhetorical positionings through which the French frontier was represented. The many historians of the French frontier, to whom I am greatly indebted, base their claims on vast unpublished archival resources—

letters and documents—that reveal more precisely the collision of French and Anglo ideologies in the American Midwest. The breadth of the published primary texts discussed nonetheless demonstrates the existence of an important and distinct but overlooked aspect of nineteenth-century American culture.

I take my title for this book from a phrase in Henry Marie Brackenridge's *Views of Louisiana* (1814): "From the gentle and easy life which they led, their manners, and even language, have assumed a certain degree of softness or mildness: the word *paisible* expresses this characteristic. In this remote country, there are few objects to urge enterprise, and few occasions to call forth and exercise their energies."[22] Brackenridge placed this model of benign agrarian anarchy alongside the emergent "American" presence and hoped they could coexist—"They are in fact both natives of the same land, and both can claim Freedom as their birth right. It requires many hands to work the complicated machinery of our government" —and he hoped that the diversity of the French frontier could persist to counterbalance the more aggressive Anglos. His emphasis is on the power of both to create a virtuous nation—not one or the other— a sentiment that demonstrates the transformative uses of the image of the French by the dissident writers in general.

But Brackenridge also understood the difficulty of asking his Anglo-American readers to find a place for the French in both his story and their nation, especially after Lewis and Clark had described so many Frenchmen as both central to their expedition's operation yet peripheral to its meaning.[23] While the captains established an image of the vanishing French, for Brackenridge, the French should not be written off so blithely. In his *Views of Louisiana*, they are then both here ("this") and not here ("remote"). Moreover, their remoteness is based on the contrast between long-standing French traditions and the incoming tidal wave of Yankee materialism and individuality. Even in this phrase, Brackenridge complicates the standard narrative of the frontier by insisting on an

American place that is neither civilization nor wilderness and a people who are "white" but not like the other whites.

The Upper Louisiana he views is a complicated and multiracial region, full of places and peoples that could broaden the nation's cultural scope and ethnic identity but that could also, just as easily, be ignored and forgotten. To accommodate all these peoples and their rights in the new nation would have taken a long time and careful consideration—demanding more patience than most Anglos had exhibited. Like Chevalier, Brackenridge implies that any nation founded by the French—or, more important, on French colonial principles—would have been smaller, slower, and more peripheral. His point is that that might not have been a bad thing: such a nation might have been happier, more virtuous, and more aligned with its founding principles. As *In This Remote Country* studies how the French frontier was both willfully forgotten and contentiously remembered, it engages the story of how the United States debated whether to become an empire or to stay remote.

The Leaden Plates

Exploration and Ownership

ONE

No nation ever had a fairer claim to a newly discovered country, than the French had to the valley of the Ohio, but a wise Providence had ordained, that the beautiful region should be possessed by the Anglo Saxon race, and not by the Gallic.

Samuel Hildreth, *Pioneer History* (1848)

In 1848, Dr. Samuel Hildreth of Cincinnati tried his hand at history writing, the profession of his more famous brother, Richard. Harper and Brothers would soon unveil Richard's eight-volume *History of the United States*, establishing him just a tier down from George Bancroft, William Prescott, and Francis Parkman in the school of American romantic history.[1] Like the others, each Hildreth engaged the emerging field of scientific racism to structure his version of events from the nation's past. By this way of thinking, beneath all the details, there is a teleological master narrative of inevitable Anglo-Saxon ascendance. Usually, versions of this romantic epic were used to justify the displacement of Indians and the enslavement of Africans, the superiority of the Anglo-Saxons doubly proved by their steadfast resistance to the urge to exterminate these "inferior" races.[2] On the national scale assumed by Richard, such narratives are worked out at length.

In *Pioneer History: Being an Account of the First Examinations of the Ohio Valley and the Early Settlement of the Northwest Territory* (1848), Samuel created a local version of his brother's story that needed to do a little extra work: an intensively researched story of the Anglo-Saxons' "civilization" of the region meant to justify their "immemorial" right to occupy the land.[3] How, then, to deal with the French? In his treatment of them, the same patterns of erasure and empire building that characterize Richard's and, more famously, Bancroft's statements about Indians and Africans are manifest. For example, Samuel explained the use of lead plates by the French to mark the rivers draining into the Ohio whose basins they had been granted by the Treaty of Aix-la-Chapelle in 1749.[4] Noting their excavations in 1798 and 1846, Samuel comments: "No nation ever had a fairer claim to a newly discovered country, than the French had to the valley of the Ohio, but a wise Providence had ordained, that the beautiful region should be possessed by the Anglo Saxon race, and not by the Gallic."[5] This distinction of Anglo-Saxon from Gallic "races" was common in American writing about the French during the 1840s. Meaningful history in the Ohio Valley begins, by implication, with the arrival of the Anglo-Saxon settlers from the east in the years following the French and Indian War. "Gallic" communities are therefore not part of regional or national history but rather just the final stage of the region's prehistory. The French—relabeled, significantly, as Gauls—are thus divested of their link to the Gothic tribe of the Franks. While this seems trivial to a modern reader, in the context of scientific racism in the 1840s, this renaming bears added weight: it severed the frontier French from direct genetic or cultural connection to the Gothic ideal at the center of Anglo-Saxonism, the only pure whiteness.

Furthermore, Samuel's description of the discovery of the plates placed by the French at the point where the Muskingum drains into the Ohio has a distinctly archaeological feeling: "In the spring of the year 1798, there was a freshet in the Muskingum river, which bore away large masses of earth from the bank at the mouth, leaving it quite perpendicular. In the summer following, some boys, who were bathing, discovered projecting from the face of the bank, a square metallic plate. By the aid of a pole, they succeeded in loosening it from its bed. On a more close inspection, it was found to be lead, engraven in letters in a language which they did not understand."[6] This plate had been there for less than fifty years, yet Hildreth's description makes it seem ancient, remote and distant from the bucolic and peaceful present of the swimming Anglo boys. Hildreth notes that the locals responsibly sent it off to the American Antiquarian Society in Massachusetts.[7] Coming out of the American earth, their artifacts could be put in museums next to Shawnee war clubs, mammoth tusks, and the other curiosities of the vanished and inferior races and species. As "ancient" members of an inferior race, the Ohio Gauls could be removed as easily and as justly as could the Indians. While the British administration of the Ohio Valley became law in 1763, the actual displacement of the French and the extinguishment of individual land titles were legally dubious; but, in this narrative, "wise Providence" had larger goals in mind. Human constructs such as laws, contracts, and treaties were invalidated by evidence of divine intervention on the part of God's favored people.

In other words, the Hildreths and others understood the shaky legal and even moral validity of the eradication of French land rights in the Ohio Valley: the French were in place sooner, they were white, and they were farming. Samuel Hildreth's strategy is simply to diminish French claims of legal ownership and occupation to a level beneath the transcendent justice of the divine selection of the Anglo-Saxons. By the same logic, and at the same time, the federal government was vacating dozens of treaties made with Indians to facilitate removal, even treaties with codicils encouraging the assimilation of the tribes. Other like-minded historians would use "Celtic" for the frontier French for the same purpose: neither Gaul, Celt, nor, of course, Indian, was as pure as the Anglos and therefore could be excluded from Anglo-Saxon America's occupation of *its* continent.

Few professional historians were as blunt as Samuel Hildreth. As a medical doctor, Samuel was more likely directly involved in discussions of craniology and phrenology, the purported disciplines that provided the so-called data for scientific racism.[8] However, George Bancroft, Francis Parkman, and Samuel Eliot espoused parallel sentiments. In reading these, the larger contexts of their composition must be reconsidered: Indian removal, industrialism, abolitionism, the Mexican-American War, and southern sectionalism. Their treatment of the French, then, reflects on each author's view not so much on the French in and of themselves but on these issues as well. For example, the New England–based Bancroft ends the third volume (1840) of his magisterial *History of the United States* with a conclusion similar to Samuel's. Upon the defeat of the French in the French and Indian War, he comments: "In America, the Teutonic race, with its strong tendency to individuality and freedom, was become the master from the Gulf of Mexico to the poles; and the English tongue, which, but a century and a half before, had for its entire world parts only of two narrow islands on the outer verge of Europe, was now to spread more widely than any that had ever given expression to human thought. Go forth, then, language of Milton and Hampden, language of my country, take possession of the north American continent!"[9] Bancroft's references to Teutonic supremacy and to the civilizing power of the English language imply a mandate for dominion that supersedes, for example, Mexican claims to Texas, since Mexico still claimed more of the "north American" continent than could the United States. Bancroft's emphasis on language dovetails with the popular notion that the spread of the language of a "civilized" people indeed spread civilization itself. Further, in the day's historically blurry taxonomy, the slaveholding South was identified with Norman aristocracy, not Teutonic republicanism, and so the reference to "individuality" implicitly narrows the power of dominion to New England. Bancroft's earlier and extended celebrations of Puritanism therefore identify the only true Americans as Anglo-Protestants.[10] Finally, Bancroft's narrative suggests that the Revolution was, at best, incidental to the longer story of "Teutonic" ascendance, a purification of the Anglo strain at most.

The Hildreths and Bancroft thus told American history as a story of Anglo-Saxon dominion over a series of lesser peoples. The last of these was the French, and the story of their removal became the final chapter to be written in support of the legitimizing narrative of an imperial nation-state derived directly from the Gothic traditions of private property, participatory government, and transcendent superiority. If Anglo-Saxon ascendance required violence and a very narrow definition of "individual" to secure itself, so be it: participation in government was limited to the descendants of the Saxons alone, and only the males at that. The French become, at best, transitional in these narratives: precursors to the Anglos, a step up from the Indians but still categorically to be swept away by the rising Saxon tide; precursors, overtures that prepare the ground for "our" settlement. The pronoun "our" takes on added significance. By reaching out to the reader with the first-person plural possessive, romantic historians created a commonality with their readers that pitted mid-nineteenth-century, white, middle-class readers and historians, as Americans, against the French and the Indians, as Others.[11]

Such divisive, oppositional rhetoric characterized romantic historiography as it reflected shifts in ideas of nationhood. A "romantic" history had become a prerequisite for national legitimacy in Europe, too, as Europeans, like the United States, pondered and practiced extraterritorial expansion throughout this era. In reference to this pattern, Bill Ashcroft notes that "the emergence of history in European thought is coterminus with the rise of modern colonialism, which, in its radical othering and violent annexation of the non-European world, found in history a prominent, if not the prominent, instrument for the control of subject peoples."[12] Cosmopolitan European historians defined "nations" as groups of people bound together by language, culture, physiognomy, and history transcending the written record. To use Ashcroft's term, they "narrativized" white, local indigeneities, creating back stories for the culturally singular nations they desired; these stories were more coherent than the capricious borders drawn by the fading aristocracies, dispossessing "subject" peoples of a role in that narrative to underwrite the dispossession of their land, labor, and cultures.

But romantic history must not be read as the only version of American history being written in the antebellum decades, just the only one that garnered eastern favor and scholarly transmission in the years since. In fact, it was only one side—and not necessarily the dominant one—in a debate concerning the historical context of a variety of issues in American life. Many white Americans—Anglo and otherwise—resisted Indian removal, the Mexican-American War, and other such imperialist gestures. Not surprisingly, then, they needed historical bases for their counterdiscursive views as well. In opposition to the Anglo-Saxon nationalists, they found in the French a counternarrative, an alternative founding myth. Samuel Hildreth's invocation of the divine right of God's elite, in this chapter, shall serve as a compass for understanding how the French model was used to challenge Anglo-Saxonist nationalism and its specific manifestation in debates concerning the occupancy of the land itself.

On the one hand, individuals such as Hildreth and Bancroft, or, to be more precise, Chief Justice John Marshall, argued for racial destiny as a historical fact and thus for the legitimacy of the Anglo-Saxon right to occupancy of the land, articulating a form of romantic nationalism that has been called "providential." Michael Warner writes that "national culture began with a moment of sweeping amnesia about colonialism. Americans learned to think of themselves as living in an immemorial nation, rather than a colonial interaction of cultures."[13] In the opening section of this chapter, this "amnesia" is traced out through the historiographic erasure of the French. More important, the "immemorial" aspect of this definition can be shown as having two effects: a backward-looking narrative of acquired indigeneity and a forward-looking prescription for empire.

On the other hand, among others, Anglo historians from western states had a less expansive narrative in mind—a "civic" nation. Specifically, Eliza Sheldon of Michigan, John Reynolds of Illinois, A. W. Patterson of Ohio, and, most succinctly, William R. Smith of Wisconsin disputed the dominant narrative to assert not only a different version of the past but also a different way of thinking about their present. By interweaving French, Anglo, and Indian stories, they described and celebrated the diversity of their states' histories, never imposing a hierarchy of races to undergird narratives of exclusion or erasure. In fact, often their books are dominated by French and Indian subjects, taking careful note of the carryover of French language, communities, and institutions long after benchmark dates such as 1763, 1776, 1787, and 1815. For these historians, both the Indians and the French exist and persist not as prehistory—remnants of a vanished past, irrelevant curiosities—but as history, parts of the past still vibrant and present in their states' communities. Specifically, for them, the French method of sharing the land with the Indians represented a far more just and thus *justified* means of settlement than the Anglo method of unilateral conquest and removal.

God thus played little role for the state historians. They resisted the romantic binary—claiming God and his Providence as *their* ally—and sought to transform the process of historical memory making by imagining—and asking their readers to imagine—history free from divine interposition or teleologically ordained mission. To understand their achievement, however, the master narrative they were compelled to rebut must be understood as it sought to shape not only the national imaginary but also actual legislative and judiciary policy.

As this conflict over American history emerged in the antebellum decades, it reflected older intraracial conflicts on how to gain access to the continent's soil without resorting to barbarism and so occupy it within the context of the rule of moral, divine, or human law, as dictated by the rationalist and ethical cores of the Protestant Reformation and, later, the Enlightenment. In the original Puritan communities of the 1620s and 1630s, the medieval right of conquest was entangled with the Reformation's concept of following universal natural law. In 1626, the Pilgrim Robert Cushman argued:

> This then is a sufficient reason to prove our going thither to live lawful: their land is spacious and void, and there are few and do but run over the grass, as do also the foxes and wild beasts. They are not industrious, neither have art, science, skill or faculty to use either the land or the commodities of it, but all spoils, rots, and is marred for want of manuring, gathering, ordering, etc. As the ancient patriarchs therefore removed from straiter places into more roomy, where the land lay idle and waste, and none used it, though there dwelt inhabitants by them, (as Gen. 13:6, 11, 12 and 34:21, and 41:20,) so is it lawful now to take a land which none useth, and make use of it.[14]

Land ownership, then, is legitimized by proper usage; in contrast, those who do not use the land might be removed like any other form of nonhuman wildlife. The most immediate resistance to the premises of this argument was Roger Williams's. In *A Key into the Languages of America* (1643), Williams seems to have anticipated the polygeneticism of scientific racism by stating, "From Adam and Noah that they spring it is granted on all hands."[15] Based on such a proto-Enlightenment tenet of human universalism, Williams disputed the Puritans' claims to Massachusetts and famously negotiated with the Narragansetts for the area that would become Providence, Rhode Island, *before* seeking a charter from the British government.

Nonetheless, Cushman's, and on a larger scale John Winthrop's, doctrine of *terra nullius* carried the day, and, not surprisingly, nineteenth-century historians wishing to carry on the Puritans' increasingly semisecularized mission (from *translatio imperii* to the City on the Hill to Manifest Destiny) cited Puritan precedents and New England contact history to legitimize various forms of land acquisition. Most cultural and legal historians cite the 1823 Supreme Court case *Johnson and Graham's Lessee v. William McIntosh* as central to the codification of the right of conquest into written law.[16] This case, involving land in southern Illinois, involved the ability of individual Indians to sell their land to individual Anglo-Americans. On one level, it seemed to have upheld the concept of treaty rights and thus tribal sovereignty.[17] However, as is so often true in controversial cases, the majority opinion went beyond the immediate concerns of the case itself. Chief Justice John Marshall, writing for the majority, while upholding the sovereignty of specific tribes and the federal government's transcendent authority in such matters, makes broad historical assumptions that supersede tribal specificity and assume an overriding narrative of racial behavioral determinism.

First, Marshall assumes the validity of pre-Revolutionary British claims to the Ohio Valley (even though the Proclamation of 1763 forbade white settlement west of the mountains) and that Indian title had never been "extinguished" through a treaty with the British.[18] Then, he rewrites regional history, indeed continental history, notably excluding the French and their intercultural settlements from a story of undifferentiated racial opposition. Suggesting that the "European" conquest of the American Indian is inapplicable to the historical precedent of conquests resulting from conflicts between two "civilized" peoples in the annals of European history, Marshall writes: "When the conquest is complete, and the conquered inhabitants can be blended with the conquerors, or safely governed as a distinct people, public opinion, which not even the conqueror can disregard imposes these restraints upon him; and he cannot neglect them without injury to his fame, and hazard to his power." Even the most conservative historians concede that the French and the Algonquian Indians lived in peace, mostly, for a good part of a century, but Marshall's oppositional racialism has no space for the middle ground. But then Marshall turns specifically to North America:

> But the tribes of Indians inhabiting this country were fierce savages, whose occupation was war, and whose subsistence was drawn chiefly from the forest. To leave them in possession of their country, was to leave the country a wilderness; to govern them as a distinct people, was impossible, because they were as brave and as high-spirited as they were fierce, and were ready to repel by arms every attempt on their independence.

> What was the inevitable consequence of this state of things? The Europeans were under the necessity either of abandoning the country, or relinquishing their pompous claims to it, or of enforcing those claims by the sword, and by the adoption of principles adapted to the condition of a people with whom it was impossible to mix, and who could not be governed as a distinct society. . . . European policy, numbers, and skill, prevailed. As the white population advanced, that of the Indians necessarily receded.

Marshall here applies two binaries typical of colonial discourse: savage/civilized and inhabited/empty. While documented history showed then and still shows the porous nature of those distinctions, Marshall's omission of the French betrays an unwillingness to allow such a triangularizing potential to disrupt his narrative. To be more precise, the state historians would refute Marshall's claim to uniformity in "European" behavior by citing French and Indian cohabitation and intercultural entanglement, as I note below. Marshall concludes that "the Indian inhabitants are to be considered merely as occupants, to be protected, indeed, while in peace, in the possession of their land, but to be deemed incapable of transferring their land to others."[19] From this ruling—and two cognate decisions (*Worcester v. Georgia*; *Cherokee Nation v. Georgia*) from the early 1830s—removal was legally justified. A fiction in history was thus transformed into a fiction of law.

Marshall was himself not writing in a vacuum. Anglo-American historians had been recycling Cushman's narrative of the Anglo land user's rightful removal of the Indian land waster for nearly two hundred years. Title was acquired by one's ability to stay on the land, as noted in Francis Jennings's comments on *McIntosh*: "Insofar as the difference between civilized and uncivilized men is concerned, the theorists of international law, whom Marshall followed, have held consistently that civilized people stay in place and thus acquire such right in their inhabited lands as uncivilized wanderers cannot rightfully claim."[20] Not staying on the land would come to refer not only to the "wandering" of the Indians as a means of invalidating their claims to land but also to the French. Further, the removal of even "civilized" tribes like the Cherokee—no longer wandering but by 1825 settled, slave-owning farmers—created a no-win situation. Either extrinsic or intrinsic reasons justified the displacement and dispossession of the non-Anglo-Saxon.

Again, Marshall's logic depends on a careful misreading of French history. The *McIntosh* ruling claims that individual natives could not negotiate the sale of land, and neither individual whites, counties, nor states could negotiate land transfers from Indians. By the same reasoning, individual claims to French land ownership were also invalidated. French land occupation mostly passed through royal grants—very few settlers "owned" the land they farmed. In addition, as I discuss in chapter 2, much land was held in common among the habitants. The systems of seigneurship and common-field farming were not based on concepts of individual private property, so the French settlers likewise become removable occupants rather than the genuine residents of the place.[21] The transposition of a single system of land acquisition imposes on the American landscape a very limited and limiting means of building communities and institutions—deeply Anglophilic and uniformly competitive and commercial.

Ironically, the dominant thinking of the Jacksonian era—and its linkage to scientific racism—were implicitly at odds with the Founders' recognition of the validity of French and Indian land claims. Richard White and Andrew R. L. Cayton, among others, however, have traced a more humanitarian attitude toward Indian humanity as late as 1795.[22] Cayton writes about the negotiations that led to the Treaty of Greenville in 1795: "Although brutal Indian-hating *machismo* predominated, there were also men who affirmed their society and claimed significant places in it by treating Indians in what they considered to be a civilized fashion." Elsewhere Cayton has discussed the French precedent and model for frontier civility and interchange among the first generation of Anglo-Americans in the trans-Appalachian regions. Furthermore, the emphasis on acquiring Indian land only through consensual contracts is central to Indian policy in documents such the Northwest Ordinance (1787).[23]

For example, in 1789 Secretary of War Henry Knox reported to Congress on the need for respecting Indian land rights: "The principle of the Indian right to the lands they possess being thus conceded, the dignity and the interest of the nation will be advanced by making it the basis of the future administration of justice toward the Indian tribes."[24] Based on Enlightenment-era monogenetic theories, such sentiments reflect the universalist rhetoric of the Revolution. However, as the external threats to national cohesion in the form of the British vanished after the War of 1812, the patience required by such a principled stand vanished, allowing more exclusive definitions to justify more efficient means of land acquisition: removal, purgation, and erasure. Although a holdover from the more humane republican 1790s, Marshall's reinscription of European/Indian oppositionalism in the 1820s and 1830s was more Jacksonian in nature. The omission of the French from Marshall's restatement of the interracial history of North America was carried on and fleshed out by like-minded historians in at least two ways.

First, the French might be simply and thoughtlessly conflated with British colonials. Marshall writes as if *all* Europeans refused "the adoption of principles" inherent to Indian culture. Typical of imperialist thinkers, Marshall views contact experience strictly along binary lines. One is either savage or civilized, European or Indian, worthy of the land or not. Along these lines, the French— outside of the explorers such as La Salle or the losers in conflicts with the British—were largely left out of antebellum histories. For example, never mentioning settlements like Kaskaskia, Detroit, or Vincennes, Samuel Eliot in his *Manual of United States History* (1858) at least bestowed upon the French settlements a striking image: "The French dominion was as weak as it was vast. It spread over America like a cloud brilliant with the morning sunshine; but, insubstantial as a cloud, it was swept by the breeze and rent asunder by the storm."[25] Yet, like the shifting mud that buried the lead plates, the sweeping away of the French—not only by American settlers, jurists, historians, and writers but also by nature itself—eliminated the possibility of a legitimate conceptualization of land rights to disrupt or dispute Marshall's apotheosis of right by conquest. In other words, the unwillingness of the French to privatize and commodify the land ultimately was a sign of their genetic unfitness for it, an intrinsic flaw that vacated their claim to it, regardless of the details of treaties between European nations or policies of assimilation proposed by the American government.

The shift in American policy from squatters' rights to a more rigid system of proprietary rights signaled a crucial transformation in the shape and function of nationalism in the United States. The Founders' ideal was constructed from what scholars of nationalist theory call "civic nationalism." In this reckoning, membership in a nation is constituted by following its laws, a forward-looking premise that willfully ignores the messiness of the past and unlinks citizenship from the accidents of birth in regard to class, color, or, in theory, gender. Although civic nationalism thrived as an ideal throughout the seventeenth and eighteenth centuries, it was overshadowed after 1800 or so. Anthony D. Smith, among others, observes its displacement in the early nineteenth century by a more tribal or genetic conceptualization of nation based on the past, not the future: language, custom, or physical attributes—"primordialism." In explaining this divergence, Smith distinguishes French and German models: "The territorial conception of belonging that formed the French tradition gave rise to a civic policy that naturalized immigrants on the basis of prolonged residence in France (*ius soli*); whereas the German conception of ethnic belonging entailed a genealogical policy (*ius sanguine*)."[26] Although Smith refers to these policies in Europe, the same patterns might be traced to the antebellum Mississippi Valley: the law itself was displaced by the law of the blood, as Anglo-Americans came to define themselves as the tribal inheritors of the Gothic legacy. As historians following Bancroft extended the divine approval of this narrative, Smith's idea of "providential" nationalism might be applied as well. The open and inclusive French communities were thus written off as inferior on account of their multiracialism, a disqualifying inferiority further evidenced by their unwillingness to "use" the land.

The second, and much more prevalent, application of Marshall's binary was simply to place the French on the other side: moving them from civilized to uncivilized, a process innately linked to their rhetorical deracination.[27] This was done in two ways. In Hildreth or Bancroft, the French could be designated a less-than-Anglo-Saxon based on European history. As non-Goths—as Gauls or Celts —they had already been pushed away westward once, and the experience on the American western frontier in 1800 paralleled the Gaulish frontier of around 800 during Charlemagne's push west into Gaul. But most historians were less concerned with the biological origins of racial destiny and more with the choices made by the French concerning race and identification as demonstrated in their behavior upon arrival in America. Their narrative is that, white or not, the French *chose* not to act like whites and so, by becoming "uncivilized" and by not using the land, they vacated their claim to rightful ownership.

Other forms of non-Anglo behavior among specific groups within the French communities are discussed in subsequent chapters, but the emphasis here must be on how behavioral deviance was linked to biological degradation. However, a passage such as this one from Timothy Flint's *A Condensed History and Geography of the Western States* (1828) is typical: "[The French] negotiated marriages, or temporary connexions with the young women of their red brethren; and the mixed races, which we now see in their settlements, were the fruit. . . . The grand business of the [Métis] young men was to navigate the almost interminable rivers, to hunt small adventures, trade and consort with the Indians to procure food. Their evenings, on their return, were spent dancing, in intercourse with the savages, and in relating long stories of their voyages, adventures, and exploits."[28] In other words, the mixed-race offspring were not using the land, outside of subsistence agriculture; they were "wandering." From such a view, they too, to recall Marshall's term, were only "occupants" and never really owners. Furthermore, individual French farmers were only renting lands from absentee owners in the French nobility, though rents were rarely collected. This fact too was brought to bear: the dispossession of the aristocracy was certainly a goal of Anglo-Saxonism. However, after both 1763 and 1787, the Anglos usually denied fee-simple land ownership to the French, even though the French had been farming the land in question for decades.[29]

In fact, French farmers—the habitants discussed in chapter 2—were often left out of the narrative altogether so that Anglo historians could focus instead on the more romantic and more easily removable and exploitable coureurs de bois or voyageurs—the subjects of chapter 3. For my immediate purposes, though, Francis Parkman's description typifies the mode of representing French backwoodsmen: "more akin to Indians than to white men."[30] Implicitly, Flint's elision of the French and "their" "savage" brethren established a context of degeneration that led to deracination. Set against the fear of the "white" backwoodsman in post-Revolutionary and antebellum America—what Hector St. John (née Michel-Guillaume) de Crèvecoeur called "the new-made Indian"—such imagery was linked to larger fears of the frontier and its destabilizing influence.[31]

Frontier conflicts such as the Whiskey Rebellion or frontier conspiracies such as the Burr Conspiracy made Anglo-Americans along the east coast fearful of either losing or losing control of their western lands. While Jacksonian democracy and universal manhood suffrage in 1824 greatly democratized and enfranchised western white males, these policies also set in motion a cultural pattern of marginalizing frontier whites to discourage their participation in their government. For example, in Morgan Neville's 1828 short story "The Last of the Boatmen," the exploits of Mike Fink, the prototype "half-man, half-alligator," are celebrated but also eulogized.[32] The era of the "boatmen" had ended rapidly with the coming of steam power to the West following the War of 1812. Moreover, while Fink and other "half-man, half-alligators" were fictionalized as white, most travel accounts record that most boatmen were French or Métis. This calls to mind Bancroft's emphasis on language: the frontier whites, not only in Neville's story but also in much of the humor of the Old Southwest that followed, are bestialized and otherwise diminished by their speech being transcribed into phonetic dialect. In contrast, eastern Anglos are given the benefit of standardization when speaking English, a language whose standard lexicography is not directly linked to its pronunciation, a telling double standard.[33]

The degeneration of the dialect-speakers is marked by their loss of the civilized and civilizing power of the Anglo-Saxon's language. That white degeneration in the colonies was a fear throughout the North Atlantic from 1500 forward goes without saying. British historian George Warburton—a thoroughgoing Anglo-Saxonist who saw the political separation of Britain and the United States as a mere triviality—initially objected only to the French reversion to "savagery," in the case of the men acculturated to the fur trade. However, significantly, he also perceived a continuation of Old World feudalism in open-field agriculture. In the American edition of his *Conquest of Canada* (1850), he comments that French leaders were "in the colony but not of it" and continues: "The mass of the population of New France were descended from settlers sent out within a short time after the first occupation of the country, and who were not selected for any peculiar qualifications. They were not led to emigrate from the spirit of adventure, disappointed ambition, or political discontent. . . . The Canadians were trained to implicit obedience to their rulers, spiritual and temporal."[34] In an effort to justify the rightful removal of such a retrograde development from North America, Warburton champions the Anglo-Saxon's triumph over the "Norman" in the person of the French. In brief, the French were peasants —"indolent," "drunken," and, worst of all, "obedient," and so their degeneration into a state of semisavagery has more to do with a change in place than a change in condition. In brief, then, there is nothing new about the French in America: they have changed neither themselves nor the land itself to any noticeable degree. Warburton traces out the French disregard for private property, the uncritical thinking intrinsic to Catholicism, and the refusal of the French to separate themselves physically from the Indians as evidence of their legacy of not "using" the land the way their Anglo-Saxon, Puritan neighbors did east of the mountains.

Writing nearly a century earlier, Crèvecoeur provided a useful articulation of what had come to be viewed as the only valid way of "using" the American continent privileged by later writers like Warburton or Flint. Crèvecoeur's definition of "American" tolerated no such retrogression: "The American is a new man, who acts upon these principles; he must therefore entertain new ideas and form new opinions. From involuntary idleness, servile dependence, penury, and useless labour he has passed to toils of a very different nature, rewarded by ample subsistence. This is an American."[35] Crèvecoeur, who had surveyed in the Ohio Valley during the 1750s and so was familiar with the French presence, carried on the deracinating oppositionalism of Anglo-Saxon nationalism as he wrote about the French in his essay "The French in America," collected in *Sketches of Eighteenth-Century Life*: "Before the last war, the character of the Canadians was altogether original and singular: they were removed from the brutality of a savage and the useless improvements of more polished society; they were as different from the natives as from their own countrymen; they were extremely temperate, happily ignorant; . . . England has found them the best of subjects."[36] Thus for him the French settlements are simply prehistory, and the French presence in the new nation is no different from that of any other European stock, just another ethnicity to be assimilated or pushed west. By Crèvecoeur's logic, as it operated both in that essay and in *Letters*, Americanness is not determined by membership in one European tribe or another—"The Americans were once scattered all over Europe"—but rather by behavior. While this concept resembles civic nationalism's forward-looking, law-based premise, in fact Crèvecoeur here articulates an almost transcendent romantic conception whereby the tribe of Americans share a deeper distinctive link that transcends even primordialist geography-based ethnic unity to identify a specially marked chosen people, a tribe within the European tribe.

Alexis de Tocqueville, another cosmopolitan French traveler, noted a similar distinction. In "Two Weeks in the Wilderness," published in the United States at the end of his visit, years before the publication of *Democracy in America*, he describes the settlers of Michigan. Of the French he writes:

> Make your way into this leafy cabin and you will encounter a man whose warm welcome and open face will from the outset herald the liking for the pleasures of human contact and the carefree side of life. In the first instance, you will perhaps take him for an Indian; in his submission to life in the wild, he has assumed his clothes, ways, and, to a degree, his customs. . . . Yet this man has remained no less a Frenchman, cheerful, enterprising, proud, glorying in his origins, a passionate enthusiast for military honors, more vain than self-interested, a man of instinct, obeying his first emotion more than his reason.

Tocqueville then switches to the Anglo:

> This man is cold, stubborn, mercilessly argumentative. He clings to the land and rips from the life in the wilds everything he can snatch from it. He engages in a neverending struggle against it; every day, he strips it of a few more of its spoils. Bit by bit, he transports his own laws, ways, customs, and, wherever possible, even the smallest benefits of advanced civilization to the wilderness.[37]

Although Tocqueville is slightly nostalgic for the French frontier and its emphasis on pleasure, his distinction is clearly the basis for a larger narrative in which the French colonials in North America would play no role in its conquest, only in its occupation. In general, therefore, in all manner of Anglo-American and other histories written in the context of European or imperial nationalism, the lack of newness in the French colonies, on account of either genetic inferiority or cultural corruption, denigrates them to the status of a false start. From the new tribe of Americans the French colonials are excluded, Europeans who came to America without becoming Americans.

In sum, then, one could be counted as less-than-American by either staying European or going native or by being accused in print of either. Once a person or group is so diminished, the rights of citizenship are forfeited, and dispossession and disenfranchisement may justly follow. The treatment of the French in antebellum American history writing provides a context or a precedent for the treatment of other groups. Indians, ethnic minorities, religious dissenters, and economic nonplayers are all thus less white—by God or by choice—and thus less American. Their relegation to a place in the national prehistory suggests a consolidation of national identity taking place in the early nineteenth century that found its model and precedent in the justification of the removal, assimilation, and displacement—in sum, the erasure—of the French in the eighteenth.

As part of the same strategy of seeking the biological and behavioral bases of their narratives of the American tribe, providential nationalist historians likewise often relegated seventeenth-century figures such as Roger Williams or William Penn to their early chapters, before the real action started. For example, Richard Hildreth belittled Penn's peaceful relationship with the Lenni Lenape during the settlement of Pennsylvania: "We must not forget the comparative feebleness of the Pennsylvania Indians, the peaceful character of the Delawares, whom the Five Nations had compelled to acknowledge themselves women."[38] While Richard was at times critical of the British—excoriating the British treatment of the Acadians, for example—he never questioned the right of the British to remove them. He still valued the Puritan model of righteous Anglo-Saxon conquest, and he put it in undifferentiated opposition to French interculturalism. Richard reimagined contact as an either/or proposition: there can be no middle ground between Indians and whites, between "civilization" and "savagery." As to resulting violence, Timothy Flint wrote: "Aggression has commenced, in the account current of mutual crime, as a hundred to one, on the part of the Indian."[39] Such is the link of providential nationalism to the discourse of empire.

However, Cincinnati-based editor and historian Benjamin Drake in 1838 refuted Flint and the assumptions behind claims like Flint's: "The justice, benevolence, and kindness which marked the conduct of Penn towards the Indians, shielded his infant colony from aggression, and won for him personally, a generous affection, that would have been creditable to any race of people. . . . Little doubt can exist, if the subject were fairly examined, that most of these sanguinary wars, of which history speaks with a shudder, would be found to have arisen less from the blood thirsty Indian, than from the gold-thirsty and land-thirsty defamer."[40] Drake's criticism of American Indian policy—as I have noted elsewhere—was rooted in his insistence on the potential for multiracial cooperation in the Ohio Valley as based on the Quaker and French models. James Hall—Drake's close friend and posthumous editor—expounded more directly in fiction and prose on the advantages of the French model over the British for the settlement of the region, as I discuss below. Drake and Hall were far from alone: other writers working in and around Cincinnati between 1830 and 1850 were more generally interested in challenging the role assigned their region in national history.[41] Especially after the 1832 nullification crisis, they foresaw the sectionalization of the eastern seaboard and promoted the development of western regional culture as distinct from that of both New England and the South, and they used the French as a basis for doing so.

Their purpose was not merely geographic localism. They also meant to bring to light alternative histories and demographics—such as the French—to define the "West" as not just *another* American region but rather as an American place categorically different from both the North and the South. In so doing they created a context for lifting regional history out of the master narratives of nationalist writers. Colonials themselves, reflecting the "cultural lag" typical of settler colonial experience, a thousand miles away from the transatlantic cosmopolitan intellectual scene of the eastern cities, they clung to eighteenth-century values of civic nationalism even as they were largely abandoned in the East: for example, they deemphasized the need for a unified or unifying national master narrative or biological likeness as a means of fabricating a nation based on interregional and intraracial cohesion. Instead, they opened up the study of the history of Europeans in America to explore versions of the past at odds with or in addition to the Puritan model, moving toward a model of what Anthony Smith calls "plural nationalism"— a precursor to twentieth-century multiculturalism. By reclaiming a civic model of citizenship, they retained the older criteria for national membership that predated the predominance of raced citizenship in Jacksonian America.

Their counternarratives are manifest in their writing, literary, polemic, and otherwise. However, issues of legitimacy and land are intrinsically historiographic—hence, my choice to use state histories. The regionalist ethos of Cincinnati—where many of these were initially published—was most publicly fostered by Benjamin's brother, Dr. Daniel Drake (an epidemiologist who rejected phrenology and its racialist aftereffects). Daniel wrote that nothing but "intellectual improvement" would result in the Ohio Valley with the mixture and cohabitation of Spanish, French, and Indian populations. From this diversity, he means to explain a local distinctiveness; he exhorts his listeners to understand that this region "has a dignity which does not belong to the early history of other nations."[42]

Local state historians took up that call to distinguish western from eastern versions of the nation's history. In the French legacy, they found ideas and institutions that would form the basis of their historiographic resistance to Anglo-Saxon ascendance. By implication, Drake saw the East's sectionalism as a form of localized tribal or primordial nationalism. By reminding westerners of the diversity of their heritage, Drake hoped that such exclusionary thinking might be mitigated by the West's adherence to an ideal of inclusion. This ideal was rooted in the civic identity the state historians observed and then established in their rewritings of the history of the French frontier. Although I will be focusing on Sheldon, Smith, Reynolds, and Patterson, Thomas Ford, John Dillon, Caleb Atwater, and James H. Lanman crafted similar histories.[43] Each makes the French central to state history, rather than the Puritans, even though each begins with the European occupation of the eastern seaboard. By implication, these historians distinguish state and regional history from national history, querying both the scope and ideology of the absorptive narratives of writers like Bancroft and Hildreth.[44]

This choice is especially enlightening given each author's self-proclaimed need to move beyond his or her state's boundaries to tell the whole story. For example, William R. Smith's *History of Wisconsin* (1854) opens with a statement that, in various forms, appears in all these texts:

The compiler is aware that, in the perusal of almost every page of the early history, observations will present themselves to the reader, which very naturally will suggest the question, "Why is so much matter devoted to the history of portions of the country in some degree remote from the immediate Territory of Wisconsin?" It is presumed that a sufficient answer may be given in this:—The history of Wisconsin in early times is essentially embodied in the history of the Valley of the Mississippi: the country was not integral, but a small portion of the great Northwest; and, as such, the events occurring in, and spreading over, and influentially operating upon the whole, became consequently important data in its own history.[45]

More than half of Smith's narrative then ranges from Quebec to New Orleans to tell the story of Wisconsin. By this same reasoning, however, the narrower Anglo version—Samuel Hildreth's *Pioneer History*—addressed the same region but omitted the French almost entirely and began with the British entry into the Mississippi Valley after 1750. For Smith, it was more important that Wisconsin was French for one hundred years than whether it eventually became American. Hence, he insists that the French, and their Indian "brethren," are part of the state's history and are not relegated to its prehistory.

Patterson's *History of the Backwoods* (1843) enacts the same strategy but explains its reasons for doing so more directly:

As far as prior discovery gave right to the country, it must be granted the claims of the French were undeniable; however ingenious and notoriously falsified may have been the statements of the English, to deprive them of this ground to rest their claims upon, as also of historians of our own country of a later day. The French, if they did not fortify their claims upon purchases from the Indians, like the English, it still must be admitted, as it even was by many of the English at the time that their rights were preeminent, from the fact that they were the first discoverers, and, in them, at least, reposed the power to negotiate first with the natives for their land.[46]

First, notice that Hildreth's "divine providence" here is supplanted by a contemplation of the rule of law, not blood. Next, Patterson notes, the French never wanted *all* the land, the way the British did. They wanted only enough for a few villages, forts, and fields. It was the English who were more concerned with the cartographic fantasy of drawing a line dividing "ours" from "theirs," "civilized" from "savage." Patterson especially addresses the intercultural figure of Jacques Joncaire, who had lived for years as an adopted Shawnee. For Patterson, the entanglement of hunting and farming lands, of French villages and Indians lands was worked out on a personal level. Nonetheless, despite their acquisition of Indian clothes and lifeways, for Patterson and the other state historians, the French never sacrificed the right of discovery. Yet the working definition of the "right of discovery" assumed by Patterson differs sharply from Marshall's. For Patterson, the right was only to negotiation and cohabitation with the Indians, not to the land itself.

This conflict characterized early Michigan history as well. Eliza Sheldon, writing her *Early History of Michigan* (1856), goes to great lengths to re-create the tension within the French colonial administration in 1704 between the Count de Pontchartrain and Monsieur de Cadillac on this issue. Cadillac—the Roger Williams or William Penn of the story—while censured and his career destroyed, sets the tone for French interculturalism, going so far as to propose a system of public education in which Indian and French students would be taught together.[47] On the other hand, Pontchartrain, more eager for profits, is put in a bad light by Sheldon by behaving like an Englishman. For Cadillac, the right of discovery was simply a right to make the first offer to share the land, not to take it. Sheldon, like the others, though clearly in favor of including the French in state history, never gilds their time in Michigan as a golden age, as William Henry Harrison did. In setting Pontchartrain and Cadillac against each other, her narrative transcends the binary established by Bancroft: what matters more is the clash of ideas rather than the clash of ethnicities, races, or nations; the conflict becomes a struggle between confrontation and accommodation.

All the state histories spend extensive time on the era of exploration and prominent figures of that era, such as La Salle, Marquette, Radisson, and Tonti. Universally as well, Hennepin is reviled for selling out to the British. Former governor John Reynolds's *Pioneer History of Illinois* (1852) moves quickly from the exploration to the settlement period, focusing especially on Kaskaskia between 1732 and 1754. In 1831, as the defeated, lame-duck governor, Reynolds and James Hall had visited Black Hawk and sympathized with the Sauk war chief's predicament before the coming war. The consistency of Reynolds's views emerges in his extensive description of Kaskaskia:

> In these twenty-two years, the whole country exhibited a scene of flourishing prosperity. With a very few exceptions, the Indian tribes, far and near, were on peaceable terms with the French and gave their trade to them. A considerable trade was carried on between Illinois and the lower Mississippi and Mobile. In return, all the necessities of life not produced in the country, and much of the luxuries of life were received and used by the inhabitants. . . . These settlements in Illinois being so weak and so far removed from any civilized communities, and amidst savage nations of Indians, that the inhabitants were forced to rely on each other for self-preservation.[48]

Reynolds depicts a population whose right to the land is established by inhabitation, stability, and growth, hardly a *terra nullius* with "no inveterate systems to overturn," in the terms of Manasseh Cutler in 1787.[49] In the terms of Henry Nash Smith and Annette Kolodny, the land was not virgin; Anglo-Americans had not deflowered it.[50] In fact, in Reynolds and the others, the land has had a French lover whose idea of love was not domination but rather cooperation, companionship rather than control.

Reynolds further connects the French to alternative nonaggressive values by describing their "teetotal temperance" as a component of a more general recipe for human happiness:

> They were ambitious for neither knowledge nor wealth, and, therefore, possessed not much of either. That sleepless, ferocious ambition to acquire wealth and power, which seizes on so many people at this day, never was known among the early settlers of Illinois. The French of these twenty-two years had exactly, almost to a mathematical certainty, a competency of worldly gear. There is a happy medium between the extremes of poverty and wealth, if mankind could settle on it, that would render them most happy. These people had, in my opinion, found the philosopher's stone of wealth and happiness. They lived in that fortunate medium, which forced itself on them rather than they on it.[51]

While Reynolds obviously overstates the case, his concern is with establishing a counterhistory to the Bancroftian ideals of Manifest Destiny and Anglo-Saxon ascendance. In his story, the French villages are settlements, rather than colonies, and therefore detached from the larger empire of which they were nominally a part, and their story is contained by their refusing to grow beyond this "competence" into something transcendent.

Once again, in closing his discussion of the French, Reynolds took the occasion to comment more generally on what he viewed as a destructive misstep in the nation as a whole as it abandoned not only the French settlements but also the cultural and economic alternative they represented: "A people, such as those in Illinois were, in sparse settlements, poor and honest, needed very little government. And it is a curse all over the earth that 'the people are governed too much.' When a people are shackled down with excessive legislation, with charters for corporations, and sometimes with a public debt, they are in a humble and degraded condition; and if no other relief can reach them, they should resort to a revolution for it."[52] Reynolds's libertarian idealism is borne out by his documentation of the influence of the French on post-1783 Illinois politics. He describes the post-1783 situation as one of constant tension between men like himself—who based their politics on the French legacy—and those who saw in the French a meaningless prehistory. In his continuation of Reynolds's *Pioneer History*, *A History of Illinois from Its Commencement as a State in 1818 to 1847* (1859), fellow former governor Thomas Ford's description of Reynolds likewise bears out Reynolds's personal effort to retain the laid-back interculturalism of the French era. Although "classically educated," "he had passed his life on the frontier among a frontier people; he had learned all the byewords, catch-words, old sayings and figures of speech invented by vulgar ingenuity, and common among a backwoods people, and had diligently compounded them all into a language peculiar to himself, which he used on all occasions, both public and private."[53] Reynolds, who had been elected by the "anti-Jackson men," like his friend Hall, found and, more important, wanted his readers to find in the French a meaningful alternative to Yankee materialism and ambition. Reynolds's adaptation of the frontier vernacular represents a step away from the notion that the pure English language—"the language of Milton"—represents in itself a personalized resistance to the master narrative his own book likewise denied.

Along the same lines William Smith closes his pre-1763 section by commenting on how, even ninety years after the close of formal French administration, Wisconsin was still linguistically diverse, a fact that in no way lessened its condition as an American place:

Not only does this friendly feeling between the Indians and the descendants of the early French settlers continue, but through all the changes in the country that time has wrought, the French language still, partially holds its place. Although Canadian dialect prevails among the French descendants, yet there is not wanting at this day, in portions of Wisconsin, instances where the pure Parisian language is spoken, and the courtly manner of a polite people preserved, notwithstanding all the changes that have occurred since the dominion of France over the Northwest was ceded to Great Britain.[54]

Smith, writing under the imprimatur of the state legislature, does nothing to erase or push into the past the French presence. Like Reynolds's assumption of the vernacular, Smith's recognition and even celebration of the linguistic diversity left over from the French era establish a paradigm wherein Anglo-Saxon political administration might coexist with the ineradicable cultural persistence of leftover patterns of inclusion and diversity.

Smith's notion that French language still has "its place" in 1850s Wisconsin belies a historiographic method and sense of national identity among the state historians that might be understood as categorically separate from that of Bancroft and the Hildreths. In fact, for all the state historians, the racial definition of the French is simply irrelevant, the distinction of Anglo-Saxon from Gaul a useless absurdity, as is any sign of providential intervention. Likewise the notion that strict lines can be drawn between civilized and savage, between American and French, between land seizure and legitimate occupation, or between the past and the present simply does not factor into their accounts of what counts as "history" in their states. For them, Marshall's binaries are inapplicable when they look back over two hundred years of cohabitation without conquest. Given the increasing diversity of their states with widespread immigration from central and northern Europe in the 1830s and 1840s, such an inclusive paradigm could only serve the interests of interethnic peace in their own states as well, but that's the subject of chapter 5.

———————————— Let me end this chapter where it started: the shifting banks of the Ohio River and the competing views of land, legitimacy, law, and values contested on such a slippery stage. Prior to the building of levees and containment walls by Anglo-American engineers, the rivers along which the French settled, and most of their tributaries, changed shape every spring: floods moved the banks, the beds, and the bars. They are new rivers, brand new in deep geologic time, dating only from the withdrawal of the glaciers after the last Pleistocene. It only makes sense, then, that the Quaker Zadok Cramer's book *The Navigator*—a reader-friendly guide to steering one's flatboat and one's fortunes into the so-called Valley of Democracy—went through eleven editions between its initial appearance in Pittsburgh in 1801 and its final edition in 1814.[55] The eleventh is more than half footnotes, addenda, and other ephemera, all of which demonstrate a truly organic text, as shifty as the rivers it describes.

Cramer foresaw the coming incorporation of the West by Anglo-Americans, and he identified their acquisitive nature as a dire threat to the agrarian values, French and Jeffersonian, that had characterized the earlier and more peaceful settlement of the valleys. In an extended footnote on the French river town of Gallipolis, Ohio, Cramer addresses the unjust and hypocritical nature of western land speculation by Anglo-Americans coming into the region after the Treaty of Greenville in 1795. Specifically, Cramer tells of how Manasseh Cutler and other Anglo land speculators dishonestly displaced the French. Although they were late arrivals—the village was founded after 1763—the Gallipolis French, as opposed to the speculators, represented precommercial agrarian ideals: they had been "willing to risk their lives and every thing they possessed, to enter the forest with axes on their shoulders, to clear fields, and make improvements, as a home for themselves and their children."[56] Foreshadowing the regret at the loss of the French presence later articulated by the state historians, Cramer cites the relationship of the French to the land as a more suitable alternative to the land greed of Cutler and those like him.

Cramer condemns absentee or corporate speculation in favor of the individual farmer, whether he has a registered deed or is renting from a distant seigneur. In addition, Cramer describes the coming of "the sheriff with a writ of ejectment, issued by a powerful land company, who, if they cannot frighten the settler off his land, frighten him into a compromise, by which he yields at least one-half his tract, a great portion of his labor, rather than be turned out of house and home altogether by expensive lawsuits." Then, bitterly sarcastic, Cramer turns back to Gallipolis as a whole: "The purchase of the people of Gallipolis *happened* to be within [the Ohio Company's] tract, and the Company, *happening* to neglect fulfilling the condition of the grant, the land reverted again to the United States, leaving the Frenchmen landless, and in many cases moneyless."[57] The local Anglo sheriff, in cahoots with the land company, is then guilty of theft of more than land: at stake in the end is the whole premise of America as a place where the sins of Europe are not repeated. Caleb Atwater affirms Cramer's account of the "swindlers calling themselves the 'Scioto Land Company'" and adds that some of the refugee French went to Philadelphia, as well as downriver to Vincennes or New Orleans.[58]

Cramer's and Atwater's analyses of the Gallipolis episode foreshadow the populism of almost a century later: valuing virtue over profit and local control of resources over centralized corporate delocalization—commonwealth over empire. But whether the accusing voice is Cramer's or the state historians', or William Jennings Bryan's, the crime is the same: the treatment of the farmers, in this case the French, is indicative of larger forces transforming the new nation from virtuous republic to commercial empire. On a microcosmic scale, the fate of the French in Gallipolis foreshadows the fate of the virtues they represented. For Cramer, the case of Gallipolis pitted the informal and improvisational nature of frontier settlement against a means of reckoning legitimacy along more legally rigid lines. Even if Penn's Pennsylvania and the Illinois country were technically the possessions of absentee landowners (Penn himself and the French seigneurs), day-to-day life in the actual settlements was characterized by benign neglect and near total liberty from any institutional obligations. The argument of this chapter has been that the very lack of structure on the French frontier enabled this liberty. In turn, their embrace of relative anarchy in the name of liberty made possible the disqualification of the French as American landowners—an extension of the same argument used to displace Indians.

To express resistance to removal and all it represented, however, the French were contrarily appropriated to extend and articulate an alternative imagining of Anglo-Americans' relationship to the Indians and their lands. The nineteenth century's emphasis on more strict subdivisions of humanity along racially specific lines extended to more than a race-based definition of citizenship: it led to a more brutal and violent means of seizing land from those less inclined toward the practice of commercial agriculture and corporate land speculation. The placement of the French among the excluded demonstrates the lengths to which the empire builders would go to attain their ends, even redefining whiteness with a behavioral codicil to a pseudoscientific definition. By holding up the French frontier in opposition to a nation bent on Indian removal, the Mexican-American War, the extension of slavery, and unchecked industrialism, the state historians reminded Anglo-Americans that their national destiny was a matter of informed choice, not biological fate. By excavating the leaden plates—symbols of an alternative past only recently buried—from the banks of the Ohio, they reminded their readers that they could be American and white without being violent and bigoted.

Habitants and the American Way of Doing Things

Open-field cultivation demanded cooperative effort and a certain sense that agricultural land to some extent belonged to the community and was not utterly governed by the laws of freehold proprietorship. These notions conflicted with an American ethos of individual autonomy, liberty, and self-reliance; in short, they were incompatible with the American way of doing things.

Carl J. Ekberg, *French Roots in the Illinois Country* (1998)

arl J. Ekberg's description of the conflict between French and Anglo land-use ideas in the early nineteenth century might be read next to Zadok Cramer's description of the dispossession of the Gallipolis Gauls that ended chapter 1. Ekberg traces and documents the French emphasis on "cooperative effort" and resistance to "freehold proprietorship" that came into stark contrast with "the American way of doing things" after 1815.[1] The Gauls' communitarian sharing of common resources—irrigation systems, fertilizer, and so on—was more directly the point of conflict for the Anglos and quite often the administrative lever used to uproot or displace French settlements. Outside habitant villages in the Mississippi basin like Vincennes, Indiana, or Cahokia, Illinois, open fields of five thousand or six thousand acres were under cultivation every summer. The fields were unbroken by fences and so were passable by Indians and other hunters. A century later, even romantic Anglos admired the picturesque expanses—even as they terminated the land-use policies that harnessed the region's fecundity to its potential for creating beauty and community. When the Yankees seized the land, the open fields were divided among individual landowners: fences went up, roads went down, and habitants' principles of collectivity were superseded by waves of privatization and enclosure.[2]

The habitants lived close together in the villages and walked to the fields each day, as opposed to the Anglo farmer, who more likely lived in solitude surrounded by privately owned fields, without access to the companionship or resources of neighbors or colleagues. Furthermore, French villages and fields did not stretch uninterrupted from one settlement to the next: each was surrounded by hunting grounds, Indian villages, or whatever else occupied the space between. Neither the habitants nor the landowners—the seigneurs in Paris, Quebec, or Montreal, stockholders in the Company of India—had any interest in occupying the land in any unbroken or comprehensive fashion—each habitant settlement was an island in the sea of prairie or forest. Yet the fate of such villages and values reflects Ekberg's observation: collectivity and heterogeneity were not characteristic of "American" values.

A further problem was the way the French distributed land and resources among their settlers farther north. In French settlements in the Great Lakes basin, where fertile meadows were harder to find, the French imported the "ribbon-farm" model. Strikingly thin strips of land—four by eighty arpents, for example—were allotted to individual farmers,each stretching, usually, from the waterline of a river or lake, up through the fertile floodplain, and up to the timberline. This way, each farm was more likely to possess all the resources needed for self-sufficiency: water, wood, living space, and arable land were equally distributed among the farms. The bothersome redistribution of life's necessities at the heart of commercial economics was mitigated—and the people got to live near one another. In contrast, the placeless rectangles prescribed by the United States' Land Ordinance of 1785—by assuring an uneven distribution of resources—implicitly promoted commercial activity: one settler might have water, another wood, but few had both. Ekberg's terminology reflects the outcome of the conflict: the equation and conflation of "American" and "Anglo-American."

In something so straightforward as the shape of farms, historical evidence bears out the difference between French and Anglo ways of food production and community building, a difference further borne out in texts that used this conflict to suggest that how a nation farms reveals much about how that nation imagines itself. In both arrangements, the French emphasis is on finding the means of land distribution that best combines the demands of local topography (fertile Illinois prairie or sandy Michigan waterfronts) with an ineradicable need for community, fellowship, and human interdependence. In addition, the habitants pooled their harvests and sold the surplus to the fur companies or downriver. In contrast, the "grid" created by the ordinance assured that farmers lived far from one another and that each imagined himself in competition with his neighbors.

But that was the whole idea. The life of the habitants was not business; it was life, "inverting the usual order," according to historian, journalist, and creative writer James Hall. This reversal struck Anglo-Americans less enamored by commercialization and industrialization as contrary to revolutionary or republican values wherein profit is subordinated to virtue, self-interest to public service—at least in theory. Ekberg cites Captain Amos Stoddard's 1803 observation that "the inhabitants of all the compact villages are . . . Creoles and Canadians. But the extensive settlements about the country have been made by English Americans."[3] French and American approaches to the land reveal a marked contrast in values: the French viewed the land as a way of supporting a way of life—neighborly, egalitarian, and village-based. The Anglos viewed it as a means to wealth—individualistic, acquisitive, and farm-as-property-based. While through the late seventeenth century the French aristocracy sought immediate profits in the regions, finding no gold, by the early eighteenth century, they had largely left the habitants to their own devices. Ekberg also notes that French families stayed in the same village for multiple generations, a pattern he contrasts with the Anglo-American tendency to stay for only a few seasons before seeking more profitable chances elsewhere, exhausting the land—and not caring that they did—in the process.

The all-absorbing nature of "the American way of doing things" obviously resulted in confrontations with Indians. The contiguous and extensive fields cleared by Anglo farmers disrupted hunting patterns, and individual land ownership meant twelve-month occupation of the same land, each system at odds with Indian agricultural and hunting practices. To do what they wanted to do, the Americans needed *all* the land; the French needed only a little. In contrast, habitant villages rarely were in conflict with their Indian neighbors, scattered as they were among Indian and, later, Métis settlements. The Anglo imagination also seemed to require a line running north and south across the continent separating Indian from American lands, civilization from savagery, a need to fabricate "zones of cultural purity" in the terms of Gareth Griffiths, to bolster fictions of civilization's progress and unmediated difference from savagery.[4] On the level of policy, French agreements with the Indians never drew such definitive borders, whereas border drawing was at the heart of Anglo treaty policy. More central is a cultural contrast between those who saw land as property from which profit must be gleaned and those who saw its cultivation simply as a means of supporting an unencumbered way of life, between commercial and pastoral values. As we saw in the struggle between civic and tribal nationalisms in regard to land ownership, this was a conflict between more than French and Anglo land-use systems.

On a larger scale, early nineteenth-century developments were seen as moving the nation away from the eighteenth-century values of the Founders, or at least the Jeffersonian wing.[5] The French, as a link to those earlier values, would again be used to remind Americans of their options beyond those of corporate and commercial materialism. This conflict was present but latent even in the drafting of the Declaration of Independence. In Thomas Jefferson's own famous revision of his original list of inalienable rights from "life, liberty, and property" to "life, liberty, and the pursuit of happiness," we can see the momentary triumph of agrarianism over commercialism.[6] That is not the same as the difference between capitalism and collectivism, however: it's a matter of prioritization. The French viewed commercial activity as a means of supporting a way of life; the Anglos viewed commercial activity *as* a way of life. Another distinction: during the antebellum decades, the slaveholding South inappropriately hid behind "agrarianism" to mask its own laissez-faire traffic in human property. Although many habitants owned a slave or two (most of whom lived in the same houses and ate at the same tables), they never aspired to the factory-style production of plantation slavery—a thoroughly nonagrarian agricultural practice. Moreover, as translated and reprinted by John Dillon in his *History of Indiana* (1859), the 1724 revision of the Code Noire established French law concerning slavery as working toward a goal of voluntary manumission and "affranchisement," with former slaves continuing to live among the habitants afterward. Moreover, slaves could sue abusive masters, terms were set for buying their freedom, and masters were legally obliged to act "in a parental manner," a gesture that at once is based in a racialist paternalism but acknowledges the need for government monitoring, a surveillance Anglo slaveholders always rejected.[7]

Hence, both radical and abolitionist Anglo-Americans found the French a useful model for critiquing the excesses and assumptions of the culture of commercialization. The fact of French slave ownership, however, was contained by placing it in the context of a more general agrarian way of life. The assumption made in the Code Noire was that agrarian experience would moderate the difference between master and slave, an assumption Ekberg, Eccles, and others find to be materially substantiated by the high birth rates and low death rates among slaves in the Illinois country. In sum, low-intensity slavery among the French could be rhetorically mitigated by abolitionist Anglo-American writers by its having been merely a component of European culture that was vanishing as the agrarian way of life cleansed itself of such corruptions over the course of a few generations. In fact, most of the French slaves came to be owned by a few aristocratic fur-trading families—the Choteaus, for example (see chapter 4)—while most habitants had little or no contact with forced labor.[8]

This chapter, then, has as its backdrop the politics of labor in the incorporation of the American economy, including agriculture, during the antebellum decades and its attendant ossification of class structure, as even freeholding farmers reinvented agriculture to meet the commercialized expectations of an urbanizing nation. During these years, the working classes—both in factories and on farms—were being defined in individualistic, competitive terms. Poor people were supposed to want to become rich, competing with one another rather than with their employers, in an isolated and ironic arena whereby assimilation into the large-scale system of bureaucratic conformity led to personal or familial advancement. In such a structure, a shame comes to be associated with the failure to achieve material wealth, and that shame is supposed to engender both competitive individualism *and* a pattern of obedience to one's employer, displacing older loyalties to church, community, or, oddly enough, self.[9]

"Peasant" was employed to describe French settlers both by those who approved of the habitant way of life and by those who used it as a term of denigration. For both, "peasantry" existed outside or, at best, on the margins of "the American way of doing things." Principles of collectivity inform peasant identity; members of peasant societies thus think in terms of group membership before individual advancement. Membership is necessarily predicated on civic rather than tribal terms: behavior rather than birth. Moreover, peasantry means long-term attachment to the land and one's neighbors—stability in the face of change—and the use of land for subsistence rather than enrichment. The most familiar peasants in early American literature are Washington Irving's Dutch in "Rip Van Winkle" and "The Legend of Sleepy Hollow." Even for the wealthy villagers, money is not the point. Pastoral noncompetitiveness defines peasantry: Herr Van Tassel would never imagine subdividing his land, selling it, and then doing the same in Tennessee, as does Ichabod Crane.[10] In "Sleepy Hollow," while Brom Bones chases the greedy Ichabod across the bridge, the story's narrative frame—a gentlemen's club in New York—distinguishes that part of America that has changed from those parts left behind. In the "Postscript," a group of wealthy New Yorkers listen to the story; among them is, obviously, Ichabod as an older and wealthier man. Each story ultimately draws its strength from the contrast between those who favor change and growth and those who value stability and sameness. In "Sleepy Hollow," the peasants are simply written off as picturesque and quaint, what "Americans" used to be. On the other hand, when Rip awakens, the Dutch have lost their peaceful picturesqueness as bucolic peasants by assimilating to the American way of doing things, noisily progressing toward petit bourgeois materialism, what "Americans" were becoming.

In both scenarios, the Dutch peasantry is either anachronized or assimilated—drained of meaning one way or another, nothing more than part of the nation's prehistory. The rags-to-riches model, although codified during the Progressive Era by Andrew Carnegie, Booker T. Washington, and Horatio Alger, had its roots in eighteenth-century models such as Benjamin Franklin's "Poor Richard" and Hector St. John de Crèvecoeur's "Andrew the Hebridean." Manual labor in these narratives is a starting point, the beginning of personal and familial trajectories toward wealth and inclusion beginning with fee-simple property ownership. Prior to the rise of labor unions, membership in the working classes in America was supposedly transient, the first step up Franklin's or Crèvecoeur's ladder. Peasants, on the other hand, rely on each other and cannot conceive of their lives in terms of individual, careerist ascent through several layers of the class structure.

That an American class structure was emerging in the early nineteenth century can hardly be denied. In this system, ascent of that usually elusive ladder was inhibited by a variety of demographic, economic, and cultural forces, starting with the de facto and often de jure grounding of women and nonwhites. Beyond that, even Crèvecoeur noted the high rate of failure among European males in the late eighteenth century; more than half of the west-moving immigrants became east-moving emigrants. For those who could not leave, membership in the working class rarely led to a schedule of ascent, either individually or in generations of a single family. While Rebecca Harding Davis's "Life in the Iron Mills" (1860) spurred agitation on class issues later in the century, the most famous Frenchman traveling in the United States during the antebellum decades recognized the ossification of class structure intrinsic to industrialization.

A French nobleman whose perspective was clearly cosmopolitan rather than colonial, Alexis de Tocqueville observed the deleterious effect of class division on republican values. As to agriculture, he writes:

> Almost all the farmers of the United States combine some trade with agriculture; most of them make agriculture itself a trade. It seldom happens that an American farmer settles for good upon the land which he occupies: especially in the districts of the [Mississippi Valley], he brings land into tillage in order to sell it again, and not to farm it: he builds a farm-house on the speculation that, as the state of the country will soon be changed by the increase in population, a good price may be obtained for it. . . . Thus the Americans carry their business-like qualities into agriculture; and their trading passions are displayed in that, as in their other pursuits.

Tocqueville omits from his analysis the downside of this way of doing things. The crashes of 1819 and 1837, as well as the resulting pattern of resales and exploitative mortgages, relegated many farmers, like factory workers, to the status of *unwilling* peasant. As to manufacturing, Tocqueville writes: "What can be expected of a man who has spent twenty years of his life in making heads for pins? And to what can that mighty human intelligence, which has so often stirred the world, be applied in him, except it be to investigate the best method of making pins. . . . In proportion as the principle of the division of labor is more extensively applied, the workman becomes more weak, more narrow-minded, and more dependent. . . . Thus the elements of which the class of the poor is composed are fixed." At the same time, Tocqueville comments that the new rich in democratic societies differ from the aristocracies in preindustrial communities: "The manufacturer asks nothing of the workman but his labor; the workman expects nothing from him but his wages. The one contracts no obligation to protect, nor the other to defend; and they are not permanently connected by either habit or duty."[11] Industrialism, for Tocqueville, brings with it a new class structure that is far less unified and stable than other social hierarchies elsewhere: even the Code Noire required masters "to act in a parental manner" with regard to their slaves and empowered local constables to arrest them if they overstepped or ignored that responsibility. Simultaneously, Tocqueville defines the "American way of doing things" as defined by the premise, if not the fact, of social mobility and dynamism, even as such options were fading.

Either way, there's no space, in factories or in fields, for nonplayers—*willing* peasants. Peasants are often materially poor but refuse to feel ashamed of it by equating comfort in life with material gain or moral virtue. The system Tocqueville described depends upon the new industrial underclasses living in denial as to their lack of social and economic self-determination; subsequently their selfbased ambition causes them to be better, less disruptive laborers. In the antebellum public sphere, the dominant cultural apparatus encouraged members of the exploitable working class by contrasting their supposed ambition and mobility with the static inertia and moral torpidity of historical peasantry. For example, enslaved Africans and "Mexicans"—actually Hispanophone Chicanos living in territories acquired by the United States—were portrayed as *willing* peasants and thus either ownable or exploitable.[12] Beyond that, to establish the white industrial working class as distinct from nonwhite peasant populations, then, nonacquisitiveness was defined as both racially inappropriate and intrinsically backward-looking.

The historical precedent used to justify social stratification in the nineteenth century was the historiographic degradation of American peasants in the eighteenth: the habitants. Negative depictions of the habitants reflected the larger cultural need to define economic nonparticipation as unwelcome in the industrializing and urbanizing nation. In chapter 1, the subject was what happened when the French colonists and settlers were reimagined along exclusionary tribal lines—biologically or behaviorally—and so written out en masse from participation in the Anglo-Saxon imperial nation. In this chapter, the subject is not just access to land but, precisely, how one imagines one's relation to that land. In exploring that specific subject, we can perceive larger patterns of how people relate to a series of other things: material goods, their neighbors, and themselves. Thus my sources reflect more interior aspects of post-Revolutionary experience. The choice to live either the "American" way or the peasant way operated at a personal and subjective level. On the whole, though, the choice has to do with insisting that there is, in fact, more than one "American" way of doing things. In the process, we must shift from historiography into the more elusive terrain of travel and literary sources.

A brief return to Gallipolis will set the tone for understanding the standard representation of the habitants. In 1812, Jervis Cutler, son of Manasseh, leader of the land-speculating Ohio Company of Connecticut, told his version of the town's demise in his

Topographical Description of the State of Ohio, Indiana Territory, and Louisiana: "These people, wholly unacquainted with clearing up forests of heavy timber, after forming some handsome gardens, and planting vineyards and orchards, became disorganized. Finding themselves hazarded by the Indian War, they began to desert the town. Some went down the river about twenty-five miles and settled on donation lands given them by Congress, opposite little Sandy Creek, but many of them went down the Mississippi to Louisiana. The town has since been on the decline."[13] Cutler makes no reference to the forced removal of the French from Gallipolis, the main point of Cramer's account (and the one confirmed by historians). In contrast, Cutler's book is mostly topography: a description of the unexploited assets awaiting the white settler upon his purchase of company lands. However, his omission of the coerced depopulation of Gallipolis reflects a critical bias at odds with Cramer's. Cramer reflects the Quaker and the eighteenth-century ideals of civic membership and preindustrial agrarianism, valuing quality of life over material gain. In contrast, while Cutler praises the settlements of Vincennes and Kaskaskia as picturesque, one must note that he had no land to sell in these places, as he did throughout the nonempty regions of southern Ohio.[14] Yet, in the Illinois and Indiana French villages, the gardens are well kept and the denizens are "indolent" and "content" —their remoteness had thus far protected them from speculators like the Cutlers, for the moment.

Cutler thus reflects one of the two ways Anglo-American writers marginalized the habitants: idealization. The other is debasement. Both terms come from David Spurr's rubric for analyzing the rhetorical processes by which imperialist writers subjugated the places, peoples, and cultures over which they sought dominion from 1600 to the present. The post-1763 Anglo-American *colonization* of the French frontier in the Ohio and Mississippi basins is a historical given: even Frederick Jackson Turner used terms like "empire" and "colony" in a 1912 essay on the subject, although he was using each in the context of the early twentieth-century rubric of benevolent, liberal imperialism, rewordings of Jefferson's oxymoronic phrase the "empire of liberty."[15] To understand how the United States not only accomplished administrative dominion in the region but also pursued a national atmosphere of social and economic unilateralism and uniformity—cultural imperialism—studies like Spurr's can be brought to bear.

Spurr identifies the practice of rhetorical idealization in nineteenth-century North Atlantic empires primarily as a means of defining each nation's own goals: "The world, in other words, comes increasingly to be classified according to a purely utilitarian logic or instrumentality and quantification." For example, when we use the word "peasant" even today, we usually associate it either with medieval Europeans or with nonwhites in underdeveloped nations: "Idealization may thus be said to provide a compensation on the symbolic level for the political and economic processes that have destroyed the traditional fabric of non-Western societies; by representing individual instances of courage, beauty, and spiritual transcendence, Western writing . . . offers a kind of substitute gratification for what would otherwise be an overwhelming sense of loss."[16] The "non-Western" status of the French, in this case, was evidenced by their voluntary peasantry and rhetorical deracination, as noted in chapter 1. As in the more standard colonial setting, then, like Samuel Hildreth's recognition of the claim of the French to their land—a claim superseded by the providential intervention of a pro-Anglo-Saxon God—idealization assumes the defeat of a worthy adversary. It allows a cathartic release, an emotional discharging of a moral debt, efficiently transmogrifying a dangerous moment of self-doubt into a salient cleansing of clinging ambiguities.

To the "progressive" way of thinking intrinsic to empire building, chronology is the primary ordering principle of human communities, and locking something away in an Edenic past is one of the most efficient techniques of idealization and, hence, exclusion. To say that any given community is behind the times is to say that, even if it is happy and virtuous, it bears no real meaning, only a nostalgic one.

This form of idealization—infantilization, really—predominated in imperialist representations of the habitants. In his 1793 novel *The Emigrants*, Gilbert Imlay makes all the crucial stereotypical observations of Kaskaskia: "It is impossible for any country to appear to advantage after you have seen the Illinois; but still there are a variety of charms at this place, and you could see the naïveté of the inhabitants, which united with it, all the sprightliness of the country, from whom they have descended, you would believe you were living in those Arcadian days, when the tuneful shepherd used to compose sonnets to his mistress, and when the charms of love, were propitiated in sequestered groves, and smiling meads."[17] Like Irving's Dutch, Imlay's French are, for all intents and purposes, children. Adams and Eves back in a "regained Paradise," they live innocently, before the Fortunate Fall—uncorrupt but also unwise. When Imlay's hero plants his own colony in the West, it is in Kentucky, and he makes no such assumption of its occupants—he brings young farmers from New England, accustomed to Puritan order, just as the real-life Manasseh Cutler had when planting Marietta in southern Ohio in 1787. That is, no attempt is made to replicate the habitants' disordered innocence in Imlay's rationalist, Rousseauvian critique of European and American communities. The habitants are picturesque, but they exist before history, while the Anglos *are* history moving forward.

George Rogers Clark's 1788 memoir of his command on the Illinois frontier during the Revolution likewise recalls an easily manipulated and guileless population in his bloodless occupation of Kaskaskia, Cahokia, and Vincennes. Excited at the thought of military training, the habitants must be constantly reminded of the seriousness of the campaign: "These new friends of ours were so elated over the thought of the parade they were to make at Cahokia that they were too much concerned about equipping themselves to appear to the best advantage."[18] While he brings them back into history by enrolling them as members of the Revolutionary Army, Clark suggests that he is dealing with children, not with fully realized adults, more interested in uniforms and parades than in the business of the war.

Other government-sponsored explorers, such as Lewis and Clark and Henry Rowe Schoolcraft, made similar observations. Before he settled in Mackinac, Michigan, in 1823, married into the most powerful Métis family in the region, and began publishing reams of poorly recorded and rewritten Ojibwa legends, Schoolcraft served as a surveyor and geologist in territorial governor Lewis Cass's expedition to the source of the Mississippi River in the summer of 1821.[19] They may or may not have found it, but the many French voyageurs employed by the Anglos were certainly not impressed with their effort, if we can read their contempt through Schoolcraft's published journal. In fact, most of the people (twenty-two out of thirty-seven) traveling with Cass were of various French and Indian extractions, but Schoolcraft assiduously evades descriptions of the Anglos' dependence on the French for resources, translation, and basic survival skills.[20]

Schoolcraft's model for publishing a very selective account of western travels among the French and Indians was undoubtedly Nicholas Biddle's edition of Lewis and Clark's journals (1814). As we know from the successive waves of reediting to which the journals have been subjected, the captains' expedition was a far more complicated, complex, and intercultural venture than Biddle represented it to be. But nineteenth-century American readers had only the Biddle edition, and that's what influenced so many later western travelers from Schoolcraft, to Thomas Farnham, to, most famously, Francis Parkman. So, here are the captains, as ventriloquized by Biddle, on habitant lifeways around St. Louis: "In their manners, they unite all the careless gayety, and the amiability of the best times of France: yet, like most of their countrymen in America, they are but ill qualified for the rude life of the frontier; not that they are without talent, for they possess much natural genius and vivacity; nor that they are destitute of enterprise, for their hunting expeditions are long, laborious, and hazardous: but their exertions are desultory; their industry is without system, and without persever-ance."[21] In other words, they are children—not really worthy of pos-sessing the land in the name of Western civilization and the progress of history. Most tellingly, they have let the land change them rather than changing the land. In the harsher hands of writers more influ-enced by scientific views of race in the 1830s and after, this repre-sents another reason why the French rhetorically lost their white-ness: they refused to dominate and acquire; they preferred to share and cohabit the land, rather than dominate it.

In Schoolcraft's own *Narrative Journal of Travels* (1823), con-cerning his experience on a second expedition, the French presence, an undercurrent, is constant and consistent. Yet the voyageurs and the Indians become interchangeable as the journey progresses, and each seems more interested in telling stories and in companionship than in Schoolcraft's more material goals. Moreover, like the cap-tains, Schoolcraft sees in the French a very limited prospect of mean-ingful participation in the nation: "The settlement of Green Bay is one of ancient standing, having been first begun by the French about the year 1670. It now consists of sixty dwelling houses, and five hundred inhabitants, exclusive of the garrison. . . . The inhabitants are, with few exceptions, French, who have intermarried with In-dian women, and are said, generally, to be indolent, gay, intemper-ate, and illiterate." Hence, he sees the village as little more than a trading post. In contrast, Schoolcraft's view of Detroit omits the French presence to focus on his real interests: "The advantages it enjoys for the purposes of commerce, are calculated to arrest our admiration, and to originate a high estimation of its future desti-nation and importance. A cursory examination of the map of the United States, will indicate its importance as a place of business." The French, as well as the various Métis and Indian populations, are thus an afterthought to the sheer materiality of the West as a source of wealth. When Schoolcraft does praise the French, it is only for their willingness to farm or trade like the Anglos and for their occa-sional ability to get the Indians to be "civilized." He also badly misreads the use of "ribbon farms" on the St. Clair River, an area where common-field farming was untenable: "Farms are laid out with a width of only four acres in front and extending eighty acres in depth, which gives a compactness to the settlement that was formerly very advantageous in defending the early settlers against the attacks of the aborigines."[22] Seemingly unaware that Europeans and Indians might live in a state of peace, Schoolcraft betrays an implicit confrontationalism. As studied by historians Leslie Choquette, Carl Ekberg, and John McDermott, the French used ribbon farms to equalize access to water and to retain community relations and neighborly connections.[23]

Finally, despite his efforts to conceal it, the voyageurs seem to have lost interest in Schoolcraft as the expedition progressed. Early on, while traveling in better-known places, they exchange stories, reflecting a moment of bonding and camaraderie. But as Schoolcraft becomes obsessed with resources, especially the copper in the Keweenaw Peninsula in southern Lake Superior, he writes very little about his companions. Sensing his detachment and contempt, they seem to have responded in kind. Later, while at Sault Ste. Marie, Mackinac, and Detroit, Schoolcraft complains constantly of the unwillingness of the French to follow his orders.[24] He writes of their being like Indians, their love of storytelling, and their reluctance to work more than was needed to satisfy their immediate needs— they don't want to get rich. But such ephemeral values are beyond Schoolcraft's material and race-based values system, as I discuss more in chapter 4.

In the Mississippi Valley, the erstwhile Boston missionary Timothy Flint extensively described the French living in St. Genevieve, Missouri. In his descriptions, Flint makes the most of the important linkages between culture, national identity, economic activity, and, not surprisingly, physical demeanor that distinguished the habitants from the Anglos; he does so through a running narrative that bridges idealization and debasement. Flint begins by distinguishing assimilable French merchants, who have "no other differences of character from the people of other Americans," from the "peasants." The peasants then complicate his narrative of the Americanization of the Mississippi Valley by clinging to Old World land-use patterns: "They generally make indifferent farmers. Their cabin indeed shows well at a distance; and the mud daubing is carefully white washed. They have gardens neatly laid out, and kept clean of weeds. Beyond this the establishments of the *petits paysans* are generally sterile and comfortless.—Their ancestors were accustomed to continual intercourse with the savages. . . . They were accustomed to the prompt and despotic mandate and decision of a commandant." The logic here is simple: because they lived like savages and never challenged the priesthood or the aristocracy, the best they can do is to keep their cabins clean. They are not the genuinely reclaimed yeoman farmers/noble savages in the Jeffersonian mold; nor do they want to be. Incessantly distinguishing "they" and "their" from "we" and "our," Flint shows what happens when "idealized" peasants are exposed to the competitive world of modernity—they become "debased," to return to Spurr. After noting their childishness, Flint returns them to nature: "On the whole there is a much nearer assimilation to Indian thoughts and habits than there is in our people. They are slow in adopting our improvements in dress and agriculture, and all that concerns their domestic establishments. They are strongly attached to the ways of their forefathers; . . . They have the national *gaiete du coeur*, the French enviable cheerfulness under all circumstances. They are generally temperate and sober; and from their manner of life better calculated to endure the extremes of heat and cold, than the Americans."[25] The habitants, in short, never stopped being peasants, and peasants assimilate toward Indianness, not Americanness. In terms of how they relate to both the land and other people, they have regained the joyful innocence of childhood but at the cost of the wisdom—and the attendant responsibility—of European privilege.

Darker aspects of this transracialization were more sinister and unsanitary, making the French even more unsuitable for assimilation. Flint's notice that the habitants are "more meagre" and that they have "more tanned and sallow complexions" and an ability to "bow with grace" implies a more cunning underside to the habitants, in whom the regression has been manifested physiologically. Spurr defines "debasement" as "uncivilized society, according to this logic, being little more than the uncivilized mind and body writ large."[26] Flint's commenting on the physical degeneration of the French typifies this pattern. Whites could be either hale and hearty, like the Kentuckians, or sallow and slinking, like the French.

The most notable debaser of the French is Francis Parkman. While setting the stage in *The Conspiracy of Pontiac* (1851), the only volume of *The French and the British in North America* published before the Civil War, Parkman railed against the boundary blurring that was a feature of French culture: "They met the savage halfway, and showed an abundant readiness to mould their own features after his likeness. Count Frontenac himself plumed and dressed like an Indian chief, danced the war-dance and yelled the war-song at the campfire of his delighted allies. It would have been well had the French been less exact in their imitation, for at times they copied their model with infamous fidelity, and fell into excesses scarcely credible." Refusing to recognize the entangled, intercultural nature of frontier experience, Parkman presents French actions as on the wrong side of the savage/civilized rhetorical binary that served imperial discourse so well: "At first, great hopes were entertained that, by the mingling of French and Indians, the latter would be won over to civilization and the church; but the effect was precisely the reverse; for, as Charlevoix observes, the savages did not become French, but the French became savages. Hundreds betook themselves to the forest, never more to return. These outflowings of French civilization were merged in the waste of barbarism, as a river is lost in the sands of a desert."[27] Just as many Frenchmen, of course, settled in ribbon farms along rivers in Illinois, Michigan, or Wisconsin. Even more settled in more inland villages like Vincennes or Cahokia characterized by open-field cultivation or, farther north, in ribbon villages like Detroit, the site of the "conspiracy." Contrarily, many Anglos "became savages" as well. But Parkman was not concerned with such details, only with establishing these debasing and essentialist stereotypes and using them to further his own imperial narrative.

Throughout his massive history of the French presence in North America, Parkman never conceded that the French living in the territorial United States were American but instead consistently identified them as "Canadian," even if they had been born fifty years after Canada's border was moved north of the Great Lakes. Of the habitants living in Detroit, like Flint, Parkman traced a singular progression from idealization to debasement: "The Canadian is usually a happy man. Life sits lightly upon him; he laughs at its hardships, and soon forgets its sorrows. A lover of roving and adventure, of the frolic and the dance, he is little troubled with thoughts of the past or the future, and little plagued with avarice or ambition." At the same time, he "could be little trusted, in the event of an Indian outbreak," and Parkman noted that Pontiac deluded himself that the French and Indian forces could together defeat "the rock-like strength of the Anglo-Saxon."[28] Throughout the seven volumes of *France and England in North America*, Parkman, like Flint, Schoolcraft, Imlay, and the others, described the French as not mature enough to value property above pleasure, too epicurean and hedonistic to be trusted with too much responsibility. Last, because property matters little to peasants, taking it from them is no great crime, since it was never really theirs anyway.

Whether idealized or debased, the frontier French loved to "frolic" —a word seen in dozens of sources—and they lacked the gravitas needed for full participation in the commercializing United States of the antebellum decades. In reference to the habitants, modern historian W. J. Eccles summarized the essential difference: "Unlike in England and its colonies, property was not sacred; it was human rights, not property rights, that were paramount."[29] To that we might add the American scout George Croghan's notion that the

French and Ojibwa had been "bred up together like Children in that Country, & the French have always adopted the Indian customs & manners."[30] The French combination of Old World notions of peasantry and Indian customs of civic nationalism melded into a way of life that resisted commercialization and ran counter to the racial and materialistic underpinnings of the Anglo-Saxon world mission.

Finally, Morris Birkbeck—a pre-Chartist Englishman seeking to establish a colony in western Illinois in which the latest industrial equipment would be used in agriculture—saw the French around Vincennes as an anodyne to his own aspirations: "They cultivate indolence as a privilege: 'You English are very industrious, but we have freedom.' And thus they exist in yawning indifference, surrounded with nuisances, and petty wants, the first to be removed, and the latter supplied by a tenth of the time loitered away in their innumerable idle times."[31] As late as Samuel Gompers's 1896 defense of the eight-hour workday, the argument was that the working poor—if given the chance—would simply waste any free time; hence eighty-hour workweeks were purportedly necessary to protect them from themselves. Furthermore, colonies like Birkbeck's were among the first of the middle-class-intelligentsia-based back-to-the-land movements that led to the formation of many experimental communities in the Midwest, attempts to re-create the virtues of agrarian peasantry without embracing its values.

However, these were usually the inventions of bourgeois Anglo town dwellers armed with a progressive intellectual agenda. Even if they sought the collectivity and peace of the habitant way of life, they would never concede to "peasantry" and so found little use for their French neighbors.[32] Anthony Smith chides such nineteenth-century romantic or pastoral nationalists for substituting the "people," a construction, for the peasantry, a natural phenomenon: "In returning to 'nature,' the intelligentsia also sought to reroot themselves in a particular historical context and sequence (the nation and its homeland), and more generally in the 'movement' and 'progress' of history itself. From this perspective, history and nature become interwoven, and even fused; the natural nation was *ipso facto* the historically evolved nation."[33] For Smith, the paradox is that historical progress is supposedly achieved through a nonspontaneous, contrived effort at refinding the indigene within. Yet most peasants and other indigenes view time as circular rather than linear. As this contradictory narrative was imposed on the habitants, they were found to be not the true *folk* but rather simply usurpers. The *folk* imagined for the Midwest were the yeoman Anglo farmers who aspired to do anything but farm—constantly trading up into other commercial ventures, according to Tocqueville—rather than the complacent habitant. Andrew R. L. Cayton and Peter S. Onuf have observed: "The rise of middle-class values and the institutions of capitalism were synonymous with the rise of the Midwest." They continue: "In the realm of popular culture, in short, the frontier and middle class values had become fused. To the Midwest bourgeoisie, they had always been one and inseparable. The wilderness had, after the inevitable demise of Indians, trappers, squatters and soldiers, become the refuge of industrious, pious, decent people."[34]

The nationalist master narrative, then, worked, and still works, along the axis of class as well as axes of race and ethnicity. The habitants were written out of the range of national and regional economic and social categories by the mid-nineteenth century simply because they never commercialized their land or themselves; there was, ironically, no French bourgeoisie in their communities.

To celebrate—without the gauzy idealization of nostalgia or melodrama—the habitants' lifestyle, then, was to remind the American reading audience of the noncommercial values they embodied and practiced. Throughout the nineteenth century, most Anglo-Americans were farmers, but, as Tocqueville observed, very few of them viewed agriculture as anything other than a business, following the model of Jeffersonian agrarianism in name only. For example, the emphasis on self-sufficiency and individualism was always more symbol than fact: public cooperation always enabled capitalism. In *Internal Improvements*, John Lauritz Larson writes that modern Americans "have been conditioned to see free enterprise and government noninterference as virtues so compelling and self-evident that they must have been the goals of our revolutionary forebears. During the course of the nineteenth century, the advocates of private-sector liberty and laissez-faire policy triumphed so completely in the United States that educated people today commonly are unaware that there ever was a contest."[35] Larson then proceeds to document the extensive role of government interposition in the economy throughout the early nineteenth century.

Nonetheless, the battle between the forces of activist government and laissez-faire was often fought over the memory of the French frontier as a means of contrasting republicanism's emphases on virtue and community with the market's stress on profit and individuality. Moreover, the slow pace of agriculture itself increasingly put it at odds with the rising commercial sensibility. In *The Yankee West*, Susan E. Gray writes that for Anglo settlers in Michigan "farm building was predicated on the assumption of the rapid profitability of commercial agriculture, but they learned quickly to defer their expectations of market integration."[36] In other words, agriculture, then as now, is neither as predictable nor as immediately profitable as other forms of production in an industrial economy. Gray notes that, unable to wait, many settlers in her Kalamazoo County, Michigan, sample population simply left. That is not to say that the sandy, clay-based soil of the Kalamazoo Valley could not to turn a profit—it was just too slow—and the "American way of doing things" was always premised on acceleration, not satisfaction.

The paradox of the iconic status of the yeoman farmer is that its power as national symbol is simultaneously premised on both a deep, sustained engagement with the land and a conceptualization of that land as commodity. Even Tocqueville recognized preindustrial agriculture as a bad fit for the opportunism and impatience of the antebellum era. Of the normal, white Anglo male, he writes: "Agriculture is therefore suited only to those who have already large superfluous wealth, or to those whose penury bids them only seek a bare subsistence. The choice of such a man as we have supposed is soon made; he sells his plot of ground, leaves his dwelling, and embarks in some hazardous but lucrative calling."[37] Once again, the process of normalization in the post-Revolutionary decades offered only opposites: the glow of success or the shame of failure. But even failure indicates that one had tried. Peasants did not even try. Habitants generally engaged in low-level capitalist activity but could be more generally identified as subsistence farmers. However, the negative connotations of "subsistence," and its usual linkage in the taxonomies of anthropology or economics to "primitive" lifeways, reflect the success of the program of denigration conducted against communities like those of the habitants that refused to focus on material acquisition and competition.

Anglos more disturbed than the rather detached Tocqueville by the negative effects on class and opportunity caused by commercial agriculture and its attendant contradictions used the habitant to celebrate alternative values. Margaret Fuller, in "A Summer on the Lakes" (1844), contrasts French and Anglo settlements at Mackinac in Michigan: "How pleasing a sight after the raw, crude, staring assemblage of houses, everywhere else to be met in this country, an old French town, mellow in its coloring and with the harmonious effect of a slow growth, which assimilates, naturally, with objects around it. The people in its streets, Indian, French, half-breed, and others, walked with a leisured step, as those who live a life of taste and inclination, rather than the hard press of business, as in American towns elsewhere."[38] Yet Fuller does not idealize the habitants, removing them from meaning. These are adults living not in Arcadia but in a complex balance of races, religions, and economics, like all Americans at the time. Unlike the others, though, they are doing so in peace with one another. Fuller had come west, like many easterners, to see if all the fantastic things being printed about the Anglo-American frontier in the eastern press were true. She found they were not. She was bored by the Anglo-based towns and the businesses and disappointed by their pervasive materialism. Only in places like Mackinac, or in a village of Irish Catholics in Illinois, does she find people capable of enjoying the western setting without thinking about how to profit from it.

In this way, though, Fuller was exceptional as regards the geographical center of the Anglo-American cultural imagination. By 1840, Boston, rife as it was with the post-Puritan movements of and reactions against Unitarianism and transcendentalism, had become —after actively seeking—the intellectual focus of creative and theological energies of the new nation. In this respect it had displaced Philadelphia, where the momentum of 1776 and 1787 had not been sustained following the demise of Philip Freneau, Benjamin Franklin, and Francis Hopkinson and the pacifist zealotry of the Quakers had been likewise watered down. Nonetheless, in figures such as Charles Brockden Brown, William Dunlap, Joseph Dennie, Samuel Stanhope Smith, and Elihu Hubbard Smith, Philadelphia still represented a formidable rival to Boston. Many of the essential differences between the two cities persisted in terms of how Anglo-American readers and writers imagined the nation—which city best represented its intellectual wellspring? Most New England writers—Bancroft, Cutler, Flint, and Parkman—valued the close transmission of their own Yankee values by defining them in opposition to habitant values. Not surprisingly—if we think of this as a debate over national identity occurring *within* Anglo-America— writers from Philadelphia were much more likely to be like Fuller and embrace the habitants as manifesting an alternative to what they found distasteful in the "universal Yankee nation."

The struggle between Boston and Philadelphia—between Puritan- and Quaker-derived worldviews—is thus often exposed in how the two groups of writers represented the French. For example, we have already seen how descendants of the Quakers—such as the Drakes and Zadok Cramer—established the displacement of the French as characteristic of destructive and hypocritical Anglo-American materialism and self-righteousness. The Quakers, whose first New World refuge was among Roger Williams's Antinomians, themselves refugees from Boston, represented a more democratic and inclusive view, less informed by a scale of vertical ascent to stabilize definitions of races, genders, regions, and classes. In regard to habitants' economics, as opposed to their religious practices, two writers rooted in Pennsylvania, not surprisingly, best countered the New Englanders: in both their public lives and their writings, Henry Marie Brackenridge and James Hall recalled French values to imagine an America less materialistic and more thoughtful.

Brackenridge's biography bears out his attempts to transfer the ideals he learned from the French and the Quakers to national and international issues and contexts throughout the early nineteenth century.[39] He came by his Philadelphia roots indirectly. His widowed father—the Pittsburgh novelist, politician, and all-around troublemaker Hugh Henry Brackenridge, who began writing by collaborating with Philip Freneau at Princeton and in Revolutionary Philadelphia—sent Henry to live among the habitants in St. Genevieve, Missouri, to learn French at age eight in 1794, the same summer Hugh was involved in the Whiskey Rebellion. Albert Gallatin, a French-speaking Swiss immigrant and later Jefferson's secretary of the treasury, brought Henry home a few months later, while returning from a failed foray into the fur trade. Henry then grew up among the Quaker relatives of his father's second wife. After joining the bar in Pennsylvania, Henry drifted west again and journeyed up the Missouri in 1811, publishing his notes and journals of the voyage in _Views of Louisiana_, published by Cramer in Pittsburgh. Next, as circuit judge in Louisiana from 1812 to 1815, Henry aided in the preservation of Roman civil law among the mostly French residents of that state, in opposition to the Yankee speculators' efforts to impose English common law, a division that still stands.

Fluent in Spanish and Portuguese, as well as French and English, Henry was next appointed secretary to the "American Mission in South America," where he argued for the American recognition of mestizo governments after Chilean and Brazilian independence, and returned to Washington in 1818 to lobby for the anti-imperialist Monroe Doctrine. Upon moving to Baltimore, he was elected to the state legislature, where in 1819 he resisted, unsuccessfully, the infamous "Jew Bill." Maryland had on its books—until 1963—laws banning Jews from the full rights of citizenship. Brackenridge led the charge to erase these legislative manifestations of the Anglo-Saxonization of the nation. Not reelected in 1820—his abolitionism also a problem—he went west again.

Andrew Jackson, the territorial governor, took Henry from St. Louis to West Florida to administer the former Spanish colony acquired by the United States in the Adams-Onis Treaty. His job was to manage the transition to American civil law and jurisprudence and to work with Spanish land and property rights cases, a complicated process. Brackenridge's break from Jackson began with his insistence on the rights of a "quadroon" to regain property taken from her father by the outgoing Spanish regime. He lost his judgeship in 1830 when his former patron, Jackson, recognized that Henry's intransigent abolitionism would always be at odds with the onset of widespread plantation slavery in northern Florida during the 1830s.[40] Brackenridge then retired to his wife's family's estate outside Pittsburgh, surfacing to serve briefly in Congress as a Whig in the early 1840s. His defense of his father's and Gallatin's actions in the Whiskey Rebellion in *A History of the Western Insurrection* (1857) put a capstone on a long career of resisting the narrowing and centralizing of identity and culture in the United States.[41] At a time when the categories of American identity were shrinking, his defense of Jewish, French, Spanish, mixed-race, and Indian rights and cultures against the burgeoning Anglo-American nation suggests an ideology of inclusion running throughout Brackenridge's career, a trait that might be traced to his time on the French frontier.

As a writer, his first foray into this arena was in *Views*. In this book, by the term "Illinoix," Brackenridge refers to lands and villages on both sides of the Mississippi, and he assigns himself the task of describing the remaining "inhabitants." After twenty pages of doing so, his final lines, addressed to the habitants themselves, however, render his meaning most clearly. Addressing their fear of losing their culture, their villages, and their land, Brackenridge reassures them with promises of American inclusion: "Louisianians, you have now become truly Americans; never will you again be transferred from one nation to another; IF YOU ARE EVER SOLD AGAIN, IT WILL BE FOR BLOOD. At the same time, let us allow, for those emotions which must naturally be felt. Like two streams that flow to each other from remote and distant climes, although at length, included in the same channel, it is *not* all at once that they will unite their contributary waters, and mingle into one."[42] The most important word here is "not." For Brackenridge, cultural distinctiveness and national citizenship are by no means mutually exclusive. At once, he promises full citizenship and pledges no immediate attempt at cultural integration or assimilation. He suggests that all Anglos would be like himself and *not* try to unite the waters, a promise that other Anglos would not keep. Brackenridge comes to this point after a lengthy description of the conflict between habitant and Yankee lifeways on the Illinoix frontier in the early nineteenth century. What sets him apart is his insistence on the use of the present tense to describe "the original inhabitants," although he uses the past tense to distinguish their lives before and after 1763.

Without idealizing them, Brackenridge depicts a community living in peace with itself, as I noted regarding this passage in the introduction to this book. Read against Hawthorne's famous opening of *The Scarlet Letter*, in which a prison house is among the first Puritan building projects, *Views* presents nearly the opposite: "From the gentle and easy life they led, their manners, and even language, have assumed a certain degree of softness and mildness; the word *paisible*, expresses this characteristic. In this remote country, there were few objects to urge to enterprise, and few occasions to call forth and exercise their energies. The necessaries of life were easily procured, and beggary was unknown. . . . Judges, codes of law, and prisons, were of little use, where such simplicity of manners prevailed, and where everyone knew how far to confide in his neighbour." Note, however, that they were "of little use," not "of no use": these are not Clark's or Imlay's frolicking children. Furthermore, Brackenridge admires that Frenchwomen "will not be considered secondary personages in the matrimonial association." He also notes that "there were hardly any classes in the society. The wealthy and more intelligent, would of course be considered as more important personages, but there was no difference clearly marked." Finally, Brackenridge celebrates the community's inclusive nature: "The number of persons excluded was exceedingly small. What an inducement to comport one's self with propriety and circumspection! The same interest at stake, the same sentiments that in other countries influence the first classes in society, were here felt by all its members." "Catholic, but very far from being bigoted or superstitious," the habitants betray none of the physical degeneration associated by Flint with moral decay: "In their persons, they are well-formed, of an agreeable pleasant countenance." As to the colonial administration, he writes, "The rod of government was so light as scarcely to be felt."[43] In brief, the habitants lived in a state of peaceful anarchy—class tensions, violence, and other sources of anxiety were lightly known.

Then the Americans show up in Brackenridge's narrative, and he concedes that, by sheer bulk and energy, the French islands of bucolic peace will be lost in the turbulent sea of American immersion: "Upon the whole, the American manners, and even language, begin to predominate." More telling is a paragraph on the absorption of the French frontier by the American way of doing things: "The idea of their becoming extinct, by dissolving before a people of a different race, and of losing their *moeurs cheries* might excite unhappy sensations. Already the principal villages look like the towns of the Americans. Are not the customs and manners of our fathers, and of our own youth dear to us all? Would it not fill our hearts with bitterness, to see them vanish as a dream? Sentiments like these, doubtless, sometimes steal into our hearts. They awake, and their HOME has disappeared."[44] Only then does Brackenridge call for retaining French lifeways, so as not to mix the streams—despite the demographic imbalance—with the American way of doing things. He recognizes that, while their loss in an industrializing age seems to be progressing inexorably, the French knew something that the Americans did not about appreciating the natural setting and fecundity of the Illinoix region and that the loss of that knowledge in the name of progress would be, in fact, a step away from wisdom and happiness, albeit a step toward progress and profit.

Brackenridge's career thrice put him a position of authority when it came to the integration of non-Anglos into the American national administrative realm: in New Orleans in 1812, in Baltimore in 1819, and in Florida throughout the 1820s. Based on his behavior in those posts, Brackenridge dedicated much of his career to finding ways to reconcile a diversity of legal systems, land tenure structures, and cultural institutions with membership in the United States. Had Brackenridge been in Illinois in the 1780s, he may have been able to retain French common laws in ways that would have protected the habitants in the same way the Napoleonic Code has protected the Cajuns for the past two hundred years. His actions reflect an idea that the folk *cultures* on the margins of the nation were being threatened with absorption, erasure, or extermination and that the nation would be lessened by their erasure. His activism and writing suggest a resistance to the Anglo-Saxonization of the nation by placing the easygoing peasant alongside—not in the place of—the commercial pioneer as the symbols of the "folk" of America. Implicitly, he recognized that more than one primordial symbol was needed to symbolize the new nation, a paradigm of pluralism.

Likewise in the case of James Hall. Hall's public work to defend and retain the diversity of the nation is replicated and re-created in his stories about the French frontier.[45] Born to an old Philadelphia literary family, Hall moved to Illinois after a controversial but honorable discharge from the navy in 1818. A published poet and journalist since a teenager in various journals edited by his brothers—most notable, Joseph Dennie's *Port-Folio*—Hall lived in Shawneetown and Vandalia as a successful editor. During those years, he was also an internationally published short story writer, cofounder of the Illinois Historical Society, and stubborn Whig politician. Hall was a longtime political ally of John Reynolds's and "a violent anti-Jackson man" in the words of Thomas Ford.[46] In 1833, faced with the triumph of the Jacksonians in Illinois and their successful ethnic cleansing in the Black Hawk War, Hall moved to Cincinnati.

Hall is best known for his short story "The Indian Hater" (1828), but he returned to French villages he had lived in and traveled through in Illinois as a source for his fiction throughout his career. As I discuss at the end of chapter 4, the addition of a central French character in his final reworking of "The Indian Hater," "The Pioneer" (1835), reveals Hall's growing alienation from the racial politics of the American frontier. From the start, however, his sympathy with and affinity for the French appeared in his short stories.[47] As a circuit court judge in the 1820s, Hall traveled extensively in Illinois, an occupation, like Brackenridge's, that brought him not only into contact with the region's demographic diversity but also into intimate contact with the legal aftereffects of the collision between French and Anglo cultures and customs. Two of his early stories, "A Legend of Carondolet" and "The French Village" (both 1828), reveal that Hall's sympathies were with the former. Each story—the first set in the late eighteenth century and the second in the 1820s—records a moment in the transition of Illinois from French to Anglo that describes the habitants' way of life as a missed opportunity.

"Carondolet" centers upon an orphaned Yankee coming west right before the Revolution. Like Hall himself, Timothy Eleazar Tompkins is bright and charismatic, genteel but poor and given to mischief. Tompkins leaves New England in wonderful Franklinian or Emersonian style: "with an elastic step, with a staff in his hand, and a small portmanteau under his arm." In every community he travels to—perhaps as much like New England con men Stephen Burroughs and Ichabod Crane as Franklin himself—Tompkins pretends to have a different profession before moving on. However, the French village of Vuide Pouche (Empty Pocket) stops him and his parvenu ways. Hall interrupts the story to tell the story of the town and to describe its fields at length:

> Although now dwindled into an obscure and ruinous hamlet, remarkable only for its outlandish huts and lean ponies, it was then the goodly seat of a prosperous community. . . . The inhabitants presented, as I suppose, a fair specimen of the French peasantry, as they existed in France, previous to the first revolution. They had all the levity, the kindness, and the contentment which are so well described by Sterne. . . . Though subject, at the date of our tale, to a foreign king, they were as good republicans as if they had been trained up in one of our own colonies. They knew the restraints and distinctions of a monarchy only by report, practicing the most rigid equality among themselves, and never troubling to inquire how things were ordered elsewhere.

In the winters, the young men of the village travel up the Missouri to trade with the Indians, "never dreaming of fatigue or danger."[48] Hall's positive and lengthy description at once answers historians like Flint or Cutler who rejected the French as indolent or wasteful. At the same time, he imagines a habitant role model that allows for political inclusion without cultural erasure—a peasant economy that was not incompatible with the principles of representative government.

To make a long story short, the story becomes the opposite of "Sleepy Hollow." The Yankee con man comes to town, tricks the peasants for a while (pretending to be a doctor), is found out, is expelled, mends his ways, and is allowed to reenter, but only after retraining as a coureur de bois and farmer, like the other young men of the village. That is, the Yankee becomes a Frenchman and is better for it in every way. Hall closes with a comment that must be read beyond the confines of the story: "With his band of adventurous boatmen, he navigated the long rivers of the west, to their tributary fountains; he visited the wigwams of tribes afar off, to whom the white man was not yet known as a scourge."[49] In the longer history behind this aside, implicitly, whites became a scourge only when they were no longer French—when they were Anglos. Having earned "enough," Tompkins retires to the village, "contented." Tompkins learns that while trade is useful, there is more to life than trade. He also learns that exchange with the Indians, as practiced by the French, might not take on the form of exploitation. Hall's story goes against the grain of unilateral Americanization and subtly critiques the master narrative that had led Tompkins west to look to get rich.

In "The French Village," unfortunately, nearly the reverse becomes the sad tale Hall relates. Most Yankees insisted on changing the land rather than changing themselves, and the French hamlet of the story is displaced, like Rip's, by a Yankee town. But the narrative serves mostly as Hall's excuse to describe the French way of life as an important alternative to the forces that predicated its destruction. After describing relations with the Indians, Hall comments:

> The French alone have won them to the familiar intercourse of social life, lived with them in mutual interchange of commerce; and, by treating them as friends and equals, gained their entire confidence. This result, which has been attributed to the sagacious policy of their government is perhaps more owing to the conciliatory manners of that amiable people, and the absence among them of that insatiable avarice, that boundless ambition, that reckless prodigality of human life, that inhuman disregard of public and solemn leagues, in which the conquests of the British and the Spaniards, have marked their footsteps with misery, and blood, and desolation.

Hall's asides, typical of the verbosity of much of the fiction of his era, allow him extensive extraliterary commentary. In this case, his critique of Anglo-American values is set against, again, a description that colors the French as more true to the values of the Revolution than the Anglos: "Here they lived perfectly happy, and well they might—for they enjoyed, to the full extent those three blessings on which our declaration of independence has laid so much stress—life, liberty, and the pursuit of happiness. . . . And as for happiness, they pursued nothing else. Inverting the usual order, to enjoy life was their daily business; to provide for its wants an occasional labour, sweetened by its brief continuance and its abundant fruit." Once again, Hall's detachment of the values of the summer of 1776 in Philadelphia from nineteenth-century Yankee acquisitiveness draws attention to what is, in his opinion, a dangerous drifting away from the nation's potential—Hall's implication is that Jefferson's excision of "property" for "the pursuit of happiness" had been reversed in practice. Hall concludes this section with a lengthy tribute to open-field agriculture. The crux of the story, though, is the infestation of the village by Yankees, a process that chases most of the French farther west or down to Louisiana. Back in the fields, "surveyors were busily employed in measuring off the whole country, with the avowed intention, on the part of the government, of converting into private property those beautiful regions which had heretofore been free to all who trod the soil or breathed the air."[50] Only one old couple remains by the end, and Hall and reader can only mourn what was lost.

In a lesser story, "Michel de Coucy" (1828), Hall weaves a fable of failure when the eponymous habitant tries to become a venture capitalist, borrowing from a Spanish loan shark to do so. In the collective economy of the village, however, most of his peasant French neighbors owe him something, but he cannot bring himself to collect from them to cover his own losses.[51] The subsequent mess he makes of his life—related in comical terms—bears more directly on Hall's linkage of greed and commercialism and, conversely, virtue and agrarianism: the paradox of the profit-minded agrarian. Hall stopped writing fiction after 1835, however, perhaps because he found his message falling on deaf ears. While Hall's other writing bears on later chapters in this book, his greatest value as a fiction writer is in his stories of the French and in his preservation of their realization of the virtues and pleasures destroyed by the greed and rush of the Yankee way of life. Though Hall was not a Quaker himself, his retention of the Quakers' essential worldview, and his recognition of their similarities to the French, represented an important voice for diversity and inclusion on the frontier, a struggle Philadelphia eventually lost to Boston.

Nevertheless, the most famous and sympathetic poem associated with the habitants was written in Boston: Henry Wadsworth Longfellow's "Evangeline" (1847). Although Longfellow's Acadians and the western habitants are categorically and geographically separate, "Evangeline" partook of the dissident rhetoric critiquing Anglo-American commercialism and acquisitiveness at the expense of the pleasures of village life. Lawrence Buell casts the poem upon the context of urbanization and claims that Longfellow spoke for "a generation of displaced persons with intense nostalgia for the kind of small, interdependent, pre-industrial village life portrayed at the poem's start."[52] Rather than in Longfellow's Boston, the poem, significantly, ends in Philadelphia, with the lovers, now an aged nun and a dying voyageur, finally reunited in death.

"Evangeline" begins in idyllic Acadia and turns on the British ethnic cleansing/pogrom of the French after 1755.[53] Like Hall's descriptions of Carondolet or Brackenridge's of St. Genevieve, Longfellow's Acadia is not idealized—pastoral, but not bucolic. Most of Longfellow's narrative then moves to the Mississippi Valley, as the displaced Acadians found their way down to Louisiana, where they became Cajuns. Nonetheless, Evangeline ultimately finds her home among the Quakers in Philadelphia:

> Something at least there was in the friendly streets of that city,
> Something that spake to her heart, and made her no longer a
> stranger;

And her ear was pleased with the Thee and Thou of the
Quakers.

For it recalled the past, the old Acadian country,
Where all men were equal, and all were brothers and sisters.[54]

Longfellow could have just as easily ended in story in his Boston, but he knew the affinitive, connecting values represented by the French were more closely aligned with Quaker openness rather than Puritan austerity, especially given the anti-Catholic riots that wracked Charlestown in the 1830s. A peasant whatever his occupation, Longfellow's habitant-turned-voyageur hero, Gabriel, dies of yellow fever, a martyr to Anglo-American close-mindedness and selfishness, of its willingness to sacrifice the principles of brotherhood for the materialist profits of gain.

Fuller, Hall, Brackenridge, Longfellow, and more pro-habitant writers than space allows mention were pretty much all white Anglo-Saxon Protestants. Furthermore, each was born into privilege in the new nation. Yet each reached out to the habitants of "Illinoix" to challenge the values they saw corrupting the principles of liberty and freedom at the core of the new nation's experiment in republicanism: the double standard of Jacksonian egalitarianism and its simultaneous antiegalitarian exclusions based on race, gender, class, and ethnicity. By demanding that political inclusion not be linked to racial or economic assimilation, they celebrate not only the ethnic diversity represented by the habitants but also the ethos of inclusion and egalitarian cooperation practiced by the habitants.

Gentle as a Woman, though Braver Than a Lion

Voyageurs, Coureurs de Bois, and American Masculinities

THREE

"Am I," I thought to myself, "the same man who, a few months since, was seated, a quiet student of *belles lettres*, in a cushioned arm-chair by a sea-coal fire?"

Francis Parkman, *The Oregon Trail* (1849)

While momentarily trapped in the murky bottom of a Black Hills gully, Francis Parkman soliloquized about his reasons for being there: "Am I . . . the same man who, a few months since, was seated, a quiet student of *belles lettres*, in a cushioned arm-chair by a sea-coal fire?"[1] This query in *The Oregon Trail* (1849) embodies in microcosm a host of anxieties that beset Anglo-American males of the middle and upper classes by the middle of the nineteenth century. Parkman is physically ill, is dependent upon his French and Métis guides, and has proved physically incapable of staying on the trail. The other men around him are physically stronger, healthier, and hardier. What sustains him, however, is that he has sat in that cushioned armchair, the literal lap of privilege, and is just a Harvard undergraduate out for his annual summer jaunt in the wilds—he will return there; these men will never sit in such a chair and will still be out in the wilderness that winter when he is warmed by the fire.

On the trail, however, he learns that he cannot have it both ways, and this is the last of his summer trips into the wilderness. In *Francis Parkman, Historian as Hero*, Wilbur Jacobs describes this conflict as a lifelong issue for Parkman:

> He seems to have had a bipolar personality. At one pole was control over personal behavior involving finances and adherence to Beacon Hill proprieties. The other pole, as seen in his early youth and manhood, involved risk-taking, adventure, Canada, the Indians, the Prairies, and the Oregon Trail. The bipolar axis required, on the one hand, "correct" behavior, gentility, and tight control over funds. And on the other side, there were the opposing elements of spontaneity and love of nature and adventure. The result was a continual inner struggle that could bring on feelings of instability. This ongoing struggle became a keynote in his life.[2]

This bipolarity is also played out in his treatment of the French that reflects the "love and theft" paradigm in American race studies. While Parkman loved the danger and freedom offered by the French ideal personified by Henry Chatillon, his guide on the Oregon Trail, he appropriated this ideal for only selfish purposes—to make his own life more satisfying, not to remedy the plight of the French. Ultimately, as privileged Anglos usually do, he chooses to be "correct" and joins George Bancroft—his mentor—in erasing the French from the frontier.

The trek recorded in Parkman's most famous book was to be his last: later summers found him safely east of the Appalachians. By ending his adventures—accentuated by his particularly bad health—Parkman internalized the paradoxical choice made by all white men who chose to support themselves in bourgeois comfort through their intellectual effort, with all its feminizing creature comforts, rather than in a natural setting by physical labor, with all its empowering material deprivations. Men like Parkman, as they retreated to their cities and firesides, therefore, needed two things: first, a narrative that validated their choices and, second, workers to do the physical labor that supported their comfort. While he chooses the armchair, and while, as an older writer, he would berate and bestialize the working classes, as a younger traveler and writer, Parkman was deeply ambivalent about closing off the physical side of his identity. That ambivalence, a sense of accession to the inevitability of middle-class emasculation, comes through in *The Oregon Trail* in his description of Chatillon.

In the armchair passage and in other places in the book, Parkman identifies a paradoxical double standard characterizing the life of American men in the wake of the nation's commercialization, urbanization, and industrialization. Parkman's query represents men's limited choices: the bestializing physicality of labor or the feminizing emasculation of privilege. Before the 1820s, such distinctions were less rigid: the mostly rural demographics and the lack of conspicuously consumable luxuries forced an integration of the physical and the cerebral for most men and put the elite and the peasants in greater contact with each other. In a pre- or nonindustrial or commercial setting, a man's physicality, stamina, and general hardiness defined masculine identity. Such men could be sensual and, in the terms of Mary Chapman and Glenn Hendler, were free to be "sentimental"—their masculinity was so abundantly proven in other ways that they could cry, publicly. After citing George Washington's unabashed public tearing-up, Chapman and Hendler then trace out the fact that, as the nineteenth century progressed, crying and other forms of sentimental self-expression became taboo.[3]

This is because, like so many cultural components of the times, the socially acceptable terms of masculine identity and behavior shrank. If Parkman cries in that gully, or over the loss of a horse, his masculinity is called into question in ways Washington's would not have been—it is not buttressed by the ineluctable maleness of physical fortitude. If Parkman is to stay in his chair, he had better not cry. Simultaneously, the physical labor needed in an industrializing, commercializing society is usually drained of its moral or intellectual dignity: routine that dulls the mind and the senses. Each option—bourgeois or laborer—represents the class-based categorization and compartmentalization of male roles in the social hierarchization intrinsic to industrial production and consumption.[4] A man at a desk was unfitted for the factory; a man in a factory was unfitted for the desk.

In 1817, Morris Birkbeck wrote that "America was born in a cabin."[5] By the 1830s, however, the sons of Anglo-American men born in cabins were born in houses, hospitals, or tenements. The men themselves were working more in offices and factories, spatially and emotionally removed from the distinct value associated with physical strength and stamina in the farm or workshop setting. The traditional, preindustrial male was supposed to be able to do anything and everything and not complain about it, but he was allowed to cry. However, with the coming of industrial capitalism came the need for intense specialization and professionalization, and the rules of manhood shifted in very confusing ways, ways that Americans on the whole were (and often still are) reluctant to discuss—men are not supposed to complain. Among the reading classes, this shift bred nostalgia for the supposedly simpler masculine identities of earlier eras. A product of this anxiety, James Fenimore Cooper's Leatherstocking—Natty Bumppo—was and is attractive because of his hypermasculine ability with the gun and his attachment to natives and nature.

However, the virginal Natty is an *isolato*—constantly fleeing the sound of the ax and finally vanishing on the prairie: his constant moves west actually enclose "natural" masculinity by displacing it to an exotic place and a fading past. More than a century later, Cooper's narrative was rephrased in Henry Nash Smith's and R. W. B. Lewis's genealogies: the last-century natural man still in touch with moral righteousness as the figure of both balance and nostalgia.[6] Yet the draw to do what Natty did—even for a moment—has always exerted a powerful pull on middle-class Anglo-American men: to "play Indian," to slum, to reconnect with the more coherent and gratifying characteristics of masculinity and emotion they themselves had relegated to the lower classes and the "inferior" races. Scholars such as Dana D. Nelson, Philip Deloria, Eric Lott, and David Roediger identify such impulses as racist appropriations of minority cultures to serve white needs. As they show, these anxieties are traceable to the beginning of the industrial era.[7]

By the 1830s, leisure-class white men often actively sought in the racially dangerous frontier setting opportunities to test or discover their manhood in ways not offered in their everyday lives.[8] They went to sea, joined the military, or accepted other challenges along those lines, where risk and exposure were still bracketed by class, whiteness, and the ability to return, at will, to the armchair. All these tourists sought what Parkman describes: "Here society is reduced to its original elements, the whole fabric of art and conventionality is struck rudely to pieces, and men find themselves suddenly brought back to the wants and resources of their original natures."[9] Testing oneself in such a context supposedly authenticates one's linkage to identifiably atavistic virtues—our original natures. But in almost every case, measures are taken to mitigate the original "wants and resources": the comforts of the fort, the forecastle, or the resort are never too distant. Parkman was the most famous of these men in his century. Three generations before Theodore Roosevelt's advocacy of the "strenuous life," young white men seeking something more than the emasculation of the office and the hearth went west looking for what they thought they had lost—their misplaced masculinity.

What the tourists found were Frenchmen: voyageurs (river men, laborers) and coureurs de bois (woodsmen, independent traders).[10] Virtually every account written in English of traveling, trading, pioneering, hunting, settling, or surveying on the early nineteenth-century frontier is saturated by men with French names. They seem to have been ubiquitous between Ohio and Oregon—and often their precise racial identity was impossible to ascertain. Many worked as fur traders during the winter season and spent the off-season as habitants. Others were descendants of habitants pushed west out of Acadia, Illinois, Indiana, and Michigan after Anglo occupation and land seizure. Many were adopted into Indian tribes, married Indian women, and split their lives between Indian villages and white towns, as Frenchmen had been doing for almost two hundred years by the time Parkman spent his summer vacation on the prairie.

Their representation in Anglo-American texts, however, reveals how Anglo masculinity sought to repair itself on the "frontier"— Anglo men venturing to test themselves on that mythic line between savagery and civilization. These tourists, that is, acted as ethnologists of a sort, participatory journalists, who in defining the French Other defined themselves as well. Many simply defined themselves in opposition to "degenerate" Frenchmen by portraying them in terms we have already encountered, white men retrogressed to savagery, and they simply imagined places for them in the class-based scale of importance they supposedly came west to leave behind. Parkman, Lewis and Clark, Washington Irving, and many others simply transferred industrial-era class-based distinctions to the French frontier through their descriptions of the divisions of labor in the camps and on the trails. Such narratives reiterate the standard hierarchizations of races, classes, and genders. Parkman and the others find their a priori assumptions about their social, cultural, and racial inferiors affirmed in the semiforeign setting of the multilingual and multiracial West—erasing its Otherness and potential to destabilize the nation as it absorbed these peoples and places.

At the same time, other writers found no demarcated frontier, no line between this and that. Instead they found and wrote about a series of communities stretching over a thousand miles from the Wabash River to the Grand Tetons in which diverse races, ethnicities, and values were hopelessly and fortunately entangled—an alternative to the constricting identity from which they sought release. Not surprisingly, these writers found in the Frenchmen models of resistant masculinity based in a refusal of the categories of industrial or commercial identity. Yet unlike Natty, and unlike the habitant peasantry, these Frenchmen were not vanishing or locked in a distant past: they fulfilled a function in the American economy, participating in the exchange and profit-based rituals of the fur trade or becoming paid guides for Anglo or European hunters and self-explorers. These Frenchmen accept the terms of professionalization and the limits imposed on their masculine freedom by the necessity of specialization in the commercializing American economy as it moved into the Rocky Mountain West in the decades before the Civil War.

However, they do so on their own terms, dipping in and out of participation in commercial enterprises to retain individual initiative and self-definition, according to their own needs and those of their families. In this way, they represent a critique of the encroaching systemization of American life in general and masculinity in particular. From these Frenchmen, Anglo readers were meant to learn that participation in the imperial nation was a choice, not an obligation, and that one could limit the terms of participation in ways that allowed the reintegration of the physical and moral dimensions of manhood. In the end, those who portray the Frenchmen as responsible *men*—and not as essentialized or polarized avatars of virtue or vice—implicitly argue that they represent a means of restoring balance to men's lives. The following sections examine voyageurs and coureurs de bois as they were used both to affirm and to critique the systematization of masculine identity intrinsic to industrial-era capitalism. Even within *The Oregon Trail*, Parkman writes on both sides of this issue.

In Chatillon, he finds a truly admirable figure whose presence resonates throughout the book. This restorative and libratory invocation of what Dana D. Nelson would call "fraternity"—based in the concept of Revolutionary brotherhood—is created between the ill and anxious but wealthy and willing young Francis Parkman and the strong and illiterate but compassionate and wise Chatillon.[11] In the book, it is a model for man-to-man relationships so elusive in the competition-based national manhood paradigm Nelson describes as permeating the United States in the antebellum decades, restoring the potential for true and constructive bonding between men. The first section of this chapter affirms Parkman's portrayal of Chatillon through the corroborating descriptions of coureurs de bois offered by Métis historian William Warren.

As I describe in the second section, however, in this same book and later as a historian, Parkman also affirmed the stratifying patterns Nelson relates as the opposite of Revolutionary "fraternity"— competition: "My argument turns our attention instead toward the antidemocratic structure of national manhood, and particularly two of its key entailments: first, that the process of identifying with national manhood blocks white men from being able efficiently to identify socioeconomic inequality as structural rather than individual failure, thereby conditioning them for market and professional competition; second and more importantly that it entails a series of affective foreclosures that block those men's more heterogeneous democratic identifications and energies."[12] By this reckoning, the poverty—material, moral, and intellectual—of the lesser Frenchmen, like that of all the lower classes and "inferior" races, is understood as the result of individual rather than structural deficiencies. Moreover, the young Parkman distances himself from the ethnic and racial heterogeneity they represent, since affirming them as equals or brothers would reveal the incompleteness of his own fragile masculinity. As Parkman turned from travel writing to history, all of his Frenchmen come to resemble the skilled and unskilled laborers of *The Oregon Trail*, Reynal and Delorier, and the absence of any Chatillon-type characters reflects his willful abandonment of the destabilizing potential the guide embodied. Both Reynal and Delorier are lower down on the book's implicit social and racial hierarchy, a view of Frenchmen in general that reflects the influence of his friend and mentor George Bancroft. For both historians, most Frenchmen were incapable of critical thought, sustained conversation, or the quiet dignity that denotes a potential for social advancement. Hedonistic and conniving, they embody an inferior breed, in need of governance by the Anglo-Saxon elite. This pervasive image found its roots not only in Parkman but also, as I discuss, in the writing of Captains Lewis and Clark and Washington Irving.

As it reflects *both* the heterogeneous Métis sensibility of Warren and the homogenizing Anglo-Saxonism of the captains and Irving, Parkman's trajectory from sympathy to exclusion set the tone for Anglo-America's transition from embracing to expelling the French frontiersman and all he represented in the larger processes of enclosing American masculinity. In the end, Parkman simply abandoned the conflicts personified by Chatillon, just as Anglo-Americans in general did not want to remember the frontier French more generally and how they had embodied a more integrated and less fragmentary masculinity in comparison with their own confined and comfortable lives.

The final image Parkman creates of Henry Chatillon complicates any false notion of Natty-like noble savagery that his readers might have expected: "On the evening before our departure, Henry Chatillon came to our rooms at the Planters' House to take leave of us. No one who met him in the streets of St. Louis, would have taken him for a hunter fresh from the Rocky Mountains. He was very neatly and simply dressed in a suit of dark cloth; for although since his sixteenth year he had scarcely been for a month together among the abodes of men, he had a native good taste and a sense of propriety which always led him to pay great attention to his personal appearance." Chatillon's ability to integrate the vitality of his experience in nature with the compromises necessary to urban socialization sets him apart from both the Anglos and the lesser Frenchmen. His ability to wear the costume of the civilized white man is complemented by Parkman's description of his strict professionalism in a concluding footnote:

Yet whoever had been his employers, or to whatever closeness of intercourse they might have thought fit to admit him, he would have never changed the bearing of quiet respect which he considered due to *bourgeois*. If sincerity and honor, a boundless generosity of spirit, a delicate regard to the feelings of others, and a nice perception of what was due to them are the essential characteristics of a gentleman, then Henry Chatillon deserves the title. . . . In spite of his bloody calling, Henry was always humane and merciful; he was gentle as a woman, though braver than a lion.[13]

Parkman's use of "bourgeois"—here and throughout—reminds us of its history: the person doing the hiring. Yet Parkman and Chatillon transcended that hierarchical arrangement to connect on the level of brothers, or so Parkman assumed. Chatillon's ability to wear a suit as well as buckskin, and Parkman's use of "gentleman," affirm him as a man who can move between the worlds of the French and Indian middle ground and the Anglo-American commercial sphere. Chatillon's experience during his summer as Parkman's hired guide tested the boundaries of each. Chatillon—while once compared to Natty[14]—is a professional hunter and guide, a married man, and a compassionate traveling companion: everything Parkman left his armchair and went west to find. While on the trail, Parkman accepts Chatillon as a brother with whom he is not in competition and whose differences are not markers of inferiority,

Early on, Chatillon learns that his "squaw"—the mother of his children—is dying. Parkman agrees to a detour, but the ill Parkman cannot accompany him to her village. Even through this, though, Parkman admires Chatillon's resolve and professionalism. The episode establishes Chatillon as a compassionate man: with the woman, he has been "connected for years by the strongest ties which in that country exist between the sexes." When he hears she is failing, "Henry's manly face became clouded and downcast." Upon returning after her death, "Henry seemed dejected. The woman was dead, and his children must henceforward be exposed, without a protector, to the hardships and vicissitudes of Indian life."[15] Nonetheless, Chatillon's ability to own and display his grief and fear—a range of emotion and sentiment inaccessible to Anglo-American office dwellers—is partner to his physicality. His emotional wealth is the envy of the materially wealthy and socially elite.

Chatillon—as both actual man and Parkman's embellishment—was a type of frontier Frenchman whose presence up through the middle of the century is confirmed in dozens of other sources. By their emotional displays and their compassion toward their children and mothers (Parkman's trip is delayed when Chatillon visits his mother in St. Louis), these men diverge from the images of fatherhood and masculinity that were increasingly dominant in the antebellum decades. In *A History of the Ojibway People* (1852), William Warren—an Anglo, French, and Ojibwa Métis—provides the most cogent description of the fur trade as a site of alternative, multivalent masculine possibilities, full of Chatillon's precursors.[16] In Warren's description of his own coureurs de bois forefathers, he constructs a version of manhood that integrates the values of the middle ground with the inevitable commercialization and specialization of Anglo-America, just as Parkman did with Chatillon.

The coureurs de bois, it must be noted, were independent traders, unaligned with any of the massive, multinational fur-trading companies whose conflicts characterized life on the western waters throughout the early nineteenth century. By the time Lewis and Clark arrived, the Chouteau family—who arrived only after 1763—had organized and in fact commercialized most of the French labor on the western waters. By the time Irving was writing, John Jacob Astor's American Fur Company had further partnered with the Chouteaus in creating a virtual monopoly. In contrast, men like Chatillon and Warren's ancestors, either by maintaining their independence or by working on short-term contracts with the fur companies, could maintain a degree of autonomy and do things like work as guides, if they chose, or stay among their wife's tribes, if they chose.[17] The eponymous mogul commissioned Irving's *Astoria*

(1836), just as he likewise employed Henry Rowe Schoolcraft, and neither had a bad thing to say about the exploitative labor practices in the fur trade, as opposed to Warren.

Like Parkman, Warren was both economically privileged and physically fragile.[18] Like Parkman as well, Warren sought in history writing—the one form of belles lettres invested with a remasculinizing transformative power—a means to reintegrate the fragmented masculinity of privileged men, especially as each wrote in the midst of eroding health. Each wrote, then, with an acute awareness of the issues of masculine identity set in the personal context of an "unmanly" illness and the physically undemanding world of belles lettres. Subsequently, the idea of reintegrated male identity is a consistent and deliberate subtext in both Parkman's *The Oregon Trail* and Warren's *History*, one reflected in the celebration of men who combine their roles as loving husbands and fathers with manly virtue and physicality.

Warren begins by taking a longer historical view of the subject. His recognition of the French model begins with the acceptance by the French of Ojibwa forms of masculinity and leadership:

> The French understood their divisions into clans, and treated each clan according to the order of its ascendancy in the tribe. They conformed also to their system of governmental polity, of which the totemic division formed the principal ingredient. . . . In this important respect, the British and American government, especially, have lacked most wofully [*sic*]. . . . This short-sighted system has created nothing but jealousies and heart-burnings among the Ojibways. It has broken the former commanding influence of their hereditary chiefs, and the consequence is, that the tribe is without a head or government, and it has become infinitely difficult to treat with them as a people.[19]

The French recognize the categories of Ojibwa masculinity and leadership without imposing their own, establishing an egalitarian basis for intercultural relations based on looser and transformable definitions of either. Warren's narrative of the decades of French-Ojibwa interchange establishes a relation of fraternity between the two.

This becomes most apparent near the end, where Warren identifies a few "Yankee" coureurs de bois that took on the French model of masculinity:

> The American fur traders, many of whom were descended from respectable New England families, did not consider their dignity lessened by forming marital alliances with the tribe, and the Ojibway women were of so much service to their husbands, they so easily assimilated themselves into their modes of life, and their affections were so strong, and their conduct so beyond reproach, that these alliances, generally first formed by the traders for present convenience, became cemented by the strongest ties of mutual affection. They kindly cherished their Indian wives, and for their sakes, as well as for the sake of the children whom they begat, these traders were eventually induced to pass their lifetime in Ojibway country. They soon forgot the money-making mania which first brought them into the country, and gradually imbibing the generous and hospitable qualities of the Indians, lived only to enjoy the present.[20]

Aware that he very visibly was the result of this cultural and genetic blending, Warren celebrates this transformation. More important, his placement of so powerful a passage so close to the end of his book demonstrates his intent to participate in more than a historiographic exhumation of the French and Ojibwa experience in the fur trade on the upper Great Lakes. On one level, this transformation is held out to his Anglo readers as a lesson in their own potential, that they too can escape the traps and trappings of material gentility and its emasculating effects.

On another level, the *History*, like *The Oregon Trail*, might also be read as a very personal struggle for the author's masculinity and legitimacy in the context of an Anglo-American culture fully set on enclosing each. Suffering from tuberculosis, Warren traveled east to find a publisher in 1852, knowing that New York publications were more present in national debates than texts published regionally. Unsuccessful, Warren died on the way back to Minnesota, leaving the *History* unpublished until the Minnesota Historical Society brought it out in 1888. Amid the slew of both antebellum and post-bellum Indian ethnographic writings, however, Warren's work stands out for its intercultural perspective. Neither wholly French, Anglo, nor Ojibwa, Warren—raised as both an Anglo Warren in a New York boarding school and a Métis Cadotte in the "wigwams" of his mother's people—confesses at one point that his book will come to focus on his families and their centrality in the region's history. Moreover, in his preface, Warren claims both the outdoors masculinity of his ancestors and an awareness of his own condition: "The following work may not claim to be well and elaborately written, as it cannot be expected that a person who has passed most of his life among the wild Indians, even beyond what might be termed the frontiers of civilization, can wield the pen of an Irving or a Schoolcraft. But the work does claim to be one of truth, and the first work written from purely Indian sources, which has probably ever been presented to the public. . . . Succeeding this, the writer proposes, if his precarious health holds out, and life is spared to him, a collection of their mythological traditions."[21] Recognizing himself, like Parkman, as a victim of emasculating maladies that mirror, for modern readers, crippled industrial-era manhood more generally, Warren represents history writing as an act of heroism. To describe the French and Ojibwa achievement of a century of multiracial cohabitation, he endeavors to integrate in his text the virtues of all three sets of ancestral traditions, doing on paper, from his deathbed, what they had done in fact, in the north woods and waters.

Warren's historiographic method—blending archival documents, interviews with natives, and personal and family history—mirrors the social entanglement of the French-Ojibwa community he means to celebrate. On an intertextual level, Warren's equation of French interculturalism and virtuous masculinity articulates a paradigm wherein open-mindedness and personal flexibility stand opposed to the Anglo model of determined individuality and unwavering rigidity. As he describes French-Ojibwa relations in the Lake Superior region as a personal family history, he carefully describes his own ancestors' balance of Indian and French behaviors. When describing his Ojibwa ancestors—such as Keesh-ke-mun, an Ojibwa chief who resisted Tecumseh's efforts to pull the Lake Superior Ojibwa into the War of 1812—Warren is careful to present them as articulate and reasonable. At the same time, his French and Anglo ancestors must be represented as fully able to embrace the strenuous and arduous conditions of village life—adapting themselves to the Ojibwa rather than the reverse. Moreover, throughout, Warren repeatedly admires Anglo men who form loving marriages based on partnership with, rather than dominion over, Indian women.

While this sounds naïve—playing Indian to mimic noble savagery—Warren seems aware of the gender-based motivation at the heart of Anglo-based violence and avarice. Of the coureurs de bois, he writes: "Their aim was not so much that of gain as of pleasure, and the enjoyment of the present life, and mainly in this respect will be found the difference between the nature of their intercourse with the natives of America, and that which has been carried on by the English and Americans, who, as a general truth, have made Mammon their God, and have looked on the Indian but as a tool or means of obtaining riches, and other equally mercenary ends." "Pleasure," as Warren establishes in many places throughout the book, is founded, even for coureurs de bois, on virtuous behavior: loyalty to one's Ojibwa wife, honest trading, and being a father to one's mixed-race children. Warren then concedes that his equation of the coureur de bois and the Indian, in the conventions of American culture, might seem anomalous: "Some of my readers may be surprised at my thus placing the Indian on a par with the laughter-loving Frenchman, for the reasons that he has ever been represented as a morose, silent, and uncommunicative being. It is only necessary to state that this is a gross mistake, and but a character (far different from his real one), assumed by the Indian in the presence of strangers, and especially white stranger in whom he has no confidence here."[22] At stake here are the principles and standards of male public behavior. The myth of the stoic Indian, the noble savage, is here written off as a mere facade, and Indian masculinity, like the French version, is based on kindness, humor, and respect for others. Warren understands that stereotypes not only misrepresent; they also misinform, creating inaccurate and oversimplified models of and for the behavior of the reader. Both the silent Indian and the laughing coureur de bois are masks—fabrications, fronts put up by marginalized, suspicious peoples from whom the dominant imperial culture has forced a choice. They can seek inclusion in the dominant culture and accept their subsequent marginality and second-class citizenship, or, like colonized peoples often have, they can simply wear the mask expected in public and embrace the privacy of the periphery, the autonomy of neglect and invisibility.[23]

Wearing the mask in public becomes a means of protecting, in private, an identity and a code of behavior outside the norms and expectations of the imperial culture. Warren describes both coureur de bois and Indian behavior in these terms: each performs the stereotype in public to cordon off the more important parts of their lives from those they consider corrupt or, more important, meaningless. This act of mimicry decenters the imperial culture and allows the presumably contained and colonized middle-ground ethos created by the French and the Indians to survive, as Parkman testifies, for at least eighty years after the fall of the French government in 1763 until he met Chatillon in 1846. Yet when he first meets him, the guide is wearing his mask: they have very little dialogue until the second half of the book. In the opening chapters, some British hunters traveling with the party capture Parkman's imagination: they represent Parkman's own lingering colonial desire for a patrimonial model of male behavior within the Anglo-American repertoire from a British source, the former colonial parent. Yet they inevitably fail to impress him, and they hunt badly. Adrift, Parkman turns to Chatillon.

Only after this does Parkman move Chatillon to the center of the narrative in the final one hundred pages. Only at this point has Parkman penetrated Chatillon's mask to understand the individualized nature of the Frenchman's masculinity and that its strength came from its disregard for the coercions of "structural" cultural or economic influences. In fact, to accentuate Chatillon's character, Parkman smudges even more the difference between French and Anglo masculinities by introducing an Anglo-American deserter from the Mexican War, whom Chatillon nicknames Tete Rouge. Although "Anglo-Saxon," Tete Rouge is everything Chatillon is not: weak, indecisive, and undignified.[24] If *The Oregon Trail* were a novel, Parkman's thematic and structural unity—his use of such a counterdiscurive foil to undermine essentialist assumptions—would be considered the mark of a fine novelist. As it is travel book, however, the credit must go to Parkman's selective use of his materials. The paired contrasts between Chatillon and the British "Captain" early on and with Tete Rouge near the end reveal that individuality and self-control are, ironically, universal rather than Anglo virtues.

Moments demonstrating Parkman's self-conscious awareness of masculinity as a vital issue in the narrative litter *The Oregon Trail*. First, his constant illness "unmans" him repeatedly, and terms like "manly" and "masculine" or, contrarily, "feminine" or "womanly" creep into his commentary at nearly every turn. For example, when describing "white" civilization to the Sioux, he begins: "All the men were brave warriors." But then he thinks to himself: "Here I was assailed by a sharp twinge of conscience, for I fancied I could perceive a fragrance of perfumery in the air, and a vision rose before me of white-kid gloves and silken moustaches with mild and gentle countenances of many fair-headed young men." Later, Parkman, while recuperating from a bout of sickness, deplores himself for reading the effeminate Lord Byron's poetry rather than the more masculine

Old Testament or Shakespeare. Byron's verse, Parkman comments, "achieved no more signal triumph than that of half beguiling us to forget the pitiful and unmanly character of its possessor."[25]

Parkman traveled west aware of the softness of Anglo manhood and meant to define his own transformative experience on the prairie as reinvesting him with his manhood without reducing him to moral or physical brutishness. In Chatillon, he found a brother upon whom he hoped, in a way, to model his own ambitions for overcoming his own unmanly cultural and personal failings. However, as much as Parkman admires Chatillon, he cannot allow the coureur de bois himself to cross the Mississippi: "A certain species of selfishness is essential to the sternness of spirit which bears down opposition and subjects the will of others to its own. Henry's character was of an opposite stamp."[26] As a Frenchman, essentially incapable of the gravitas needed for leadership, Chatillon must remain marginal, a lesson in dignity, but ultimately not a role model. It is important to note that this statement comes in a footnote, as if Parkman finally could not take full ownership of its cowardice.

Just as he had in the gully, Parkman expresses the paradox of Anglo masculinity: he assumes as inevitable the Anglo conquest of the West—since even a Frenchman as strong as Chatillon will not do it—but he asserts that doing so will require the Anglos to reassemble the traits of mature masculinity Chatillon personifies, combining them with the sternness, selfishness, and restlessness of the Anglo. While Chatillon's weaknesses are part of his Frenchness, his strengths must be accessible to both Parkman and his readers. Parkman's initial introduction of Chatillon had already made any other outcome impossible. After a long litany of his virtues, Parkman concludes: "His manly face was a mirror of perfect uprightness, simplicity, and kindness of heart; he had, moreover, a keen perspective of a character, and a tact that would preserve him from error in any society. Henry had not the restless energy of the Anglo-American.... I have never, in the city or the wilderness, met a better man than my noble and true-hearted friend, Henry Chatillon."[27] Written retrospectively, this passage must be matched with the description of Chatillon in a suit discussed earlier in this chapter. The Frenchman's "manly" face bears striking significance for understanding the depth of Parkman's initial conviction that masculine identity be universal. What holds Chatillon back is his Frenchness, that is, his lack of "sternness of spirit" and "restless energy," the virtues—burdens, perhaps—he identifies as distinctly Anglo.

On the level of method, like Warren as well, Parkman sought in writing a book rooted in both documentary sources and arduous personal experience the authorial equivalent of Chatillon's ability to thrive "in any society," in buckskin or in a suit, in the gully or the armchair. Each sought to make the reader forget the sickly, "pitiful and unmanly" condition of the author by linking himself— genetically or fraternally—with men more directly able to reintegrate the physical and moral dimensions of full manhood. Both writers commonly recognized that the demythologized coureur de bois transcended the categories of "civilized" and "savagery" by setting the terms of his involvement in the systems of specialization as Anglo-America crept westward. Again, the goal is transformation—both Warren and Parkman write aware that their readers are unlikely to run off to the wilderness and become coureurs de bois: in fact, in their very interest in reading, their readers are always already part of the bourgeoisie.

For Warren and Parkman, the coureur de bois's principles of dignity, sociability, adaptability, fraternity, and compassion matter most. Each found in the behavior of the coureurs de bois virtues transferable from the wilderness to the city, where they might engender a more holistic and less fragmented way of imagining manhood. Once individual men resist the structural threats to their masculinity and take responsibility for their roles as leaders or followers, the coureur de bois might then exist in a bond of egalitarian, valuesbased brotherhood with the bourgeois, a relation that supersedes notions of employer and employee, conqueror and conquered, management and labor, to find a model of male-to-male relation based on something other than competition. Unfortunately, Parkman's intellectual and moral ability to sustain this egalitarian vision was as weak as his arthritic body.

Despite his articulation of the fraternal model, Parkman more often reconstructed Anglo masculinity in *The Oregon Trail* by placing it above other versions of French manhood. Against these, he gleefully compares himself and finds himself superior, abandoning masculine brotherhood for the conventions of hierarchy. *The Oregon Trail* is usually described as a travel book, and most travel books primarily describe the place to which the traveler has gone. Perhaps, then, misnamed, *The Oregon Trail* is really about Francis Parkman, as his narrative intrusions and biases intervene in the text even more than those of most Victorian travelers.[28] To use Anne Tyler's well-known phrase, he is an accidental tourist in that his goal is not knowledge of the exotic but rather an expansion of the familiar.

The biggest baggage Parkman brought west was his ideas concerning class and hierarchy. The mostly individualized Chatillon becomes the exception that proves the rule, and Parkman spends even more time making sure every other Frenchman he meets is his inferior. Just as a factory owner imagined himself as superior to his workers, Parkman likewise elevated and affirmed himself by denigrating his other *engagees*. It has been noted that Parkman's description of the eastern woodland Indians in *France and England in North America* is inaccurate, that he simply transposed his memory of the Sioux from *The Oregon Trail* onto the Iroquois in a sweeping stereotypical conflation.[29] If he did so, then he also treated the French the same way: the French soldiers of *France and England in North America* are based on *The Oregon Trail*'s servants, the other, lesser and unindividualized Frenchmen of the rank and file, both doomed to vanish before Anglo-Saxon inevitability.

Most voyageurs and soldiers in *France and England in North America* bear little or no resemblance to Chatillon, a coureur de bois, and this class-based distinction matters greatly in Parkman's later work. Rather, they seem more like the lesser Frenchmen from his earlier book: Delorier, an annoying cook, and Reynal, a lesser voyageur with none of Chatillon's dignity or wisdom. If in Chatillon Parkman had found a "brother," a means of reinvesting male-to-male relations with egalitarian fraternity, in Delorier and Reynal Parkman simply returns to the received hierarchies of the competitive industrial model he supposedly went west to escape. The pattern of transposing industrial class identities onto the French was established in at least three other preceding and well-known sources. Parkman had undoubtedly read the Biddle edition of *The History of the Expedition of Captains Lewis and Clark* and the three western adventures of Washington Irving, *A Tour of the Prairies* (1835), *Astoria* (1836), and *The Adventures of Captain Bonneville* (1837), before his summer on the trail, and he simply extended their stereotypical representations, signaling his reversion to "structural" forms of verticality and his rejection of the horizontal model of individualized fraternity.

In fact, a striking pattern emerges in each: paired sets of lower-class Frenchman—hunters and cooks, skilled and unskilled laborers. The pair in Parkman consists of Reynal and Delorier; in Irving's *Tour*, Antoine and Tonish; and in Biddle's *History*, Toussaint Charboneau and the expedition's many "Frenchmen." Dana Nelson's comment on Biddle's edition of Lewis and Clark summarizes the narrative the editor built atop the captains' journal and might be applied to Irving and Parkman as well. In crafting an "accumulating theme about disciplined and disciplinary manhood," he "offered a space for U.S. men to imagine dominance—over women—and to enact dominance—over Indians."[30] And, I would add, Frenchmen and other ethnic minorities. The lesser Frenchmen stand in need of discipline and so are in no position themselves to discipline women and nonwhites. In turn, these Anglo writers discipline and police the lines of class distinction at the expense of ethnic distinction or value. An examination of how industrial class identities were transposed onto the nonindustrial French in publications universally well received by the antebellum American readership reveals much about how ethnic and class identities could be simultaneously distinguished and then merged in the same processes of social and economic "Americanization."

First, the common assignment of the voyageurs—Charboneau, Antoine, and Reynal—to the role of skilled laborer draws the essential line that would inform class relations throughout the industrial era. Although this group represents the upper echelon of the laboring classes, it is still in need of the discipline and guidance of the Anglo elite. The inability of these men to become "gentlemen" reveals an early version of the glass ceiling—the elevation of Chatillon notwithstanding—that limited the terms of social mobility and contributed to the solidification of the upper class by further constricting the terms of membership. This group's inability to change and develop through time and across generations troubled the progressive stories the Anglos wanted to tell. In these decades, the United States exploded westward, and contact between the French and the Anglos became at once both commonplace and an event that occurred farther to the west every year. Despite that change, each of the Anglo texts tells something of the same story: the transference of difference based in ethnicity to discipline based in class. The point is, despite the intimacy of living and working in close contact with the Anglo bourgeois, the voyageurs remained unchanged and incapable of self-government: because they are nonassimilable as Frenchmen, intractable and so in need of some kind of categorization or narrativization, they were reimagined as workers. As such, they have a place in the structural monolith of Anglo-America's story about itself, albeit a subordinate one, disciplined rather than different.

Nicholas Biddle, with some help from Paul Allen (associate of William Dunlap and Charles Brockden Brown), spent about five years editing the journals of Lewis and Clark, a process complicated by Lewis's suicide in 1809.[31] To explain this failure in Lewis's masculine identity, Biddle opens with Thomas Jefferson's minibiography, "A Life of Captain Lewis." Jefferson explains that, while he had noted Lewis's depressive tendencies as a family pattern, "during his western expedition, the constant exertion which that required of all the faculties of body and mind, suspended these distressing affections; but after his establishment in St. Louis in sedentary occupations, they returned upon him with redoubled vigour."[32] Jefferson's distinction of the life of "exertion" from the sedentary life of the administrator sets the pattern Parkman would continue—the gully or the armchair. Once Lewis's masculinity was confined, his life was over. Yet Jefferson never did anything to put Lewis back into the field of exertion, which might have saved his life, even as he commissioned further western expeditions.

At the same time, a life of unchecked brutal exertion alone is likewise disparaged. This is the captains' description of habitant lifeways in Missouri: "In their manners, they unite all the careless gayety, and the amiability of the best times of France: yet, like most of their countrymen in America, they are but ill qualified for the rude life of the frontier; not that they are without talent, for they possess much natural genius and vivacity; nor that they are destitute of enterprise, for their hunting expeditions are long, laborious, and hazardous: but their exertions are desultory; their industry is without system, and with perseverance." Likewise, Charboneau— obviously skilled as a hunter, interpreter, and frontier diplomat— joins the expedition only reluctantly. The captains hold fast in their offer to him, and he is disciplined: "This morning he sent an apology for his improper conduct, and agreed to go with us."[33] The Frenchman, that is, can be made to work only when he agrees to the terms and hence the discipline of the Anglo overlords. In this relation, the captains neither seek nor find a brotherhood such as Chatillon and Parkman's: Charboneau is an employee.

While Charboneau and Sacagawea are obviously and immensely helpful to the expedition, and while the interpreter and his wife are often noted as dining and traveling with the captains, the Anglos make it clear that their dominance is ascendant. Clark has to rescue Charboneau from a flood, and Charboneau is "unable to proceed" at least twice when the company would otherwise keep moving. Although Charboneau is useful for his sophistication as an interpreter, his "sedentary" specialization as a translator seems to lessen his masculine survival skills. Near the end of the expedition, the captains' final description of Charboneau perhaps best represents him as a liminal figure, unable to attain the position of prominence in Anglo society that he had among his in-laws: "Charboneau, with his wife and child [was induced] to remain here [among the Minnetarees], as he could be no longer useful; and notwithstanding our offers of taking him with us to the United States, he said that he had there no acquaintance, and no chance of making a livelihood, and preferred remaining among the Indians. This man has been very serviceable to us, and his wife particularly, among the Shoshonees. . . . We therefore paid him his wages, amounting to five hundred dollars and thirty-three cents, including the price of a horse and a lodge purchased of him."[34] In the end, Charboneau seems to understand that, so long as he interacts with Anglos, he will always need the employment of men like Lewis and Clark, ever an employee and never an employer, at best. However, as an "interpreter" (rather than as a hunter or a guide), Charboneau had momentary access to a clerical-level, sedentary social mobility at the cost of a fragment of his masculinity.

The captains set him off from the other Frenchmen not only on account of his multilingual abilities but also on account of his inability to turn those skills into something more productive. Like the habitants, Charboneau embodies the unrealized potential of the entirety of the French experience in North America: the white man who could become a Yankee if only he chose to be a conqueror rather than a collaborator. There can be no scene of him in a suit in St. Louis: he is irreversibly intercultural and incapable of the internal discipline and balancing that would characterize Chatillon. Moreover, while the reader never sees Chatillon's wife, Charboneau is rarely seen without his. The reader is never allowed to forget that Sacagawea is an Indian girl purchased by her husband. He will never, therefore, cross the line of class, no matter how skilled he is or how well he has been paid: he is "useful" as skilled labor, but he is also circumscribed to a subelite position in Anglo society because of his lacking the necessary discipline to meld the sedentary to the strenuous.

In *A Tour of the Prairies*, Washington Irving imagines and narrativizes Antoine and other "hunters" they hire as skilled laborers who assist tourists like himself along the same lines (as he would Pierre Dorion in *Astoria*) as had Biddle. The lead guide, the Métis Pierre Beate, is set off from men like Antoine by race more than class, and so the categories and the logic of his exclusion differ (see chapter 4). Irving never individualizes Antoine as he does Beate, for example. In fact, Irving draws Antoine's type before he introduces the Frenchman himself: "Beside these, there was a sprinkling of trappers, hunters, half-breeds, Creoles, Negroes of every hue; and all that other rabble rout of nondescript beings that keep about the frontiers, between civilized and savage life, as those equivocal birds, the bats that hover about the confines of light and darkness." From this crew, the Count, a "lesser" nobleman from Europe who has joined Irving's hunting party, hires Antoine. He is chosen mostly for his looks: "He was to be a jack-of-all works; to cook, to hunt, and to take care of the horses; but he had a vehement propensity to do nothing, being one of the worthless brood engendered and brought up among the missions. He was, moreover, a little spoiled by being really a handsome young fellow, an Adonis of the frontier, and still worse by fancying himself highly connected, his sister being concubine to an opulent white trader."[35] Subsequently, Irving mentions Antoine very little. When mentioned, he appears working as a peer with both Pierre Beate, the Métis Chatillon-type guide, and Tonish, the comical servant. Irving, a far more polished writer than Biddle, Lewis and Clark, or Parkman (in 1849), introduces Antoine only to abandon him, and that is no accident.

The extensive buildup Irving creates for Antoine foregrounds his erasability. Antoine's virtues are animal virtues, all surface and lacking substance. Like Charboneau, Antoine could have no function on the other side of the frontier. Although Antoine is occasionally described as a "half-breed," he is just as often described as "French"; in other words, Irving has no idea of his race, and he does not think the distinction in this case matters—his subordination matters more: he needs not only Anglos to motivate him but also superior frontiersmen, such as Beate. Never tested by some inner drive to become more, like so many other Frenchmen in the texts of Anglo writers, he never becomes more. By existing in a liminal space, like Irving's bats, between red and white, partially professional and partly primitive, Antoine, and what he represents in *A Tour of the Prairies*, "hovers" in the book but cannot and will not, ultimately, be brought into the light of civilization—he remains undisciplined.

The final figure in the transformation of semiprofessional French frontiersman into industrial skilled laborer is Parkman's Reynal. Taking his cue from Irving, whose *Tour* is mentioned more than once in *The Oregon Trail*, Parkman likewise introduces Reynal as a type: " 'Mountain men' completed the group; some lounging in the boats, some strolling on shore; some attired in gayly painted buffalo robes, like Indian dandies; some with hair saturated with red paint, and beplastered with glue to their temples; and one bedaubed with vermilion upon the forehead and each cheek. They were a mongrel race; yet the French blood seemed to predominate: in a few, indeed, might be seen the black snaky eye of the Indian half-breed, and one and all they seemed to aim at assimilating themselves to their savage associates."[36] Forgetting that his beloved Chatillon's children would be among those untrustworthy "half-breeds," Parkman reverts to the stereotype and denies the mountain men the benefit of individuality. His use of the term "race" also makes this passage important: a race can be made through adaptation rather than birth, and this "mongrel" one is clearly inferior, despite the varied blood quanta of its members.

Nonetheless, Parkman is forced to travel with one of them, Reynal, "an Indian in most things but color" and "an image of sleek and selfish complacency." Despite all this, Reynal is "adept at this work" and serves as a functional hunter and guide for Parkman when they temporarily part ways with Chatillon and Shaw, Parkman's traveling companion and fellow Harvard undergraduate. Parkman cannot accompany them because of illness and so is left with Reynal and the Sioux. At this point, Parkman witnesses a California-bound wagon train—soon to be the famous Donner Party—that employs "three of the grandsons of Daniel Boone." The grandsons "had clearly inherited the adventurous character of that prince of pioneers; but I saw no signs of the quiet and tranquil spirit that so distinguished him."[37] That is, they have degenerated to become part of the undisciplined "mongrel race," Irving's frontier "rabble," a narrative, again, that esteems class over race as a means of discerning and stabilizing identity.

Other such French or semi-French trappers and hunters cross paths with Parkman, and, to varying degrees, all fall short of the standard set by Chatillon. What they share is a lack of organization, foresight, and self-restraint. Whether they have become more like Indians or more like the animals they hunt, the message for Parkman's readers is the same: on the frontier, there is a group of men who are willing to work for money, who have useful skills, and who will not challenge their Anglo bourgeois for control of the continent. Although Other in terms of ethnicity, geography, language, and maybe race, they are just skilled laborers most likely transferable to the industrial or commercial setting: Parkman domesticates and assimilates them by finding slots for them in the class system familiar to the reader. In *France and England in North America*, this type predominates in Parkman's descriptions of French soldiers and scouts. In those books, the French foot soldier differs from the Anglo-American one in that the latter will rise from his station; the former, the desultory, Catholic, and maybe "mongrel" Frenchman, lacks the energy to seek a personal stake in the wars.

The Anglos win the continent because their armies are composed of men who are both disciplined and ambitious; the French lose because they are meant to be governed, not to govern themselves. By defining themselves in opposition to even the skilled French frontiersmen, by extending a model of fraternity to their own Anglo readers, rather than a model of competition, the captains, Irving, and Parkman—and their readers—can feel better about themselves as men. The frontier French provide no meaningful alternative or threat to the categories of manhood prescribed by commercial capitalism. Thus they use the French only to affirm the place of the Anglo male atop the national hierarchy.

When proposing a difficult side trip in *The Oregon Trail*, Parkman and Shaw run the idea by their hired men: "The men themselves made no objection, nor would they have made any had the journey been more dangerous; for Henry was without fear, and the other two without thought."[38] The "other two" represent the soon-to-be absorbed working class. One, Reynal, as noted above, is strictly functional in the book and so is mostly silent—an obedient and pliant employee. The second, Delorier, gets far more space. Delorier is drawn from the literary trope of the dunce or the fool and can be traced to earlier figures in American literary history such as Hugh Henry Brackenridge's Teague O'Regan in *Modern Chivalry* (1792–1815) or James Fenimore Cooper's many humorous characters in the Leatherstocking series.

Further back, the ultimate model for these characters is in William Shakespeare's plays. Structurally, Shakespeare's plots often alternate between the low comedy of the lower classes and the high tragedy, drama, or comedy of the elite, policing the boundaries between the classes, creating dignity and distance for the elite. The ubiquity of Shakespeare's plays in the antebellum United States assured Biddle, Irving, and Parkman that both the content and the form of the narrative reinforced each other as they reinforced class boundaries. In sum, these characters provide comic relief through their pretensions to social mobility and self-reinvention. In doing so, they represent conservative critiques of democratic and egalitarian ideals. Cleansed of such aspirations through satire and ridicule, they become workers, still in need of supervision and surveillance but generally able to provide the brute labor in the factory, on the farm, or on the frontier. In Irving's *Tour*, the French "cook," Tonish, and the various Frenchmen in Lewis and Clark's expedition are depicted as protoproletarian unskilled laborers. These men embody all the negative stereotypes noted in the earlier chapters of this book: reduced to a state of either bestial or Indianized subhumanity, they are, at best, the subject of humor. They are not fully men because they are either children or animals; in fact, this group's racial identity is by far the most smudged and confused. That, however, overlooks the larger issue: race was only one factor in determining membership in the working class in the industrial North. During these decades, African Americans and lower-class white immigrants shared the most demanding physical labor, free or otherwise.

In Biddle's edition of Lewis and Clark, this conflation of race and class is on most visible display in the characterization of York, Captain Clark's "negro slave" who accompanies the expedition. On the most superficial level, his labors are the same as those of many of the nearly anonymous "Frenchmen." Most of the Frenchmen who traveled with the captains were hunters, bearers, and boatmen and are named only once, as they set off upriver in 1805, but many others come and go from the expedition.[39] With the exception of Pierre Cruzette—who misreads the source of the Missouri and who later accidentally shoots Captain Lewis—these Frenchmen are anonymous and interchangeable both among themselves and, more important, with York.

One incident particularly establishes their existing on a level with York. The captains refer to how "the men"—and only the Frenchmen are never individualized—"found no difficulty in procuring companions for the night by means of the interpreters" while sojourning with an Indian tribe, the Ricaras. Sexual indulgence among the lower races does nothing to lower the character of these men in the eyes of the captains because, as laborers, they are already bestialized. Not surprisingly, the journal entry ends with an extended and somewhat salacious description of York's sexuality: "The black man York participated largely in these favours; for instead of inspiring any prejudice, his colour seemed to procure him additional advantages from the Indians, who desired to preserve among them some memorial of this wonderful stranger. Among other instances of attention, a Ricara invited him into his house and presenting his wife to him, retired to the outside of the door; while there one of York's companions who was looking for him came to the door, but the gallant husband would permit no interruption before a reasonable time had elapsed."[40] The hypersexualized black male—a long-standing object of fear and admiration in white texts going back to *Othello*—here embodies the sexualized existence shared by the lower red and black races, breeding with the Indians to leave a "memorial" in the form of a mixed-race child, but one safely removed from the "civilization" in which it could have no place.[41] While the captains observe this as one more ridiculous misadventure of the lower classes and races, the race-blindness of the Ricara goes unnoted and undervalued.

In terms of class, this episode reflects the Anglo distinctions: while the captains observe and describe, the interpreters pander, and the boatmen—black and white—get laid. In this episode, in microcosm, Biddle dramatizes the hierarchy of the expedition. Each group has a role, and each step down toward pure labor is less white, more bestial, and more in need of discipline. The captains' allowing the "men" time with the Indian women is simply a way of keeping order by giving vent to the carnal desires members of the lower classes and races cannot check, while they themselves do not indulge. Standing apart from the race mixing, the captains affirm their role as elites and as models for their readers' own concerns about the frontier's potential to mix the received hierarchy of races and classes, contaminating the "whiteness" of the nation. No problem, the captains and Biddle implicitly reply: the only "whites" that indulge are

French workers and other lower-class denizens, and they are not really "white" anyway.

Also lower down the social ladder, Irving's Tonish and Parkman's Delorier are virtually identical, begging the question of Parkman's debt to Irving. That issue aside, each Anglo author uses comical Frenchmen to place himself closer to the true frontiersmen—Beatte and Chatillon, respectively—and to make his book, quite simply, more fun for his Anglo readers by affirming their ethnocentric expectations. Irving introduces Tonish in this way:

> I must not pass over unnoticed, a personage of inferior rank, but of all-pervading and prevalent importance: the squire, the groom, the cook, the tent-man, in a word, the factotum, and, I may add, the universal meddler and marplot of our party. This was a swarthy meagre, French creole, named Antoine, but familiarly dubbed Tonish: a kind of Gil Blas of the frontiers, who had passed a scrambling life, sometimes among the white men, sometimes among Indians. . . . We picked him up at St. Louis, near which he has a small farm, an Indian wife, and a brood of half-breed children. According to his own account, however, he had a wife in every tribe; in fact, if all this little vagabond said of himself were to be believed, he was without morals, without caste, without creed, without country, and even without language; for he spoke a mingled French, English, and Osage.

Tonish is subsequently often described in bestial images: a "monkey" or a "roasted polecat." These images bear none of the fleeting and dignified picturesque connotations Irving created for the skilled laborers—the bats in the twilight. More important, so long as he stays within the terms of his employment, Tonish is useful and entertaining. When he pretends a degree of social or professional mobility, however, his true inferiority emerges. While the party is hunting, abandoning the horses he was assigned to watch, Tonish picks up a rifle: "No one, however, was more unmanageable than Tonish. Having an intense conceit of his skill as a hunter, and an irrepressible passion for display, he was continually sallying forth, like an ill-broken hound, whenever any game was started, and had as often to be whipped back."[42] Tonish's subsequent incompetence and absurdity result from his pretensions to join Antoine, Beatte, or Irving himself. Not only is he put in his place, but the rest of the party (and the reader) can laugh at his humiliation. Despite Irving's claim to the contrary, in fact, no one is more manageable than Tonish, and that's the whole point: managing those who cannot manage themselves.

Parkman's Delorier's striking similarity to Irving's Tonish reminds us that "travel books" were, in fact, finely crafted texts in search of popular audiences, and the employment of familiar images only helped their readers place themselves on the frontier with the authors. Such a concession compromises authenticity for the sake of public acceptance, but the nature of that concession often reveals much concerning authorial intent. Delorier, like Tonish, leavens Parkman's narrative with humor that comes, unfortunately, at the Frenchman's expense: "Our muleteer, Delorier, brought up the rear with his cart, wading ankle-deep in the mud, alternately puffing at his pipe, and ejaculating in his prairie patois: '*sacre enfant de grace!*' as one of the mules would seem to recoil before some abyss of unusual profundity. . . . Delorier was a Canadian, with all the characteristics of the true Jean Baptiste. Neither fatigue, nor exposure, nor hard labor could ever impair his cheerfulness and gayety, or his obsequious politeness to his *bourgeois*." Again, the working-class Frenchman lives for the moment. He is loyal, works when pressed, and is good company. At the same time, unlike Irving, Parkman is careful to characterize Delorier as domesticated and feminized. Repeatedly, the "men" return from the hunt to find "Delorier's fire." To praise him, Parkman observes that he "had all the skills of an Indian squaw." In another telling incident, Delorier responds to Tete Rouge's criticism of his cooking: "At this Delorier's placid face instantly flew into a paroxysm of contortions. He grinned with wrath, chattered, gesticulated, and hurled forth a volley of incoherent words in broken English."[43] Delorier's inability to control himself or his language, and his taking offense at such a seemingly trivial event, foreshadow Parkman's later critique of the women's suffrage movement along the same lines: women cannot maintain a rational state of mind for Parkman, and neither can the feminized proletarian Frenchman. By way of contrast, the sickly yet steadfast and rational Parkman is more of a man.

Parkman leaves Delorier preparing for a feast upon his return home to his mixed-race family, dancing on a rock in the river.[44] From his trip with the Anglos and from the virtuous Henry Chatillon, Delorier learned nothing. Whatever discipline he had acquired had been temporary, restricted to the term of his employment, and, that having passed, he returns to undisciplined hedonism. Ultimately harmless, no moral, physical, or material threat to the progress or legitimacy of Anglo civilization, Delorier and those like him lend an exotic air to western adventure and conquest, one easily assimilated or removed as "civilization" comes west. Frenchmen like Delorier reappear ad infinitum in numerous other texts critical of the French: George Bancroft, Timothy Flint, the Hildreth brothers, the Cutlers (Manasseh and Jervis), Zebulon Pike, Stephen Long, Thomas Farnham, John Fremont, and others too numerous to mention.

In all, these Frenchmen of the working class are simply (and perhaps simple-mindedly) awaiting the arrival of the Anglo elites to discipline their lives and behavior. Consistently, they are represented as being too familiar with the Indians, the pope, or other sources of uncritical affiliation to be trusted with self-governance— as were the white working classes. Their discipline and containment must be understood as components of a more general pattern to corral preindustrial masculinities into industrial slots. By switching an unfamiliar form of Otherness (French) for a more familiar one (worker), these writers set the stage for what would come to be called "Americanization" after the Civil War. European ethnicities are "Americanized" by learning the functions, language, and, most important, the expectation to start, and most likely stay, at the bottom of the economic hierarchy.

As he stayed in Boston for the rest of his career and chose to live "correctly" on Beacon Hill, Parkman seemed to have needed the French to be increasingly less worthy or relevant. Like Meriwether Lewis, once he was "sedentary," Parkman changed his ideals and neglected his memories. In his multivolume *France and England in North America*—so popular and so often used by historians for so many generations—Parkman writes about long-dead Frenchmen he had not known, and he never bestows on them the virtues he found in Chatillon. To bring Chatillon and what he represented into his reading of the French in North America more generally would complicate his narrative of Anglo-Saxon ascendance by creating a symbol of French masculinity and legitimacy whose defeat, disenfranchisement, and displacement could never be justified.

Had Chatillon been appropriated from the nineteenth century to the eighteenth and transferred from St. Louis to Quebec—as Parkman transposed the Sioux and the Iroquois—in the textual reconstruction of a virtuous and intelligent French common man, Chatillon's necessary death could only have been called martyrdom, a sacrifice on the altar of Anglo materialism and competition. No, Parkman sought rhetorically to kill off only nonassimilable Catholics and peasants in his narrative of "the ancient war." What Chatillon represented as a coureur de bois—power over the level of one's participation in the incorporation of the United States—was by 1870 considered dangerous and antisocial, even traitorous, a sign of resisting the "melting pot's" powers of Americanization. In terms of both ethnic and economic identity, Chatillon will never "melt in." Instead of giving himself over to Anglo systems of economic or racial dominion, he dictated the terms of his relationship to each and so retained his manhood when those around him lost theirs, including Parkman.

A similar selective amnesia struck Irving as well, a figure whose slippery masculine and sexual identity has long been in dispute.[45] In *A Tour of the Prairies*, Irving employed the Chatillon type as well. His guide, Pierre Beate, however, was half-Osage Métis—and so slightly removed from discussions of white manhood. Beate and his type, however, are absent from Irving's follow-ups to *A Tour*, *Astoria* and *Captain Bonneville*. In *Astoria* Irving tells the story of the colony the company founded in Oregon in 1808. *Captain Bonneville* mostly just retells the same stories Timothy Flint and others had established as standard grist for the popular adventure genre. Like Parkman, when Irving abandoned firsthand experiences to write from published sources in the Anglo archive, the politically and culturally inconvenient Frenchman vanishes—the pressures of cultural conformity and authorial popularity clouded both their memories.

In place of the authority of personal experience, each historian chose to echo and reinforce the established representations of the emasculated Frenchman, a misrepresentation that better served the perceived needs of his audience and, for Irving, his patrons. The later texts are built on other texts, shifting the writerly perspective from the gully to the armchair. In the end, not only the subjects but also the authors are emasculated. What do we think of when we think of frontiersmen now? Davy Crockett, Daniel Boone, and Kit Carson are all Anglo reiterations of adventures more characteristic of French experiences, with one crucial exception: they all kill Indians while the French lived in peace with them. In the disappearance of the Chatillon type from Anglo texts, we can perceive the shutting down of alternative masculinities. The unreconstructed backwoodsman who fought Indians rather than marrying them replaced the coureur de bois who could wear a suit in St. Louis. As we also saw in the displacement of the habitant with the commercial farmer, a potential symbol of an American folk identity based in egalitarian and noncommercial ideals is superseded by a more progressive and aggressive prototype for American myth making.

His biographers often refer to Parkman as representing the "patrician" class in Victorian America. For example, Wilbur Jacobs describes his resistance to women's suffrage in this way: "One reason Parkman seems to have been so effective in stating his views is that he could fall back upon the romantic, chivalric position that assumed women's dependence and helplessness. He successfully masked his contempt behind an appearance of admiration. In the battle with the opposition, his voice had a distinctly patriarchal tone. . . . Thus Parkman's patrician social attitudes were increasingly out-of-date."[46] "Patrician" shares the same Latin roots as "paternity." To assign oneself the position of collective "father"—as patricians do—is to stratify and to place oneself atop the social ladder. On the prairies, Parkman had found a brother, and maybe a father, in Chatillon. However, for Frenchmen in general, the image of Chatillon as the exception rather than the rule allowed Parkman to do the same for ethnic minorities and the working classes as he would for women: to hide contempt beneath the mask of benevolence. When he abandoned his frontier brother for more acceptable Anglo fathers, Generals Wolfe and Howe—building his ascendance on theirs—he changed from a paradigm of brotherhood to one of competition, a competition in which he ardently proclaimed himself and those like him the victors. Anglo masculinity could be established and affirmed only in its dominance—rhetorical or actual—over all the alternatives.

In selecting the metaphor of the stratified, patriarchal family— both domestically and more generally—Parkman, as well as Irving and Biddle, compelled men to be rulers rather than friends, autocrats rather than companions, constricting rather than expanding their liberty. For Parkman's Chatillon and Warren's coureurs de bois, fatherhood and family membership are important. Russ Castronovo has addressed the symbolic weight of fatherhood in the early Republic: "As the sons returned to the figures of the fathers for solace and confirmation of their own political righteousness, they discovered that the fathers themselves were hardly consistent enough in their beliefs and practices to legitimate a stable mid-nineteenth-century America."[47] Rather than embrace the libratory inconsistencies of the Revolutionary age—the tearful George Washington—Parkman selects a national masculinity built upon stability rather than sentiment, on exclusion rather than inclusion, on "sternness" rather than compassion.

But he had momentarily flirted with another narrative, another patrimony: the younger Parkman contemplated an alternative American father, one not based in the Revolution's patricidal violence. The images of Chatillon and Warren's forefathers remind us that the nation also had French fathers who loved their wives and cared for their children, even if their wives were Indians and their children had brown skins. The models of intercultural and republican masculinity they represent are based in Enlightenment values of compassion and toleration. However, as Parkman aged, and as Warren's book went unpublished until Helen Hunt Jackson's *Ramona* created a more sympathetic audience for such a racially complex text and way of imagining Indians, such alternative American fathers were actively forgotten and erased from the national familial memory.

Monstrous Exceptions

*Anglo Patriarchs, French Families,
and Métis Americans*

FOUR

The literature of frontier settlement is dominated
not by the solitary woodsman in the tradition of
Natty Bumppo but by the frontier patriarch—the
American Abraham—who leaves the society of his
forefathers to establish his family in the wilderness.
Like the famous *isolatos* of our literature, the
American Abraham strikes out for the West, but
for him the migration is strategic rather than an
essential part of his being.

> Warren Motley, *The American Abraham:
> James Fenimore Cooper and the Frontier
> Patriarch* (1987)

In *The American Abraham*, Warren Motley
describes how James Fenimore Cooper's novels place the community-founding, property-
owning Anglo male at the center of the national
mythology rather than the fleeing *isolato*, as
R. W. B. Lewis had argued in *The American
Adam*.[1] Other scholars have followed this line
productively: Russ Castronovo, Dana D. Nelson,
and others have explored the role of fatherhood
in the construction of a national imaginary and
shifted the focus from Adam to Abraham.[2] Doing
so, however, compels a closer examination of the
function—domestically and publicly—of the Anglo

patriarch and his role in the reshaping of the nation's life in the decades following the patricidal Revolution. In turn as well, the cultural articulation of the patriarchal model catalyzed a ripple effect of more general subordination and stratification that structured other, only indirectly domestic or economic institutions such as factories, poorhouses, Indian reservations, and slave quarters. Patriarchs were expected, as we saw in Lewis and Clark's treatment of their workers in chapter 3, to discipline and govern, to indulge and rescue—to balance "authority and freedom"—from a stable vantage point of moral, material, and intellectual righteousness, fulfilling their role in the "strategic" colonization of the continent.

Not surprisingly, then, both proponents and critics of the models of public patriarchy or paternity in the new nation found in the French a synecdoche of debate and departure. This was especially prickly because most of the children sired by French fathers were Métis—embodying the father's European and the mother's Indian identities, languages, cultures, and genes. Because the patriarchal model was premised on a strict principle of categorization (a son is privileged; a servant is not), the Métis, in their very existence, complicated and challenged the imposition of the patriarchal model on the diversity of cultures and peoples in the West. To extend a metaphor, the Métis represented free radicals in the American nuclear family. Their existence thus threatened to disrupt the national domestic model being so anxiously deployed to stabilize both the frontier and the nation itself. This chapter focuses on the Métis and how their differing roles in French and Anglo familial models reflected how this threat was both articulated and policed.

The patriarchal national model and the anxieties that made it so contentious have their roots in the eighteenth century, especially in the disruption of family-based authority in the symbolic patricide of the British king.[3] To replace the "sire," the Founders positioned themselves as the source of both public *and* domestic authority, the household the microcosmic template of and for nationwide stabilization. From their famous letters in the spring of 1776, Abigail

Adams's "Remember the Ladies" admonition to her husband, John, is cited as an urtext of American feminism. Yet her statement also reflects a more general challenge to social order throughout Anglo-America, appropriating his rebellion-specific language for her universal purposes. While Abigail's letter is stirring, John's response has far more telling and chilling implications for post-Revolutionary developments, ones that became all too true, despite the only semi-nuclear condition of the Adams clan.[4]

John, like most of the Founders, was away from home a great deal. Abigail, born to an old New England family, managed the Adams family farm. As a businesswoman, Abigail developed an interest in politics. She saw in her own frustration with John a parallel to his frustration with the king, hence her claim to rights. John's response reflects a keen sensitivity to the true stakes of the Revolution:

> We have been told that our struggle has loosened the bands of government every where. That Children and Apprentices were disobedient—that schools and colleges were grown turbulent—That Indians slighted their Guardians and Negroes grew insolent to their Masters. But your letter was the first Intimation that another Tribe more numerous and powerful than all the rest were grown discontented. . . . Depend upon it, We know better than to repeal our Masculine systems. Altho they are in full Force, you know they are little more than Theory. We dare not exert our power in its full Latitude. We are obliged to go fair, and softly, and in Practice you know We are the subjects. We have only the name of Masters, and rather than give this up, which would completely subject Us to the power of the petticoat . . .[5]

For our purposes, John's response does two important things. First, he limits participation in the democracy to the heads of households—the property-owning white males ("Us")—and empowers them with broad discretionary powers ("our Masculine systems"). For John, the man's home is his castle, if castles are where kings live. A look ahead to Chief Justice John Marshall's 1832 request that Indian tribes look to the federal government "as a ward to his guardian" expands the household model to a national scale.[6] John Adams and Marshall transpose domestic and political family metaphors, allowing individual white males to establish dominion over unindividualized members of racial minority groups. By this thinking, there was no distinction between a family living together under one roof and a set of peoples living together in one nation: each needed the same leader, the white male capable of the self-restraint characteristic of republican self-denial, public-interestedness, and personal asperity.

Second, John implies that white women, in both households, shared much with other, lesser family members. Later, he refers to similar trouble with "Canadians, Indians, Negroes, Hanoverians, Hessians, Russians, Irish Roman Catholicks and Scotch Renegadoes."[7] All these represent, implicitly, disruptions of paternal order by those who merit only indirect representation in public affairs through the mediating discretion of the patriarch. John affirms that ethnicity, class, race, age, and gender differences disqualify anyone other than men like himself from full citizenship. As both president and father, John policed the borders of membership. His stewardship of the Alien and Sedition Acts, then, might be seen as mirroring his refusal to allow his son—future president John Quincy Adams—to study poetry. Reflecting a post-Puritan ethos transferred from church to civic life, John, like a minister, requires orderly compliance with and filial respect for the stern but necessary discipline of a loving parent governing those for whom he is responsible, while they themselves are incapable of self-government. In turn, John Quincy, as president, removed the multiracial Métis from the Treaty of Fond du Lac (see below) and made them eligible for removal; like his father, he exercised parental authority to maintain order in the national house by removing disruptive elements just as he had, following his father's decrees, purged his poetic ambitions. For each Adams male, in his own century, the employment of civil and domestic forms of patriarchal authority engendered stability, coherence, and cohesion—making the nation as safe and as ordered as the home.

Linking these—compelling the subordinated to accept subordination and creating a ruling cadre of white males worthy of discretion and empowerment—required a strong and coherent cultural component to enable and communicate compliance. In the 1790s and the 1820s, the popularity of conduct books reflects a general desire for social order among the reading classes—Anglo children, workers, and women.[8] In each decade as well, novelists such as Tabitha Tenney and Charles Brockden Brown in the 1790s and, in the 1820s, Lydia Maria Child and James Fenimore Cooper commonly dramatized the restoration of order in otherwise disordered colonial or Revolutionary American communities through the restoration of coherent, white patriarchal families to their rightful, elite status. Their popularity reflects a nervous desire among the growing middle classes to consolidate their primacy and to use the model of the extended household to do so. The middle classes positioned themselves to resist the growing forces of democratization set loose by, among other things, the destabilized and destabilizing western frontier.

Because the "West" lacked the social, ecclesiastical, and economic institutions that bolstered the Anglo elite in the East, it was viewed as a source of deviance in need of containment prior to its inclusion in the nation—the cultural institutions used to teach the young Anglo males the workings of responsible patriarchy were missing.[9] Brown and Cooper were especially nervous about the frontier. In his preface to *Edgar Huntly* (1799), Brown identifies "the perils of the western wilderness" as a central theme, yet the story travels no farther than the eastern foothills of the Appalachians. Nonetheless, the eponymous Edgar fears that, in telling his story, "emotions will not be re-awakened by my narrative incompatible with order and coherence."[10] Cooper makes his own promises to police the West in his introduction to *The Prairie* (1827). For Cooper, in the Louisiana Territory, national security required a trans-plantation of "our language, our religion, our institutions, and it is also to be hoped, our sense of political justice."[11] Cooper used "our" in the same manner and with the same meaning as John Adams. Both have in mind a removal of all threats to what is "ours."

In *Removals*, Lucy Maddox studies the link between the literary removal of women and the removal of nonwhites from the nation's public sphere in the antebellum decades. In particular, she observes how Lydia Marie Child and Catherine Sedgwick "assert the claim of the female novelist, whose fictional domain is still limited to the places that women and children inhabit, to invent Indian charac-ters who can be brought out of the woods—the domain of the male novelists—and into the domestic place. In this regard, both women can be seen at least tentatively attempting to dislodge the categorical distinctions that had, by the early nineteenth century, separated gen-der out from issues or questions that might be termed political."[12] Maddox argues that, while these authors reinvent women's history in America, they go along with the same "categorical distinctions" that led to Indian removal. At the same time, such women were aware that they too faced a threat of removal, one less physical but just as meaningful intellectually and culturally. In their novels, the inclusion of white females hinges on establishing their suitability as opposed to nonwhites.

Cooper, like Child and Sedgwick, singled out race mixing as a source of disruption. In *The Last of the Mohicans*, the figure of Cora—a mixed-race woman from the Caribbean—is triply a source of tension along these axes. First, the Huron Magua repeatedly seeks her as a wife. While she resists him, the white males, as well as the benevolent Mohicans Uncas and Chingachgook, rebut his at-tempts at miscegenation. Second, at one point, Cora's father, Gen-eral Munro, thinks Duncan Heyward—the novel's nascent Ameri-can and implied post-Revolutionary patriarch—is asking him for Cora's hand. He tells the story of her mixed-race parentage to a confused Duncan, who had been after the purely "white" Alice instead. Finally, between Cora and Uncas there seem to be the seeds of romance, and Cooper kills them both off to stop such an unsanctioned union. In Cooper's master plot of restored order, Cora can have no mate. Miscegenation was a sign of the colonial epoch's decadence and instability. Duncan and Alice's implied union will put things to right in the raced nation.

More direct, Cooper found French ideas about families and communities far less rigid and structured and so viewed them as threats with the potential to contaminate all forms of social order. In *Mohicans*, the failure of Montcalm to control his Indian "children" during the massacre at Fort William Henry signals him as a failed father.[13] More general, on the frontier, Cooper, finding the French at odds with the virgin-land myth he so wanted to nationalize, simply ignored them in book after book, choosing to focus instead only on military characters from the French and Indian War who all, presumably, left after their defeat, ignoring the dozens of French settlements that persisted well after 1763. In *The Prairie*, he cleared the space needed to do so: "Time was necessary to blend the numerous and affluent colonists of the lower provinces with their new [Anglo-American] compatriots; but the thinner and more humble population above was almost immediately swallowed in the vortex which attended the tide of instant emigration."[14] Although Cooper's wishful thinking about a French disappearance from Upper Louisiana is refuted by most antebellum texts, his point is that the French underbred, again a sign of unsuitable patriarchal behavior, and so are vanishing. Perhaps Mark Twain could have added Cooper's blindness to all things French to his list of "Cooper's Literary Offenses." Even the Francophobe Timothy Flint conceded the ubiquity of the French in "above" provinces like Missouri, Illinois, and Wisconsin in the late 1820s. However, he maintained that their ability to sire progeny was not matched by their ability to act like responsible fathers and raise their children as "whites."

More to the point is that "the thinner and more humble" French lived at odds with Cooper's and most Anglos' notion of "our" ideas of class, race, gender, and, for my immediate interests, family. In the national family, they were imagined as lazy, bachelor uncles—useful for entertaining the children and, fortunately, out of the gene pool. My use of male terms for French colonials—both here and in the preceding chapters—reflects two facts: first, Anglo writers almost always used male characters or persons to represent the French as a whole; second, strictly in terms of demographics, there were very few Frenchwomen north of New Orleans or west of Toronto. What evidence there is suggests a nonpatriarchal template. A few fictional Frenchwomen are noted in chapter 2 and are briefly touched on in *Views of Louisiana,* in which Henry Marie Brackenridge admires that Frenchwomen "will not be considered secondary personages in the matrimonial association."[15] James Hall, Henry Wadsworth Longfellow, and a few others saw greater gender balance in French marriages, but such references are few and far between. Almost all Anglo writers note that most Frenchmen "allied themselves" with Indian women, a fact borne out by modern historians.

In Anglo writing, the women imagined and depicted as the wives of Frenchmen are either Indian or Métis, themselves the products of interracial couplings. Both primary and secondary evidence demonstrates that most Frenchmen formed lasting families with women from various Algonquian and other allied tribes. The children, grandchildren, half children, and such from these unions, in the areas of French influence, were Métis, a term meaning more, I argue below, than simply mixed-blood quanta. By the time most Anglos came west after the War of 1812, 150 years of interbreeding had so smudged the lines between the races in some places that many Anglos gave up trying to calculate precise racial percentages and inaccurately used "Canadian" for all the mixed-race peoples they found, as Francis Parkman did in *The Conspiracy of Pontiac* (1851), a mislabeling that also conveniently categorized the French as foreigners.

This chapter examines conflicts over race and gender as they were revealed in the depiction of the French-Indian family in opposition to the bourgeois Anglo family. William Handley has observed the rhetorical function of marriages in texts addressing the American West: "The relationship between marriage and nation demonstrates how allegory operates in literary and historiographic retrospect, by putting one set of narrative terms ('this story is about these two people') into metaphorical relationship with another, often larger set of terms ('this story is abut the West'), transforming the personal into the political, the literary into the historiographical, and vice versa."[16] While the Anglo family removed women and nonwhites from social or culture relevance and privatized the nuclear family—an exclusionary practice and model—the French family was depicted as a model of inclusion and collectivity. As such, it came to be a rhetorical weapon to resist parallel removals based on race and gender, especially in texts by the supposedly already-spoken-for members of the Anglo family: women and nonwhites. Each called for a reduction in patriarchal empowerment by narrating the intercoupling of the French, the Indians, and the Métis as an alternative based on more balanced and satisfyingly intimate intrafamilial relations.

The first section addresses Henry Rowe Schoolcraft's efforts to impose the ethnic, gender, material, and racial features of Anglo-American patriarchy on a Great Lakes fur trade community. In his efforts to establish dominion over all those around him in northern Michigan, Schoolcraft sought to erase the intercultural middle ground based in more than a century and a half of French and Ojibwa intermarriage and cohabitation by imposing the Anglo family model—both privately and publicly—on the diversity of peoples and practices he found in Sault Ste. Marie and Mackinac. His efforts are particularly visible in his treatment of mixed-race people, including his wife, Jane Johnston Schoolcraft (Bame-Wa-Wa-Ge-Zhik-A-Quay).[17] However, not all Anglos were so dictatorial: John H. Kinzie (Shaw-Nee-Aw-Kee), whose wife, Juliette, wrote *Wau-Bun: The "Early Day" in the North-West* (1855). In her book, she not only asserts female self-determination but also, unlike Child and Sedgwick, refuses to put down the "savage" to elevate the female. To her, gender- and race-based removals are products of the same domineering system, and each is shown as immoral and inadequate in her narration of life in the Great Lakes fur trade. Her positive depictions of French and Indian marriages, as well as her complex depictions of full-blooded Indians, show her seeking an alternative to male-based Anglo-American values in general. In particular, she features the functional partnerships of Indian women with Frenchmen in contrast to Anglo marriages, engaging the French model to question the patriarchal Anglo family's sexist roots.

Finally, I discuss how certain Anglo writers used the French model of the multirace person—Métis—to challenge the "household" model articulated by most Anglo texts. They challenged the patriarchal norm's refusal of mixed-race peoples as a distinct and unique presence. The section features part-Anglo Métis writers William Warren and Major John Richardson and full-blood Anglos Thomas McKenney, Washington Irving, and John S. Robb. All express positive views of the Métis by creating positive characters that either retain or learn the French era's interculturalism. By insisting that the Métis were neither wholly Indian, wholly white, nor tragically fragmented "half-breeds," they articulated a more diverse vision of individualized membership in the nation.

Each part of this chapter is interlinked, biographically, with the others. The Kinzies and the Schoolcrafts knew one another; Richardson worked from Kinzie's account of the Chicago Massacre and traveled with Michel Cadotte, William Warren's cousin; William's father, Lyman Warren, translated for Schoolcraft, who traveled to Fond du Lac with Thomas McKenney to sign a treaty intended to protect, by name, the land rights of the Cadottes, the Warrens, and the Johnstons—Schoolcraft's in-laws. In a way, the world of the fur trade was a family itself—some men aspiring to patriarchy, like Schoolcraft, and others, like John Kinzie, to a less exalted but perhaps more satisfying or honorable role. In the end, what emerges is an impression that the French model was used subtly to destabilize Anglo-American notions of gender and marriage, just as the patriarchs feared.

Timothy Flint insisted that, although Frenchmen fathered children with Indian women, they were never really fathers to them, in the sense of guiding them toward Anglo manhood and leadership. His argument begins with a denial of Anglo sexual attraction to Indian women but moves on to a subtler analysis of divergent concepts of marriage:

> I have already hinted at the facility with which the French and Indian intermix. There seems to be as natural affinity of the former people for them, as there is repulsion between the Anglo-Americans and them. Monstrous exceptions sometimes occur, but it is so rare that a permanent connexion is formed between an American and an Indian woman, that even the French themselves regard it as a matter of astonishment. The antipathy between the two races seems fixed and unalterable. Peace there often is between them when they are cast in the same vicinity, but affectionate intercourse never.

In this passage from *Recollections of the Last Ten Years* (1826), Flint refers to a previous account of two interracial couples in Illinois: "No words can describe the filthiness and apparent misery of this wretched place." Flint cannot account for why "the man persisted in declaring himself happy in his condition and in his wife." Flint also notes that these mixed families live among other such families in communal villages up and down the Mississippi. Such communities, however, would of necessity give way, according to Flint, with the coming of patriarchal Anglos like himself and their emphases on racial purity and material comfort. Finally, his biological distinction between the French and American "races" reflects the same pattern of deracination we have seen throughout this book.

Still, the French and Indian marriages fascinate him: "The French settle among them, learn their language, intermarry, and soon get smoked to the same copper complexion. A race of half-breeds springs up in their cabins. A singular cast is the result these intermarriages of these half-breeds, called quarteroons. The lank hair, the Indian countenance and manners predominate, even in these. It is a singular fact, that the Indian feature descends much farther in these intermixtures and is much slower to be amalgamated with that of the whites, than that of the negro."[18] Flint reduces the difference between the French and Anglo colonial models to opposed attitudes toward racial interbreeding: Anglos are repulsed by it; the French accept it. In the end, interbred or not, the French become "copper complected," while the Anglos stay white. Worse yet, Indian genes seem to persist longer than "negro" genes, posing a more lingering threat to uniform whiteness in the settlements.

For Anglos, patriarchal marriage was purportedly based on a sentimental bond rooted in individual attraction and intimacy, a pairing off that resulted in the couple's (and especially the wife's) removal from the community rather than a joining with it, a distancing that put the female's subordination to the male above the family's subordination to the community. On the other hand, as Flint attests, for the French, intermarriage comes *after* acculturation. Sexual intimacy with a spouse becomes more the result of joining the tribe and less the by-product of personal attraction: marriage with Indian women did not make Frenchmen the patriarchs of nuclear families. Rather, marriage primarily allied them with their spouse's extended tribal family. The difference between the Anglos and the French therefore has more to do with opposed views of what constitutes a family and the man's role in its construction. The ensuing conflicts between Anglo and French models are revealed in the career and writings of Henry Rowe Schoolcraft.

During his first trip through the Great Lakes—as a geologist with the expedition of Lewis Cass to the source of the Mississippi in 1820—Henry Rowe Schoolcraft passed through Sault Ste. Marie,

Michigan, where Lake Superior drains into Lake Huron. While there, he met John Johnston and his daughter, Jane. A Scots-Irish fur trader, Johnston had married Oshaw-guscoday-wayqua (Green Prairie Woman) in the informal French-Ojibwa tradition, and they forged a hybrid of French and Anglo marriages: while she took the English name Susan, she left Johnston every spring to supervise her family's maple sugar crop on La Pointe, and she insisted on speaking only Ojibwa in their home, forcing their children to be bilingual. At the same time, John raised the children after the Anglo fashion, in his home as half-breeds fully acculturated to North Atlantic standards of behavior and culture.

Jane in particular he attempted to have educated back in Ireland. Although she traveled to his homeland, the schooling never happened. Nonetheless, upon her return, despite living in a remote setting, she was accustomed to middle-class values and concepts of marriage. Not surprisingly, then, Schoolcraft was attracted to her. In contrast, on his first trip west, to Missouri in 1818, he had observed the French and their mixed-race offspring: "Children are wholly ignorant of books, and have not learned even the rudiments of their own tongue. Thus situated, without moral restraint, brought up in the uncontrolled indulgence of every passion, and with out a regard of religion, the state of society amongst the rising generation in this region is truly deplorable."[19] At the same time, his bias was based not on racial identity but rather on cultural adaptation, or assimilation to Anglo values. In *Narrative Journal of Travels* (1823), an account of his 1820 expedition, he wrote of the mixed-race population of Prairie du Chien, Wisconsin:

> The early settlers, according to the principles adopted by the French colonists in the Canadas, intermarried with Indian women, and the present population is the result of this connexion. In it, we behold the only instance our country presents, of the complete and permanent civilization of the Aborigines; and it may be doubted, after all that has been said on the subject,

whether this race can ever be reclaimed from the savage state, by any method. The result, in the present instance, is such as to equal the most sanguine expectations of the philanthropist, in regard to a mixed species. They are said to exhibit evidences of enterprise, industry, and a regard to order and the laws.[20]

Schoolcraft limits the potential for "civilization" to mixed-race populations exclusively; pure-blood Indians fall outside the scope of inclusion—and half-breeds are to be included if and only if they act like Anglos. When the Cass expedition passed through the Sault, they stayed in Johnston's whitewashed house and enjoyed what Schoolcraft called "the blandishments of refined society," another sign that genetic race mixing could be erased by thorough and sincere bourgeois behavior or mimicry.

By 1823, Schoolcraft was Indian agent at the Sault, a position supplemented by John Jacob Astor's simultaneous employment of him as a "manager." A year after that, he married Jane. Just as important, he compelled the formal marriage of John and Susan Johnston. John, that is, was insufficiently patriarchal in his son-in-law's eyes and was forced to abandon the informality of the French model for the Anglo emphasis on contractual obligation. Susan seems to have gone through the ritual without changing her behavior in any way. Henry, on the other hand, had in mind a more patriarchal arrangement, and Jane seems to have complied. Marjorie Cahn Brazer, in *Harps upon the Willows*, rereads Henry's and Jane's letters and comes to this conclusion: "Jane Johnston typified the genteel woman who has come to be described as 'Victorian.' . . . A husband, like a father, was to be revered for the superiority of his knowledge, his moral judgment, and his strength of character. The female, brilliant and intelligent though she may be, represented the weaker sex in all things." Brazer adds that Jane "did not consider herself an Indian."[21] When he picked up Henry on his way to Fond du Lac for treaty negotiation in 1826, Thomas McKenney described her: "You would never judge, either from her complexion, or language, or from any other circumstance, that her mother was a Chippeway, except that her moderately high cheekbones, her dark and fine eye, and breadth of the jaw, slightly indicate it—and you would never believe it, except on her own confession."[22] In the summer of that fateful treaty, then, Jane was everything Schoolcraft wanted mixed-race individuals to be: interchangeable with Anglos and an obedient part of his family. Her role as nonwhite and as woman thus makes her doubly subservient to him, a subordination her own mother had never observed with her father, nor one he had imposed.

During his time at the Sault, Henry brought his own brothers and sisters from New York to work in the trade he controlled. Moreover, he was constantly finding jobs for Jane's brothers, who found "half-breed" existence troubled by their inability to "marry white," as Jane and her sisters had. In brief, Henry spent the 1820s positioning himself as a patriarch, governing a broadening sphere of dependents—he wanted to be everything the French patriarchs had not been. He remade not only his home but also his entire community in his own image. Yet as he did so, his marriage seems to have been dissolving. As traced by Brazer, Jeremy Mumford, and Richard Bremer, some kind of alienation concerning race and marriage set in around the fall of 1826. That summer, Schoolcraft simultaneously sought mixed-race treaty rights for his newborn son by Jane, William Henry, under the Treaty of Fond du Lac—amounting to 640 acres of prime hardwood and sugar maple—and, as Michigan became a state, he tried and failed to champion the right of mixed bloods to vote, wanting it both ways for his son. Each was denied—John Quincy Adams erased Métis treaty rights (see below), and Michigan banned nonwhites from voting. Schoolcraft's frustration seemed to have hardened his attitudes toward race and affirmed his drive to consolidate his own patriarchal authority.

William Henry died in March 1827, so the conflict was moot, but cracks in the Schoolcraft marriage had already appeared at the textual level in *The Literary Voyager or Muzzeniegun*, a circular that Henry and Jane handwrote for the iced-in settlement. In it, Henry's familial and racial patriarchal views were clarified, and Jane's subtle resistance was initiated. Henry begins by chastising the French for not assuming patriarchal authority or responsibility:

> Civilization is a system of restraints, by which old habits and opinions are put off, and new ones taken up. To enter the private dwelling; to put on the clothing of the civilized man; to take meals, retire, wash the hands and face, attend stated duties or labors, every day at fixed hours; or to become familiarized to the dwellings, fields, and ordinary economy of civilized life, are among the essential elements of civilization. . . . Yet civilization without Christianity may be a failure. The lessons of experience on this subject ought not to be forgotten. No sects were ever animated with more zeal, in this pious work, than the Jesuit fathers. They followed the Indians in their hunting excursions, and attended them in their seasons of feasting and fasting, want and warfare, enduring perils and hardships, which prove a total abstraction from all selfish or personal considerations. But they effected no radical change in the vital moral habits or custom of the Indians. They imposed but few restraints; they taught no new methods of economy. . . . They left the Indian where they found him a savage of the forest.[23]

In 1830, Henry converted to evangelical Protestantism, after which his feelings on Indians and mixed-race peoples became even more negative as his adoration of all things bourgeois as seen here only intensified. Throughout his writings, his linkage of spiritual and material assimilation represents his efforts to establish himself as the patriarch of both his family and the Ojibwa who came to the Sault and to his agency.

In the *Literary Voyager*, as well, Jane's resistance took a number of small forms. Writing as "Rosa," Jane contributed the poem "Invocation to My Maternal Grandfather on Hearing His Descent from Chippewa Ancestors Misrepresented." Here, Jane rebuts Henry's perpetuation of stereotypical and racialist "Vanishing Indian" and "all Indians are alike" tropes in their matched accounts of Waub-Ojeeg, Jane's grandfather. In his account, Henry furthered a rumor that Waub-Ojeeg, an Ojibwa leader, had been born a Sioux—the Ojibwa's inveterate enemies—and captured into the Ojibwa nation. She responds by insisting on intertribal difference:

> Thy deeds and thy name,
> Thy child's child shall proclaim,
> And make the dark forests resound with the lay;
> Though thy spirit has fled,
> To the hills of the dead,
> Yet thy name shall be held in my heart's warmest care.[24]

The poem makes no reference to the authoress's half-blood status; she is simply a granddaughter and so may as well be full-blood. The poem assumes not only racial continuity and survival but also tribal distinctiveness. In contrast, throughout Henry's massive *Algic Researches* (1839), as Joshua David Bellin has noted, Henry consistently sought to erase tribal distinctions and to impose an essentialist master narrative of vanishing.[25]

During the early 1830s, Jane began terminal battles with tuberculosis and opium, and Henry initiated his ill-fated Indian Civilization Program, an early draft of the paternalistic Dawes Act, and the two were usually physically separate.[26] At this point, the former chaplain at the agency, Edwin James, and others began accusing Henry of nepotism, conflicts of interest, incompetence, anti-Catholicism, and general incompetence. On a familial level, Henry insisted on sending their surviving children to New York for schooling, despite Jane's stated objections—a division again revealing a clash between French and Anglo values. Both personally and professionally, the aspiring patriarch was failing to maintain order in either his own home or the extended home or community of the Sault. In 1833 the Schoolcrafts moved to Mackinac and in 1836 from Mackinac to Detroit. In 1841—his Jacksonian friends out of office—he was fired as superintendent of Indians in Michigan, and Jane died while Henry was in Europe on a tour promoting *Algic Researches*. When he remarried, his new wife was Anglo and betrayed his new alliances. He married Mary Howard from South Carolina, who later, as "Mrs. Henry Rowe Schoolcraft," trading on her husband's fame, authored the proslavery novel *The Black Gauntlet* (1860), one of whose subplots fictionalizes the self-destruction of her husband's "mixed" family, the result of "so suicidal an experiment as to amalgamate in marriage with a race as inferior to his own as an ape is to a Napolean Bonaparte."[27]

In *Personal Memoirs* (1854), Henry blamed the French-based legacy of racial cohabitation for his failings. Unlike his acquaintances Thomas McKenney and Edwin James, he was never able to incorporate the multiracial or intercultural identities of the French into his vision of a raced American frontier. By his own account, this started early; Henry reflected on the state of trade upon his arrival in Mackinac: "The very thin diffusion of American feeling or principle in both the traders and the Indians, so far as I have seen them, renders it a matter of no little difficulty to supervise this business.... It will require vigilance and firmness, yet mildness, to secure anything like a faithful performance of the duties committed to me on a remote frontier, and with very little means of action beyond the precincts of the post, and this depends much on the moral influence on the Indian mind of the military element of power." That is, the recalcitrant coureurs de bois insisted on being independent traders, so Schoolcraft means to bypass them and use the army to scare the Indians into trading with Astor directly. Schoolcraft's blending of governmental and corporate presences nicely epitomizes the role of the military in the manifestly destined nation: divergent peoples are absorbed or removed, and local trading systems quashed, by force, if necessary. Another passage reaffirms his rhetoric of assimilation and patriarchy. Recalling a visit with the Métis Madame La Framboise, a friend of Judith Kinzie's, who relates the story of Chicago's founding by Bonga (also known as Jean Baptiste du Sable, an African manumitted by his French owner and married to an Ojibwa woman), Henry simply erases such alternative narratives to reinforce the older and imperial binaries: "The Great Lakes can no longer be regarded as solitary seas, where the Indian war-whoop has alone for so many uncounted centuries startled its echoes. The Eastern World seems to be alive, and roused up to the value of the West. Every vessel, every steam-boat, brings up persons of all classes, whose countenances the desire of acquisition, or some other motive, has rendered sharp, or imported a fresh glow of hope to their eyes."[28] No Africans or Frenchmen, no space between East and West trouble this story. Like so many Anglo empire builders addressed in this study, Schoolcraft simply ignores the French and their legacy of intermixing and open-mindedness. Above all else, Schoolcraft champions "the desire of acquisition," which compelled the extermination of the Indians and the erasure of the French.

Schoolcraft's inability to understand the diversity of the French-Algonquian alliance and its persistence despite his efforts to impose his own patriarchal authority led to a grave misunderstanding of the racial and gender politics of the fur trade. His myopia began at home, though, in his inability to understand his wife or, perhaps more significant, his mother-in-law. After John Johnston's death in 1828, Susan took over his fur trade business and improved it, all the while maintaining her maple sugar plantation at La Pointe. In the end, she, Oshaw-guscoday-wayqua—a full-blooded Ojibwa woman —persisted and succeeded in both maintaining and continuing the processes of hybridization and improvisation innate to the French frontier. Neither her gender nor her race nor her son-in-law could remove her.

Henry Rowe Schoolcraft's nemesis, Dr. Edwin James, relates an episode that reflects the difference between Anglo and French notions of intermarriage. James occasionally worked at Schoolcraft's Sault and Mackinac agencies as a chaplain and medical doctor. Furthermore, each had been employed as a geologist on a federally funded expedition: James accompanied Stephen H. Long's expedition to the Rocky Mountains between 1818 and 1821; Schoolcraft was with Lewis Cass's expedition to the source of the Mississippi in 1820. Upon returning to New York, each successfully published a narrative of his journeys. However, the two often clashed on a variety of issues, and James clearly resisted Schoolcraft's efforts to establish patriarchal dominion over the various French, Ojibwa, and Métis populations on the Great Lakes. By means of revealing his character in his earlier narrative of Long's expedition, James recorded a disastrous marriage—showing the contrast between French and Anglo values—in ways that foreshadowed his later resistance to Schoolcraft.

In what is now Nebraska, James recalls an Anglo who exploited the traditions of intermarriage established by the French to gain favor as a trader with his wife's tribe. James describes a "squaw's" expectation that the Anglo would treat his vows to her as seriously as Frenchmen had: her Omaha family contracts with the Anglo trader for their daughter, and he is to be considered a son. However, he soon begins to seek patriarchal dominion in his marriage instead. Every winter, he impregnates her before returning to a white wife in St. Louis, unbeknown to his Omaha in-laws. Eventually, like Schoolcraft, he seeks to take his children from their mother and her tribe, as was the Anglo custom, and to raise them in the "settlements." With this, the Omaha woman is surprised, since Frenchmen did no such thing. What stands out in James's account is her articulate and righteous defense of her parental rights and legal autonomy. Returning to her husband's camp, "with the feelings of a wife and a mother to plead her cause before the arbiter of her fate," she speaks: "When you married me, you promised to use me kindly, as long as I should be faithful to you; that I have been so, no one can deny. Ours was not a marriage contracted for a season; it was to terminate only with our lives. . . . Is not my right paramount to that of your other wife; she had heard of me before you possessed her. It is true her skin is whiter than mine, but her heart cannot be more pure towards you nor her fidelity more rigid."[29] In his fictionalization of James's account in the short story "The New Moon," James Hall repeated this speech verbatim (and footnoted it), well aware of its multiple weapons for challenging the empire-building assumptions of patriarchal behavior. In his narrative, James then applauds Long's return of the child to its mother. The trader's attempts to exercise the unquestioned patriarchal authority granted by his whiteness and his maleness are thus rejected by the standards established by the French and applauded by James, Hall, *and* Long. While Long momentarily assumes patriarchal authority to resolve the conflict, it is limited: he leaves and takes the trader back to St. Louis. Moreover, leaving the mixed-race child with the Indians might be construed as implying a segregationist agenda. However, the saturation of both James's and Hall's versions of the story with Frenchmen denies any such binary distinction: the child will be raised (not raced) among the diversity of groups populating the Missouri River frontier.

The Anglo's duplicity, moreover, reveals a systemic flaw in the assumption of the Anglo patriarch's responsible exercise of discretion. As a patriarch, armed with the Anglo model of marriage, the trader assumes that, in marrying, the Omaha woman had forfeited such power. On the other side, the Omaha woman's recognition of their "contract" in marriage, however, implies an assumption of personal sovereignty regardless of her race, gender, or marital status. She assumes she had not forfeited these by marrying and resists his attempts to change the terms of their contract unilaterally. That is, she refuses to be removed from her rights, refusing to be any less than any person with whom a public contract had been made—and broken. James's and Hall's identification of the irresponsible use of patriarchal authority in this story points up the advantages of the French model, wherein power is less concentrated and individual rights more protected.

Along the same lines, the persistence of "squaws" like Susan Johnston in resisting patriarchy by maintaining both her Métis family and her tribal culture is corroborated more generally by a tremendous volume of research on the fur trade published since the rise of feminist scholarship in the 1970s. Jennifer Brown, Nancy Ostreich Lurie, Sylvia Van Kirk, Tanis Thorne, Colin Calloway, Lucy Eldervseld Murphy, Carol Devens, and, most recently, Leslie Choquette and Susan Sleeper-Smith have moved the entangled politics of race and family to the center of our understanding of how the French and Indians interacted in the century and a half before the Anglo-Americans dominated and then displaced the Indians and the Métis.[30] For these historians, the French willingness to accept and join extended Indian families—to put aside their patriarchal desires or expectations—was at the heart of the middle ground's premise of intercultural and interracial cohabitation. Sleeper-Smith especially discusses Catholicism's capacity for merging with Indian kinship systems as a means of empowering women:

> Because villages incorporated Frenchmen and rejected the possibility that Indian women "married out," marriages either sacramentally sanctioned or in "the manner of the country" transformed French traders into Indian husbands, fathers, and brothers. The western Great Lakes region was a highly complex kin-related world where individuality was subsumed by larger collective identity. . . . Catholic kin networks paralleled and were enmeshed in those of indigenous society. The fictive relationship created by god-parenting bridged the social boundaries between the French and the Indian worlds.[31]

In *Roads to Rome*, Jenny Franchot has also pointed out how Catholicism's diversity of family relations was viewed as a threat by Anglo-America.[32] In the fur trade, the collective identity at the heart of the extended family disempowered the patriarchal male and instead spread authority more broadly within a dense web of relations, fictive and genetic. Within this model, then, these historians find evidence of women being empowered in ways unavailable in either traditional Indian or European structures. That is, the trade's interculturalism is not simply Frenchmen "playing Indian."[33] On the contrary, each historian documents complex processes of adaptation and flexibility.

One Anglo-Ojibwa marriage modeled on the French paradigm was that of John and Susan Johnston. Their union lasted until his death, for forty years, and John seems to have recognized and respected Susan's rights as an Ojibwa woman. That their marriage lasted long enough to be so sanctified is testimony to John's adaptation of the French model of a husband's role, something his son-in-law never learned. However, despite Flint's claims of mutual repulsion, the sexual exploitation of Indian women by Anglo men was ubiquitous and well documented. As opposed to the typical French husband (such as Sacagawea's husband, Touissant Charboneau, who insisted his wife accompany him), most Anglos observed these marriages only seasonally and often returned to their white wives "at home" in the spring. Anglo men exploited the sexual opportunities offered by Indian women who thought themselves wives but who were, in fact, concubines.

During these same decades, Anglo-American women themselves were, in a way, also being *removed* from cultural viability and visibility, though not to the same degree as the Indian and the Métis. While their displacement was not physical, their increasing confinement to domestic spheres of activity, especially among the emergent bourgeois, is evidenced, correspondingly, by a rise in feminist resistance to their enclosure during the 1830s and 1840s. The new model woman, as dictated in conduct books by writers such as Catherine Beecher and Lydia Sigourney, deferred to her husband and fought her battles privately, subtly, within the domestic sphere, as Jane Johnston Schoolcraft attempted. This generation might be usefully contrasted with Revolutionary-era women such as Judith Sargent Murray, Anna Eliza Bleeker, Philis Wheatley, and Mercy Otis Warren, all of whom sought and found meaningful places in the public sphere, a place increasingly harder to find as the nineteenth century progressed.[34] In response, women such as Margaret Fuller,

Lucy Stone, and Elizabeth Cady Stanton energized a feminist movement with strong ties to the abolitionist and temperance causes. Fuller's admiration for the French has already been noted. The feminists' efforts at reform queried patriarchal marriage, and many early feminists experimented with unconventional domestic partnerships. Others redefined marriage and family in ways that did not reduce them to propertyless children. Like both Abigail Adams and the Omaha woman described by James, they sought legal equality with men and challenged the virtually unlimited discretionary patriarchal power of white husbands. One Anglo-American woman who found in the French-Indian extended family model an acceptable alternative was Juliette Kinzie.

Kinzie closes the main narrative of *Wau-Bun: The "Early Day" in the North-West* (1855) with an anecdote much like James's: an Anglo who takes advantage of the French model of interracial marriage and then abandons his squaw. Agatha Day-Kau-Ray, a Winnebago, enters the story after saving a group of voyageurs lost in a snowstorm on a mission to bring medicine to a sick woman. Agatha's family is rumored to have French blood, and she has lived with her tribe before working in the house of the Métis Paquette family, a family with whom Kinzie's readers were familiar. An Anglo "young officer" then impregnates and abandons her to marry a white woman after he is transferred back east. Kinzie notes and endorses the Winnebago response: "He will never dare show himself in this country! Not an Indian who knows the Day-Kau-Rays but would take his life if he should meet him." Following this, Agatha decides to raise the child as a Métis: "She attired it in the costume of the French children" and converts to Catholicism—all improvisations both Juliette and the community centered around her husband John's trading post find perfectly acceptable.[35]

Such mergings, splittings, and movements between and among a broad range of ethnic and racial identities are quite common in *Wau-Bun*, Juliette's chronicle of her life among the Wisconsin Winnebago between 1830 and 1833. Virtually all the other "whites" are

French, but she usually cannot tell whether they have Indian blood. In addition, she records meetings with the Winnebago chiefs named "Yellow Hair" and "Curly Head"—that is, whites or mixed-race people living tribally. Kinzie herself was a New England woman who moved west after marrying into an Anglo family that had largely acculturated into the intercultural paradigm of the fur trade. John Kinzie had been raised among the traders of southern Lake Michigan and had been appointed Indian agent first at Fort Winnebago in western Wisconsin in 1830 and later at Chicago in 1833. Unlike Schoolcraft, he had no links to Astor or any of the other multinational fur corporations. Nina Baym, in her introduction to *Wau-Bun*, comments on John's role as agent: "When such men became Indian agents they saw themselves as doing good for the Indians they supervised. Very few perceived the US government policy as a deliberate strategy to extirpate the Indians; and many of them, given their knowledge of intertribal warfare and settler greed, truly believed they were protecting the Indians from extinction." Moreover, the Kinzies' efforts were not to assimilate the Indians, and they openly acknowledged the right of individuals to make a wide array of choices concerning racial identity and cultural self-assignment. Although Juliette went west with the hope of informal Protestant proselytization, she quickly abandoned it, recognizing the "cultural imperialism," according to Baym, at its heart.[36]

While the Kinzies "kept apart from the Indians," John seems to have done little to position himself as their white "father," although that term is used for him in his capacity as agent, as was the custom. In *Wau-Bun*, Kinzie describes a community as a diverse set of familial possibilities and arrangements: some whites—French and Anglo—live as Indians, some Métis families live among the Anglos, and no one seeks to impose a single standard. Moreover, Juliette— far more than fellow Anglo women from the East who lived (albeit briefly) in the West such as Caroline Kirkland and Eliza Farnham— respects western women of all racial categories and classes and bases her comments on their behavior in that setting, refusing to measure them against the standards of the Cult of True Womanhood. In fact, the communities of women she encounters provide a less confrontational and race-obsessed means of dealing with this difficult moment in the region's history: the post-1815 era when the "Yankees arrived and dominated,"[37] in the terms of Richard White. Through their storytelling and exchange of traditions concerning the role of women in Winnebago, French, and Anglo cultures and economies, they achieve a greater intimacy than the men she describes, even her compassionate husband, John. In fact, Juliette's own story of her becoming an authoress is rooted in preserving the oral culture of the women she knew.

Juliette opens the book by claiming that John's mother inspired her to write. Juliette's transcription of her mother-in-law's story of the Chicago Massacre of 1812 was published in 1836 and is reprinted in chapters 18 through 22 in *Wau-Bun*. That massacre had been cited in a number of histories of the War of 1812 as revealing the true "savage" nature of Indians. In contrast, Kinzie's account establishes it as a far more complex affair involving different tribes, mixed-race populations, and the hostile Potawotamis' deliberate sparing of the Kinzie family. Juliette included it in *Wau-Bun* twenty years later aware of the controversial nature of her account: "Some who read the following sketches, may be inclined to believe that a residence among our native brethren and an attachment growing out of our peculiar relation to them, have exaggerated our sympathies, and our sense of the wrongs they have received at the hands of the whites. This is not the place to discuss that point. There is a tribunal at which man shall be judged, for that which he has meted out to his fellow-man. May our countrymen take heed that their legislation shall never unfit them to appear 'with joy, and not with grief' before that tribunal!"[38] Like Benjamin Drake in his sympathetic account of Black Hawk, Kinzie clearly believes many of her compatriots will not be joyful at Judgment Day. As to the Black Hawk War in 1832 itself, Juliette writes from the Winnebago perspective. John Kinzie and his cousin, Thomas Forsyth—agent at

Peoria and acknowledged as a friend by Black Hawk—try and fail to prevent the war by defending Black Hawk's right to reoccupy land in Illinois according to the 1816 treaty.[39] Juliette also goes to great lengths to prove the treacherous nature of the government's contrivance of those treaties as well (again following Drake). As the war commences and Black Hawk flees north toward Wisconsin, Juliette and the other women at the post flee to Green Bay, a removal she resists when ordered by the army but complies with when asked by her husband.

After the war, the U.S. Army captured a few Winnebagos and accused them of collaborating with Black Hawk, a fabrication used to remove the Winnebagos to Iowa as well. Juliette and John are both clearly disgusted at such behavior. When the captured men escape, Juliette writes: "It would be compromising our own reputation as loyal and patriotic citizens, to tell of the secret rejoicings this news occasioned us." Proud of being disloyal to a government she views as reprehensible, she records that John gladly accepted the Indians' "promise to return the young men *if they saw them.*"[40] Soon, even Juliette sees them, but she never turns them in. In brief, the Kinzies condemned the Black Hawk War and all that it represented as revealing the barbarous and selfish behavior of most Anglo-Americans toward the Indians. Moreover, the Winnebagos understand that the Kinzies can be trusted, viewing them as the inheritors of the long-standing French paradigm for intercultural relations.

Juliette married into a family that had been on the northwestern frontier since the end of the French dominion in 1763. Initially the British tried to regularize and regiment the fur trade. That failed, and they soon hired back the coureurs de bois and voyageurs and sought out men like John Kinzie père to represent their interests in an otherwise mostly unchanged middle ground. John fils was raised at his father's post in Chicago, and, as with Henry Marie Brackenridge, his views concerning gender—as well as race—seem to have been influenced by the many French and Métis among whom he grew up. *Wau-Bun* is saturated with French and Métis families, individuals, and entire villages. His treatment of the Winnebagos has already been noted as informed by a sense of fraternity, not patriarchy. This is can be traced out through Juliette's comments on his family's history and on his own treatment of his wife.

In *Wau-Bun*, John's mother and father seem to have played equal roles in his assumption of inherited French-based values. This becomes especially clear in the account of the massacre. Throughout, the Kinzie family and its familiars were deliberately ignored and thus spared by the British-paid Potawotamis: they mean to attack only the army. Of course, the French are spared as well—they were not considered American and therefore not part of the problem. The Kinzies save a number of other Anglos by dressing them as French servants—known as Weem-Tee-Gosh.[41] The Kinzies are taken out of Chicago by a series of Métis individuals—some tribal, some voyageur *engagees*—who address them in French for added protection. During their exile in St. Joseph, Michigan, John Kinzie père put himself fully under the authority of three tribal men: Black Partridge, a Potawotami chief; Billy Caldwell, a tribal Métis; and Ke-Po-Tah, a full-blood Winnebago who winters the family at the erstwhile French trading post. In brief, John understands that his family's survival was foregrounded by his French-like respect for the Indians, and it is sustained by his willingness to follow their lead. That is, he survives because he is not a patriarch.

Simultaneously, the women of Chicago reflect great strength and resilience. In the main text, Juliette emphasizes the role of women more generally in the fur trade. Of Madame La Framboise—the same woman Schoolcraft so badly misunderstood—she writes:

> There was the dwelling of Madame La Framboise, an Ottawa woman whose [French] husband had taught her to read and write, and who had ever after continued to use the knowledge she had acquired for the instruction and improvement of the youth among her own people. It was her custom to receive a class of

young people at her house daily. . . . She was a woman of a vast deal of energy and enterprise—of a tall and commanding figure, and most dignified deportment. After the death of her husband . . . she was accustomed to visit herself the trading-posts, superintend the clerks and engages, and satisfy herself that the business was carried on in a regular and profitable manner.[42]

One can begin to see why Henry Schoolcraft was befuddled by the world of the fur trade: the French and the Indians simply disregarded the rules of gender and race most basic to Anglo practices. Like Susan Johnston, Madame Le Framboise was not dependent on her husband or his whiteness to secure either an identity or a living for herself. Having been raised in this environment, John Kinzie—Juliette's husband—seems to have been made a better life partner for her than Henry Schoolcraft was for Jane.

First of all, John expects more from Juliette than most patriarchs expected from their wives: she is expected to ford icy swamps, to sleep in dilapidated shanties, to entertain Indian women, to manage the agency when he was away, and to supervise their *engagees* and their wives. John, multilingual and well versed in the ways of the trade, expects her to sustain herself not like a sheltered child but rather more like Susan Johnston or Madame La Framboise—Métis women for all intents and purposes. Once, while lost with her husband on a wintry journey, Juliette ponders her situation in a way not unlike that of Francis Parkman in the gully: " 'What would my friends at the East think,' I said to myself, 'if they could see me now? What would poor old Mrs. Welsh say? She who warned me that *if I came away so far to the West, I should break my heart?* Would she not rejoice to find how likely her prediction was to be fulfilled?' These thoughts roused me. I dried up my tears, and by the time my husband with his party, and all his horses and luggage, were across, I had recovered my cheerfulness, and was ready for fresh adventures."[43] In fact, when he expects the most of her, John playfully refers to her as "wifie," an ironic inversion of the infantilization of the patriarchy's reduction of women. Later, after giving birth, Juliette is visited by all the Winnebago and Métis women and allows them all to hold and touch the child. That is, her "fresh adventures" carry her far from the patriarchal expectations of her fragility and purity, and, unlike Parkman, she embraces them. Juliette becomes a woman, rather than a lady, on the frontier, and her husband gladly forgoes whatever other authority might have been available to him for the sake of her happiness and growth as a person.

Thanks to some fortunate real estate investments along the river in Chicago, the Kinzies became very wealthy after 1833. Juliette published *Wau-Bun* not for personal or financial benefit but rather for the sake of asking her Anglo-American readers to remember that there was a time when whites and Indians lived together, so long as the whites either were or acted like the French. *Wau-Bun* closes with Kinzie's inclusion of Thomas Forsyth's—John Kinzie's cousin and husband to a Potawotami woman—broadside condemning the Black Hawk War: "What right have we to tell any people, 'You shall not cross the Mississippi river on any pretext whatever'? When the Sauk and Fox Indians wish to cross the Mississippi, to visit their relations among the Pottawattamies, of Fox River, Illinois, they are prevented by us, because we have the power!'" For Forsyth, family relations transcended politically brokered borders meant to separate one race from another. The region was not just multiracial but inter-racial, a complexity the removalists could not decipher. To Forsyth's comment Juliette adds, "There is every reason to believe that had his suggestions been listened to, and had he continued as Agent of the Sauks and the Foxes, a sad record might have been spared."[44] Men like Forsyth and John Kinzie had lived on the middle ground and knew its advantages. The powers such men could have wielded over both the nonwhites and the women in their lives were great. That they did not reflects the lasting legacy of the French paradigm of friendship and exchange rather than the Anglo model of power and control.

In *Countering Colonization* (1992), her powerful account of the cultural intractability of Ojibwa women in fur trade communities, Carol Devens repeatedly observed that tribal women not only resisted assimilation but also served as the primary conservators of Indian lore: "David Thompson, a seasoned veteran of the bush married to a mixed-blood Ojibwa . . . noted, moreover, that, when villagers gathered around the fires on a winter's evening it was women who awed and intrigued them with tales of the creation and the exploits of trickster heroes—of times when people were stronger, animals more numerous, and humans could converse with the bear and the beaver."[45] Like the women in *Wau-Bun*, the women Devens studies preserve cultural integrity in the face of numerous challenges. In both, communities are built by women's preservation and perpetuation of common memories. With these she contrasts the documentary or romantic historiographies that buttressed male dominance by claiming the men's histories—such as Schoolcraft's—were far less accurate.[46] Devens claims that, in male-authored Anglo writings about the Ojibwa, "there appears, rather, to be invented tradition of male supremacy" and that "gender dichotomy is a phenomenon of colonization."[47] Yet in the hands of empire builders—like Schoolcraft—such a misrepresentation justified the transposition of their own patriarchal standards for exploiting Indian women and infantilizing white women.

As transcribed by Edwin James, John Tanner's account of thirty years as an adopted Ojibwa in the western Great Lakes region affirms Devens's findings. Tanner repeatedly finds men and women—Ojibwa, French, and Métis—serving separate but genuinely equal functions in the maintenance of the tribes and families. Many of the husbands and fathers among the Ojibwa are French or Métis, some men are culturally transgendered—doing what Anglos would call women's work—and some women assume the powers of chieftainship. In Tanner's own experience, his marriages are happy so long as he, in Sleeper-Smith's terms, becomes, like a Frenchman, an

"Indian's husband" rather than making his partner a "white man's wife."[48] Kinzie's and, implicitly, James's approval of the supple nature of gender roles and family structure in the French-Indian fur trade demonstrates a marked discontent with marriage within Anglo-America. Each communicates a subversive hint that the frontier's destabilizing effects on racial and gender relations were good things for the nation.

Kinzie places gender and family at the center of her book to show that, in adapting to the French family model, the fur-trade-based population provided a marriage paradigm not circumscribed by patriarchy or male desire. In the world of the trade, there were nuclear families, extended families, and matriarchal and matrilineal as well as patriarchal and patrilineal customs. The French and the Indians improvised according to local needs and traditions, and the French, by not imposing their needs, were more collaborators than colonizers. In her own writing, then, Kinzie carries on the longer tradition of female cultural conservatorship—countering the colonization of both women and Indians.

In James's aforementioned anecdote of the Omaha woman abandoned by her Anglo husband, the initial conflict arises over where and how their children were to be raised and educated. The Omaha expected the French custom to continue: the children would be raised in her tribe; the Anglo expected to take "his" children to St. Louis or points farther east to be educated in "white" society. At the level of terminology, she expected her children to be "Métis," and he expected them to be "half-breed," a distinction to which I want to call attention. As Métis, the children would have filled a long-standing role as transcultural "brokers" or intermediaries, if they chose, or they might have chosen to live in traditional tribal ways: the French and Indian paradigm allowed for a choice of identity alien to Anglo notions of social categorization and biological predestination.

"Métis" is *not* a synonym for "half-breed" or "half-blood," regardless of the trivia of genetic contributions. "Half" implies the fragmented and ultimately impossible cobbling together of distinctly "white" and "Indian" characteristics: a combination of old things rather than the creation of something new, an affirmation of the intransigence of racial difference—a perpetuation of incompleteness. The difference also permeates the Anglos' selective adoption of French place-names and other vernacular terminology as they came to dominate the French frontier. For example, William Cullen Bryant's "The Prairies" (1832), like most Anglo-American literature, mostly ignores a century of French settlement in Illinois in its revisionist ahistorical gaze over Illinois landscape. Yet Bryant does note that he will use one French word: "These are the gardens of the Desert, these / The unshorn fields, boundless and beautiful, / For which the speech of England has no name— / The Prairies."[49] A euphonic and mellifluous word, "prairie" lent a slight exoticism based strictly on topography, without identifying the land as anyone's possession. The word underscored the *terra nullius* or tabula rasa myth that gave the region no history to erase: the lands were Anglo-America's by "right of discovery" without the Augustan formality of the Latin. When Anglo-Americans entered the lands where the colonial French had been or still were, they encountered other peoples, places, and things, like intermarriage, for which a functional place-based vernacular had been improvised, and, like Bryant, their choice to adopt or ignore these terms reveals more than an episode in American taxonomy.

They rejected "Métis" as both a term and a way of intercultural or transcultural existence. Most Anglos imprecisely assigned "half-breed" or "half-blood" labels to all peoples of indeterminate multiracial parentage, a careless categorization typical of the racial ossification and biologization in the early nineteenth century. This was reflected in their literature, as it reflects profoundly, yet succinctly, on the racial politics of American imperialism. For example, the emphasis on blood quanta—"half"—reveals the Yankees' obsession with quantification and commodification, even as they imprecisely used "half" to refer to any amount of nonwhite blood along a fixed continuum: all mixed peoples were labeled "half-breed/blood."[50] In addition, the implicit accentuation of the biological basis of racial difference—"breed" or "blood"—indicates a reductive pseudoscientific assignment of bestial qualities to nonwhites in colonial settings.[51]

Most of the literary representations of "half-breeds" or "-bloods" in Anglo-American writing tell stories about how they failed to combine "white" and "Indian" characteristics. The authors of those stories always assumed that the two essential racial identities, even within the body of the individual, could be neither mixed nor hybridized and usually reflected the worst of each. Perhaps the most egregious example of this is Walt Whitman's "The Half-Breed," in which the deformed title character seeks to destroy Indian and white alliances in a frontier community. More often, scholars have focused on indeterminately part-Anglo, part-Indian "half-breeds" or "half-bloods" such as Mark Twain's "Injun Joe" from *The Adventures of Tom Sawyer* (1876) or the Bloney family of William Gilmore Simms's *The Partisan* (1835).[52] In fact, the Anglo version of the "half-breed/half-blood" prominently appears in notable antebellum writers James Fenimore Cooper, Lydia Maria Child, and John Neal.[53] Their historical fictions depict the removal (through either Indianization, emigration, or death) of mixed-race peoples historically set well before their stories' conclusions and consumption by antebellum readers. For those readers, this solved retroactively, as if by fiat, a contemporary problem: half-blood may as well be full-blood and so is tragically fated for the same extinction, and, by that logic, all nonwhites are unsuited for continued membership in the nation. While "half-breed" characters certainly complicate the "frontiers" imagined by Anglo writers, they essentially embody the triumphalist white/nonwhite dichotomy on which white dominion was established and narrated.

For example, although its title borrows a French synonym for "Métis"—"The Bois Brule"—William Snelling's novella dramatizes the inevitability at the heart of the "half-breed/blood" narrative dichotomy.[54] Gordon—a "half-blood" Scotsman and Algonquian— has his two sides, one Indian, one white. After an injury, the physicality based in his Indian nature is precluded, so he partners in his travels with another "half-blood," and each moves toward the opposed racial poles. Eventually, the "half-blood" whose Indian side has become dominant dies, and Gordon, the one whose white characteristics have become ascendant, marries the white heroine and moves to Europe, where his racial identity would be a nonissue, a common removal for writers like Child, Harriet Beecher Stowe, and Thomas Mayne Reid. For these Anglo writers, racial ambiguity had no place in Anglo-America, with its insistence upon more narrowly and knowably defined roles and hierarchies. In the Anglo model, there are no choices: a pre-Darwinian determinism forces the action of the story—the multiraced person contains two natures, and life on the frontier brings out latent race-based traits, each race's inevitable essence. To reject such racial determinism, then, would be to accept racial diversity and to base citizenship and social and political inclusion on behavior rather than biology. Although some Anglo writers who did so continued the use of the term "half-breed," even as they stripped it of its negative connotations, I would suggest that their positive representations of mixed-race people or individuals reflect a tacit acceptance of the conceptual distinctiveness of Métis identity.

These writers' use of the concept or consciousness of "Métis" (if not always the word) strips away the negative connotations of incompleteness in "half" and articulates a distinct presence for mixed-race peoples in Anglo-American writing. In mapping out the difference between Métis and "half-blood" experiences, John Tanner's children might serve as models.[55] His older children by his first Ojibwa wife, born prior to the Americanization of the fur trade after 1815, remained outside Anglo-America and eventually settled on the White Earth Reservation; they were Métis. His later children, by his second Ojibwa wife, were "half-breeds": they were raised at the Presbyterian Mission at Mackinac and acculturated as Anglos. One even served in the Union army. Tanner's children found at White Earth a Métis community based on French and Ojibwa habits and traditions from the pre-1815 era.[56] The point is, after 1830, to be Métis meant to live among Indians, and it had not before then.

However, just as the French-Indian model included the nuclear family as one of many options, it also allowed Métis to live as they chose, the transformative transcendence of the binaries, to recall Bill Ashcroft. Some Métis chose to assimilate to Anglo cultural standards; others chose the Indian ways of their mothers or transcultured voyageur or coureur de bois fathers (or both). Métis making this choice appear repeatedly in writing by Francis Parkman (as we have seen) and also Alexander Mackenzie, Zebulon Pike, David Thompson, and many others. The White Earth Reservation also produced William Warren—the French-Anglo-Ojibwa historian—a number of articulate and insightful Ojibwa leaders and spokespeople, and, more recently, novelists Louise Erdrich and Gerald Vizenor. When each recalls his or her time in the white schools and such, they write critically of "Americanization" and describe how it brought destructive moral values and hypocritical versions of national culture to the Ojibwa. As writers, they represent the Métis perspective, one that "counters colonization" by resisting the imperial terms of racial identity. While each could have self-identified as exclusively Ojibwa, each instead chose the more complex perspective of what Vizenor calls the "crossblood," an oblique reference to Cooper's Natty, who boasts his blood had never been "crossed."[57]

Such individuals embody a selective blending of a diversity of cultural characteristics in ways appropriate to the setting and circumstances of the individual Métis. For example, Antoine Le Clair—Potawotami-French Métis from southern Wisconsin—is best known as Black Hawk's interviewer, transcriber, and translator. For his services as translator during treaty negotiations, he was also granted lands east of the Mississippi in 1824 and 1826, lands lost when he and his Potawotami relatives were removed to Iowa after 1833.[58] Yet in Iowa, Le Clair established himself as a trader and intermediary.

Under the French model that long outlasted French administration, Le Clair was a Métis, rather than a half-breed, in that he refused to be either tribal or assimilated. Margaret Connell Szasz defined someone like Le Clair as a "broker": "Intermediaries become repositories of two or more cultures; they changed roles at will, in accordance with the circumstances. Of necessity, their lives reflected a complexity unknown to those living within the confines of a single culture. They knew how the 'other side' thought and behaved, and they responded accordingly." R. David Edmunds's study of the Métis depicts them, before 1826 and the government's relabeling them as Indian, as forming a community of intercultural "brokers," perhaps even moving toward the identity and homeland sought by Louis Reil and the Canadian Métis (Francophone) and half-bloods (Anglophone) in Manitoba in the late 1860s.[59]

Yet after 1826 in the United States, the transracial, transcultural, and transnational Métis' claim to distinctive identity was rejected. In the family metaphor, they were treated as bastards and thus unsuited for full family membership. Edmunds addresses why Anglo-America rejected them:

> The answer lies in the ethnocentric viewpoint of the Americans, and in their vision of the future development of the United States. . . . Although American leaders complained that they were indigent, many Metis maintained a standard of living comparable to that of American settlers. But, to the Americans, they had accepted the *wrong* European culture, that of the creole French. Moreover, their close ties with the remaining Indian communities made them doubly undesirable. . . . Although the new United States prided itself upon becoming a melting pot, settlers demanded that the crucible forge models in their own image. The Metis were made of a different subject.[60]

Edmunds also studies agrarian, assimilationist Métis communities where, although the *right* European culture had been chosen, removal was still imposed. From this, the cultural work of fictions like

Whitman's or Snelling's can be observed as foreclosing not only the Métis' options for self-determination itself but also the racial and cultural open-mindedness they represented.

_____ As I have alluded, the 1826 Treaty of Fond du Lac represents a crucial switch from accommodationist French to imperial American values. Thomas McKenney included both the treaty and a narrative of the negotiations in his *Sketches of a Tour of the Lakes* (1828). McKenney was a supporter of President John Quincy Adams and was working against the political ascendance of Andrew Jackson, famous as an "Indian fighter" and keen to remove them by force. As treaty commissioner, McKenney wrote the treaty with the best outdated Federalist intentions, reflecting the same Enlightenment values of consent and sovereignty Richard White has identified as characterizing the Treaty of Greenville in 1795.[61] At Fond du Lac in 1826, the American goal was not to remove the Ojibwa but rather to affirm the Ojibwa's right to lands east of the Mississippi in the upper peninsula of Michigan, rights established the summer before in the Treaty of Prairie du Chien.

For my purposes, Articles IV and V of the treaty are more significant. Article IV discusses "half-breeds":

> It being deemed important that the half-breeds, scattered through this extensive country, should be stimulated to exertion and improvement by the possession of permanent property and fixed residences, the Chippeway tribe, in consideration of the affection they bear to these persons, and of the interest they feel in their welfare, grant to each of the persons described in the schedule hereunto annexed, . . . six hundred and forty acres of land, to be located, under the direction of the President of the United States, upon the islands and shore of the St. Mary's river [the Sault], wherever good land enough for this purpose can be found.

First on the "schedule" is Susan Johnston—Oshaw-guscoday-wayqua—whose inclusion assured William Henry Schoolcraft, her grandson, of a profitable inheritance, one his father sought for himself. Henry Rowe Schoolcraft thus signed the treaty as a witness out of self-interest. McKenney's text of it, however, reflect values distinctly at odds with Schoolcraft's: "It is the intentions of the parties, that, where circumstances will permit, the grants be surveyed in the ancient French manner, bounding not less than six arpens, nor more than ten, upon the river, and running back for quantity."[62] That is, these are to be French-style ribbon farms, not Anglo-style rectangles. While he means to convert the Métis to farmers, McKenney clearly means to extend middle-ground values of community and neighborly cooperation in the process, as opposed to the distance and individuality of the Anglo model. Virtually all the names on the schedule (save for John Tanner's children) after Oshaw-guscoday-wayqua's are French, revealing that McKenney valued and recognized the functional and positive effects of French-Ojibwa interculturalism and saw no reason to remove it.

Nonetheless, his political patron John Quincy Adams did. The treaty was ratified by the president, "with the exception of the fourth and fifth articles," the fifth being an insistence on the fertility of lands selected for what would become the White Earth Reservation.[63] Learning of these crucial excisions, McKenney wrote to Michigan territorial governor Lewis Cass, "How hard is the fate of the poor Indians! We proposed to give them bread out of their *own* ground, & those who knew they were dying for lack of food will not let them have it!!!"[64] While Adams's excision may have been an effort to placate the Jacksonians, the Democrats used the split to expose Whig inconsistencies. Adams's betrayal reflects the growing "one drop" feeling of American racial identity; McKenney's effort, in contrast, reflects a hope that the Métis could bring Indians and whites closer together, as had been the case with the French.

A number of Cadotte family names also appear on McKenney's "schedule," members of an entangled French-Ojibwa family that might be considered the most important Métis family of the northern fur trade. The first Cadotte—originally Cadeau—came to western Lake Superior around 1671 and married into the Ojibwa nation. Various sons and grandsons (sometimes with Ojibwa mothers, other times Métis) were considered both French traders and Ojibwa chiefs by 1750. Over the next one hundred years, various sons, daughters, and grandchildren of the Cadottes embodied Szasz's idea of cultural brokerage. Over the years, the Cadottes were visited and described by Anglo writers including Schoolcraft, MacKenzie, and Henry. For them, the Cadottes represent the final Métis presence as the Anglos assumed control of the region from the French. Their role therefore has been narrated as transitional, a symbol of what had been rather than of what would remain.

More telling than these are the accounts of two Métis writers who knew the Cadottes as living and exciting people: William Warren and Major John Richardson. In their texts, the Cadottes offer an intriguing way of understanding the continuity of intercultural cooperation up through the middle of the nineteenth century. In various Cadottes, these multiracial writers—each working within the context of Anglo print culture—found a vehicle for rediscovering in themselves and preserving for posterity Métis values and economics in antebellum America to combat the pervasive presences such as Astor's corporate fur trade and Schoolcraft's patriarchal family. Neither Warren nor Richardson finds in the male Cadottes aspirations to patriarchy, and instead each finds men who understand their role in unifying their fragmented communities in the face of its coming dissolution.

Warren, only one year old in 1826, was on McKenney's erased "schedule" through his status as Jean-Baptiste Cadotte père's great-grandson (born c. 1730). However, as a son of Lyman Warren—a Yankee trader—he would be sent first to the Mission School at Mackinac and then to Oneida, New York, for schooling—both a Métis and half-breed, so to speak. Nonetheless, as I argue elsewhere, when he wrote his *History of the Ojibway People*, he expressed a decidedly non-Anglo perspective, articulating instead a perspective more reflective of the many cultures to which he was heir.[65] In his maternal great uncle Jean Baptiste Cadotte fils and grandfather Michel Cadotte (c. 1800), he finds the most prominent Métis characters of his book. Warren foregrounds their stories with the story of the elder Jean Baptiste, quoting at length from Alexander Henry's account of his salvation by Jean Baptiste and his Ojibwa wife during the massacre at Mackinac in 1763. Henry writes that, after the end of official French administration, "they considered Cadotte their chief, and he was not only my friend, but a friend to the English. It was by him that the Chippeways of Lake Superior were prevented from joining Pontiac."[66] While Cadotte fought with the French during the war, he considered Pontiac's insurrection pointless. Warren then relates how the Cadottes saved Henry—the same way the Kinzie family saved a few Anglos at Chicago in 1812— by cross-dressing him as French.[67]

In Warren's *History*, the next generation of Cadottes comprised the most prominent Métis traders prior to the coming of the Anglos and Astor. Unlike the later-coming Chouteaus in St. Louis, however, the Cadottes pursued their trade without Indian or African slave labor. In fact, Warren relates two episodes illustrating their problematic engagement with the overwhelming commercial values of the incorporated fur trade. In the fall of 1792, Jean Baptiste Cadotte fils, with Henry, proposed to open the headwaters of the Mississippi for beaver skins. Trouble was, the Sioux considered that area their hunting and trapping grounds. Although the Ojibwa considered Cadotte a tribal person, he appealed to the Sioux, when confronted, as a white man and brokered a functional (and very temporary) peace. Warren describes Jean Baptiste's negotiation of intertribal tensions as a masterful manipulation of his experience as an intercultural broker. After Jean Baptiste announces his momentary "whiteness" by hoisting a British flag, the Sioux back down: "The Dakotas replied to the effect, that, considering them to be a party of Ojibways interloping on their best hunting grounds, they had collected their warriors to destroy them; but as they had now discovered them to be white men, with whom they wished to be friends, they would shake hands with them, and smoke with them from the same pipe, intimating that they wished to enter his dwelling."[68] Jean Baptiste in this scene takes into account four distinct ethnic presences: French and British, Ojibwa and Sioux. As a Métis, he can move among each and all, and, in the end, a successful trading season is the result and the usual seasonal strife between the Sioux and the Ojibwa avoided.

Warren's text, however, by no means idealizes the Cadottes or even enacts a full transcendence of old prejudices. Revealing his own tribal biases, Warren, like Jane Johnston Schoolcraft in her rejection of Waub Ojeeg's Sioux roots, concludes the episode with Jean Baptiste warding off an attempted Sioux treachery. Next, Jean Baptiste then drinks away the winter's profits in Montreal, like so many other coureurs de bois, and Warren concedes the seemingly essential danger of alcoholism among the Indians and the Métis.[69] However, in the Anglicized incorporation of the fur trade, this exposes him to a new danger. Alexander MacKenzie, of the Northwest Fur Company, buys Jean Baptiste's subsequent debt from the also bankrupted Alexander Henry, and Mackenzie forces Jean Baptiste to become an employee, operating a post at Fond du Lac, ending his career as a coureur de bois, an independent trader—the small businessman swallowed by the corporate giant. On the old French frontier, such debts might have been allowed to wait until the next winter; as the Anglos come in, the Métis and the Indians could no longer rely on such informal arrangements.

In contrast, Warren discusses Michel, Jean Baptiste's brother and his own grandfather, as more aware of the changes occurring around him. Warren begins this transition by marking his own shift from oral to documentary sources. Prior to this, he relied on secondhand sources. Now, he finds he can be more reliable: "We have now arrived at a period in the history of the Ojibways, which is within the remembrance of aged chiefs, half-breeds, and traders still living amongst them . . . the greatest trouble will now consist in choosing from the mass of information which the writer has been collecting during several years past." Michel's career reflects a parallel modernity, an awareness that, if the ways of the French frontier are to survive, they must be pursued with greater sobriety and adaptability. To do this, Michel emphasized his role as Ojibwa chief: "The memory of this man, the marks of whose wintering posts are pointed out to this day throughout every portion of the Ojibwa country, is still dear to the hearts of the few old chiefs and hunters who lived cotemporary with him, and received, his unbounded charitable disposition. Full of courage and untiring enterprise, he is mentioned to this day as having not only placed the weapons into the hands of the Ojibways which enabled them to conquer their enemies, but led them each winter westward and further westward into the rich hunting grounds of the Dakotas."[70] Michel's goal was the expansion of Ojibwa territory, as he understood that the Ojibwa's ability to control the Mississippi would force the fur companies (Astor's *and* MacKenzie's) to subcontract the region's furs through the Ojibwa and allow the traditions of the ancien régime to continue in isolation.

Warren then traces his own disappointment with the intratribal conflicts that led to Michel's removing himself from the fur trade. In 1808, tensions were high because of the influence of Tenskatawa, the Shawnee prophet, and his demand that Indians recover pre-Columbian lifeways, refusing all contact with "whites."[71] Tenskatawa's reactionary position clearly represented the polarized racial atmosphere introduced by the Anglos, yet, almost as much as Anglo racism itself, this left Métis like Michel in a difficult position. As a whole, the Ojibwa were split between following and rejecting the prophet. The Cadottes mostly wanted to ignore him but admired his views on temperance. When Michel refused alcohol to a chief of an anti-Tenskatawa band, his storehouse was trashed, and he left to live with his wife's more moderate band. However, recovering these losses proved impossible, and Michel sold out to his Anglo son-in-law—Lyman Warren, William's father—in 1823. Warren eulogizes Michel in this way: "Like all other traders who have passed their lifetime in the Indian country, possessing a charitable heart and an open hand, ever ready to relieve the poor and suffering Indian, he died poor, but not unlamented. He was known among the Ojibways by the name Ke-che-me-shane (Great Michel)."[72] When Michel dies, symbolically, for Warren, the hope of racial conciliation and cohabitation withers and dies in the face of coming Anglo dominance and commercialization. While he admires his Anglo father and his Ojibwa "relations," he is clearly most interested the Cadottes' complex existence between, among, and apart from both races—the last bastion of the French frontier, as corporate pressures forced whites to act more like Anglos and Indians to protect their traditions more defensively.

In Warren's book, the Métis are the first victims of Anglo dominion and subsequent racial polarization. As a Cadotte on his mother's side, Warren understood the threat posed by the Anglo redefinition of race not only to the Indians but also to the Métis, and he traces out their decline in the story of the waning power of the family. Like other French and Métis, the Cadottes did not reckon their relationship to their opposites by biology or race. In their stories, Alexander Henry and the other cross-dressed Anglos are protected because they are willing to play by the rules written by the French and the Ojibwa, instead of writing their own. For Warren, Michel Cadotte was the father—but not the patriarch—of a family that retained its French and Ojibwa characteristics long after the end of French administration. As his grandson, Warren, a member of the Minnesota Territorial Legislature representing the White Earth Reservation, sought new means—through politics and history writing—to sustain that legacy.

Warren's cousin, Michel Cadotte fils, lived more like a traditional Métis, even after 1836 and the removal of most of the Métis and Ojibwa to White Earth or Red River. For example, in 1848, returning from Montreal, he traveled with Major John Richardson from Toronto to a distribution of treaty goods to Michigan-based Ojibwa and Potawotamis in Sarnia, Ontario. An officer in the

British army since he was fifteen years old, Richardson had fought alongside Tecumseh in the War of 1812 and in 1828 had published a long poem about the Shawnee leader. The aging Richardson—known as a Canadian poet, novelist, soldier, and administrator—had long ignored his own mixed Odawa-British birth but was now alienated from the corporate fur trade interests taking control of Canada in the wake of the uprising of 1837. He had been removed from his editorship of a provincial magazine for his insistence on editorial autonomy, and Canadian and British readers ignored his efforts at Cooperian fiction, *Wacousta* (1832) and *The Canadian Brothers* (1840).[73] His trip with Cadotte seems to have made him want to leave Canada for the United States and to self-identify as a mixed-race American rather than as a white Canadian.

Resettled in New York, he wrote for Ojibwa editor George Copway's *American Indian Magazine* and commenced a trilogy of novels set against the Chicago Massacre of 1812. Working directly from Juliette Kinzie's 1836 pamphlet, Richardson fictionalized John Kinzie père as a source of intercultural wisdom that might have prevented the tragedy had the American army only heeded his advice. *Hardscrabble* and *Wau-Nan-Gee*, the first two novellas, establish Richardson's main theme: a love story between a Potawotami warrior and an Anglo woman.[74] However, Richardson's death in 1852 left the third part of the story unwritten and the lovers fleeing to Detroit at the end of the second. The intercultural and French sympathies in these novels represent a radical departure from the marked anxiety to affirm his Anglo-British identity that characterized his earlier fiction.

Between the earlier and later parts of his career as a fiction writer, Richardson's time with Michel Cadotte, his biographers concur, seems to have spurred an internal transition from assimilated half-breed to ambivalent Métis. In the account he published in Copway's paper, "A Trip to Walpole Island and Port Sarnia in the Year of 1848," Richardson describes Cadotte:

Cadot[te] is a half-breed, and a tall and well proportioned fellow, capable, like a second Maximilian, if one may judge from appearances, of knocking down an ox with a single blow from his fist; yet like many strong men, he is of mild and unassuming manners, and altogether such a one as may well account for the passion entertained for him, by the accomplished English lady, who it will be recollected, eventually became his wife. As is the case with many of those who have Indian blood in their veins, Cadot has much of the polished manner of the courtier and is imbued with high and honorable sentiments—sentiments which may serve as a lesson and a reproach to those who make great hypocritical displays of morality, and seem the very incarnation of virtue.

Richardson's envy of Cadotte might be contrasted with his own disappointment, as expressed in his memoir, *Eight Years in Canada* (1847), with the Jackson-style Canadian Anglos who forced his removal from office, even if employment in the office kept him, like Parkman, from the outdoors virtues of men like Cadotte. Furthermore, Cadotte's marriage to an Englishwoman speaks to further race mixing, a pattern Richardson endorses and Cadotte obviously considers a nonissue. After mediating the payment, Cadotte returns to the Michigan woods across the St. Clair River with the Ojibwa, and Richardson clearly wishes he could have gone with him: "Among them was Cadotte, who, having received his presents, here left us, for the purpose of riding home a horse he had just purchased, paddled swiftly to the shore, uttering the shrill and significant *yep-yep-yep*—which was answered at intervals, and in tones rendered softer, in proportion to distance, by their departing friends on shore."[75] Like both Jane Johnston Schoolcraft and William Warren, Richardson did not live long enough to expand and articulate the Métis sensibility he apparently sought to express following his subsequent move to New York in 1850. In *Hardscrabble* and *Wau-Nan-Gee*, French characters are no longer the villains, as they had been in his

Wacousta and *The Canadian Brothers*—and his positive fictionalization of the Kinzies signals his reembrace of the intercultural accommodation on the part of the Anglos, a policy he had earlier denigrated. For both Warren and Richardson, the Cadottes represented
the retention of Métis identity despite intense pressure, from both
Anglos and Indians, to become half-breeds.

Sympathetic Anglo accounts of Cadotte-type Métis
affirm both the pervasive presence of the negative stereotype Warren
and Richardson resisted and the resilience of the Métis. Such Anglo
texts establish their critique of Anglo domestic institutions by recognizing distinct Métis abilities and identity. First, Washington Irving's guide in *A Tour of the Prairie*, Pierre Beatte, is held apart from
the lower-class *engagees* and the other marginal figures: "He was
cold and laconic; made no promises nor professions; stated the terms
he required for the services of himself and his horse, which we
thought rather high, but showed no disposition to abate them, nor
any anxiety to secure our employ. He had altogether more of the red
than the white man in his composition; and, as I had been taught to
look upon all half-breeds with disgust, as an uncertain and faith-
less race, I would gladly have dispensed with the services of Pierre
Beatte."[76] After this early passage, much of what follows has to
do with Irving unlearning this prejudice, learning that a "half-
breed" is not a Métis. Beatte turns out to be for Irving much like
Henry Chatillon would be for Francis Parkman. One difference, of
course, is that Beatte is "a half-breed of French and Osage parentage," whereas Chatillon was more purely French, although George
Catlin claims Beatte sought him out to claim that Irving was mistaken: Beatte claimed to be entirely French.[77] What matters, however, is that Irving *thought* Beatte was a "half-breed." In *Tour*, Irving
describes his own transition from thinking of Beatte as a fragmented
half-breed to reconceiving of him as a fully distinct Métis, a man
neither white nor Indian but instead one wholly of his setting and a
virtuous and humane leader in that context. While Parkman's admi-

ration for Chatillon is based on a model of white masculinity and fraternity, Irving's respect for Beatte opens up far more interesting possibilities concerning the limits of racial inclusion in antebellum America, even if the potential inclusion of multiracial men such as Beatte in Irving's elite circle is predicated on the exclusion of the lower classes.

John S. Robb's *Kaam; or, Daylight: The Arapahoe Half-Breed* (1847) also ponders this dichotomy but presents its rejection as a tragedy. The orphaned title character—half Arapahoe, half British—is placed by his Anglo trapper stepfather under the care of a French "Padre" in St. Louis. With the Padre, Kaam becomes a multilingual, kind-hearted, and handsome gentleman in local social circles, even if he's a little too fond of "historical romances" in the Padre's library. When his entirely Anglo half brother breaks up his engagement to a white girl by claiming Kaam is full-blood and then seducing his beloved, Kaam goes west with his stepfather, joins his Arapahoe family, and establishes a trading post to be operated by Métis intermediaries. On a return visit to St. Louis for supplies, Kaam saves, befriends, and then slays his half brother.[78] The Padre then leads him to his broken-hearted beloved, who dies in his arms. Kaam returns to the Arapahoe, saves them from a Pawnee ambush, and forgoes the ways of the white man entirely.

Amid all the very typical intrigue—interracial coupling, seduction, and violence—almost lost are two key elements: Robb's abolitionism and his depiction of the foreclosure of Kaam's choices by systemic social forces in antebellum America. First, what alienates Kaam most about "civilization" is slavery: "The thought that his white father, whose blood ran in his own veins, had contemplated selling him into hopeless slavery, but strengthened his hate towards him as well as created a feeling of dislike to the whole system of civilization under which such distinctions could exist, or such wrongs be perpetrated."[79] Further, had Kaam stayed in St. Louis—the old French town at the heart of the fur trade—and operated his trade with the Arapahoe, his Métis identity would have been no impediment to his social and economic inclusion, just like Billy Cald-well and other mixed-race chiefs in *Wau-Bun*. His dream of a dis-tinct Métis identity is crushed by his brother's imposition of the racial polarization central to Anglo concepts of identity, chang-ing Kaam from Métis to half-breed. In the end, unlike Snelling's Gordon—for whom race determines destiny—for Kaam, race is made fate only by racist Anglo intervention. In the end, Anglo greed and lust cause Kaam to reject American citizenship in favor of Arap-ahoe chieftainship.

Like James Hall, Robb was a frontier journalist and business-man, editor of the *St. Louis Reveille*. In "Kaam" and in his other fiction (most of it newspaper grist), Robb described St. Louis as a constantly changing mix of cultures, languages, peoples, religions, and stories that is nonetheless part of the American nation despite its diversity in language, religion, demographics, and race.[80] While Hall, in his adaptation of Edwin James's anecdote in "The New Moon," and Robb represent the European occupation of the West, their means of imagining and constructing a western community is neither homogeneous in nature nor imperial in method. Their model is the French one of cohabitation and pluralism, the extended and collaborative family, against which they pose the Anglo ethos of unilateral conquest, raced opposition, and patriarchal singularity. In what is arguably his final story, Hall returned to this theme. When "race mixing" was imagined in the antebellum period, the coupling was usually imagined as a white man with a nonwhite woman. In fact, enslaved female African American concubines/rape victims and Indian "squaws" mothered most first-generation multiracial Americans. Not only was this accurate as a matter of demographics, but in the popular, middle-class imagination, the image of the in-creasingly victimized and infantilized white woman being "de-bauched" or "ravaged" by the hypersexualized African American or Indian male was a volatile means of inciting the bitterest of racist antagonisms. In that context, the depiction of a nonwhite male cou-pled with a white female would be especially inflammatory, and purposefully so, as Richardson likely had in mind, in the final, unwritten novel of his Chicago trilogy.

In *Tales of the Border* (1835), James Hall ventured into the same volatile arena. He rewrote his most famous story, "The Indian Hater" (1828), as "The Pioneer." In the earlier story, the focus had been on the narrator's encounter with a psychotic frontiersman, bent on avenging the massacre of his family by "a group of Indians" when he was a boy. Hall ends the story ineffectively, letting the title character ride away, not doing enough to condemn the practice, leaving himself open to criticism by Herman Melville, who, in *The Confidence Man* (1857), pilloried Hall, according to Brian Drinnon, as a charlatan and an Indian hater himself.[81]

However, between writing the two stories, Hall had witnessed the Black Hawk War and had come to see Indian hating as a national sickness rather than as an anecdotal aberration, and his rewriting of the story reflects a much greater sensitivity. In 1833, Hall had moved to Cincinnati and was working with Benjamin Drake, whose 1838 biography of Black Hawk stands even now as the most eloquent excoriation of that war.[82] In "The Pioneer," the Indian Hater himself is given the narrative voice, and from the start it is remorseful, reflecting Hall's transformation. Of more immediate importance, the Indian Hater spends a few years in the woods with an old coureur de bois—Peter—who teaches him about woodcraft and racial tolerance. Nonetheless, the Indian Hater gives in to one final impulse for revenge when, while hunting, he espies an Indian family camped by a creek, a scene described by Hall as a tableau of domestic bliss and intimacy. However, the Hater soon recognizes the "squaw" as his long-lost sister, captured and never killed. Now a happy wife and mother, she rejects his offer to return her to "civilization"—laughing at the thought. The Hater returns to his farm, thinks it over, and puts on the hair shirt, ending his life wandering the forests of southern Illinois, trying to repair the damage he had done. The real-life Indian hater on whom Hall based both stories—Captain John Moredock—died a wealthy man, never repenting his murderous ways.[83]

Hall's rewriting his story, however, speaks to his own evolving reconsideration of race and gender. The fictional Frenchman is a source of nearly lost interracialism who reminds Hall's white readers that there were alternatives to Indian hating. The French had shared the land with the Indians, and "hating" had never occurred to them. Finally, the use of the image of a white woman living happily as a squaw demonstrates a deliberately transgressive rhetoric. Hall's implication that white women could be just as hardy, independent, and steadfast as "savage" women ran counter to prevailing attitudes concerning white women's need for enclosure and comfort. In "The Pioneer," the Frenchman and the squaw/sister rebut not only the Anglo males in the story but also the image of each constructed in the patriarchal American public sphere.[84]

In the story, the Métis children playing in the water have precisely the same right to play in the water as do the Anglo boys who find the French leaden plates in the Muskingum River described in chapter 1. Hall deliberately shocks his readers by approving of the white squaw and her mixed-race children to ask his own readers to rethink two parallel and simultaneous processes operating in antebellum America: the removal of Indians and the enclosure of women. On the scales of both the domestic sphere and the figurative family of the nation, the Métis presence enabled writers like Kinzie, James, Hall, Warren, and Richardson to imagine a diverse and inclusive means of community and nation building.

Nous Autres Catholiques

Nativism and the Memory of the Jesuits

FIVE

Without the power to protect themselves, in the
enjoyment of the ordinary rights of citizenship, and
with a current of prejudice setting so strongly against
them, that they find safety only in bending meekly to
the storm, how idle, how puerile, how disingenuous
is it to rave as some have done, of the danger of
Catholic influence!

James Hall, "The Catholic Question" (1835)

From the preceding chapters, James Hall's
efforts to combine French colonial and
"American" national values are familiar. In
an 1835 essay, he sarcastically rephrased Lyman
Beecher's anti-Catholic sermon *A Plea for the West*.
"The Catholic Question" reflected the same values that characterized his fiction by admonishing
Beecher for imagining "no law, no charity, no bond
of Christian fraternity" with Catholics.[1] The conflict between Beecher and Hall informs Jenny
Franchot's comment on similar conflicts in antebellum America: "An unintended irony of this reductive process was its eventual disintegrative impact, for the attack on Roman Catholicism, in its
enumeration of Rome's suspicious charms, often
led to an uncomfortable recognition of the spiritual
deficiencies and psychological pressures of Protes-

tant culture. . . . At issue were political questions over allegiance, hierarchy, tradition, and reform." Franchot's allegorization of the struggle between Protestantism and Catholicism, between nativism and pluralism, concludes with the comment that "the Protestant invective against and fascination with Rome were clearly symptomatic of the modern West's withdrawal from a cohesive spirituality."[2] Franchot's study of the antebellum period focuses on the paranoid Protestant response to recent waves of Catholic immigration from Ireland and southern and central Europe. However, while other antinativist activists defended these immigrants and their faith in the context of historical European Catholicism, Hall used a historical American Catholicism: the colonial French. His use of their history to defend and define a more inclusive American identity through his exposure of the "spiritual deficiencies" of American Protestantism make his contribution to the struggle particularly interesting.

Moreover, Hall's essay reveals that his conflict with Beecher involves more than simply questions of faith: at stake were issues of identity, nation, and citizenship. Although the conflict indeed represents an episode in the "withdrawal from a cohesive spirituality" in the United States, it should not be equated with a withdrawal of spirituality itself or even a secularization of American life—nor was Hall arguing for either. Instead, the struggle over Catholicism served as a kind of mini-Reformation of American Protestantism, one that relinked it to its birth in tolerant Arminianism, Quakerism, and Antinomianism as well as in less tolerant, but more historically vaunted, forms of Calvinism. Again, the emphasis of writers like Hall is transformative rather than reactionary: in defending the Catholics, he has no plans to catholicize the nation. Rather, in defending the Catholic historical record in America, he intended to diminish the "cohesive" power nativists like Beecher claimed for their faith. More like Jefferson or Franklin, that is, Hall asked Americans to remember that their cohesion was rooted in a unity of civic consensus rather than in the "interposition" (Jefferson's term) of a single religious denomination or faith.

Beecher had come to Cincinnati in 1830 from his family's long-standing home in the New England Puritan establishment to direct the Lane Theological Seminary, a Calvinist institution whose explicit mission was to combat Catholic influence in the Ohio Valley.[3] Before heading west, he wrote to his soon-to-be-famous daughter Harriet that "the moral destiny of our nation, and all our institutions and hopes, and the world's hopes, turn on the character of the West, and the competition now is for that of preoccupancy in the education of the rising generation, in which Catholics and infidels have got the start on us."[4] In addition, in an 1830 sermon, Beecher had already announced his anti-Catholic sentiments, and when he got to Ohio, he found plenty of Catholics, most of them Irish and German. In them, he saw a threat to the American nation he viewed as guided exclusively by Calvinist and Saxonist principles of individuality, critical thought, and democracy. In the summer of 1834, Beecher returned to Massachusetts to raise funds for the seminary and delivered his sermon *A Plea for the West*. In the sermon, Beecher described Catholics as unfit to be Americans, sleeper-cell conspirators in plots of papal imperialism and despotism. In sum, he defined it as intrinsically treasonous to be Catholic, a view Hall, when the sermon was printed in Cincinnati, found preposterous, ignorant, and absurd. In addition, Hall would imply that Beecher also found Jews, "negroes," and Cherokee in the West, presumably, but never saw them as viable threats to the blissful marriage of covenant and imperialism Calvinists viewed as central to the United States' status as millennial nation.

Nonetheless, Beecher's audience left the meeting hall and burned down a Charlestown nunnery, a response he would disown and disparage when the sermon was printed, albeit without retracting the remarks that provoked the violence.[5] The violent bigotry exposed and maybe inspired by Beecher reflects the rise of nativism in the United States between 1830 and 1860, a movement that produced the anti-immigrant Know-Nothing Party. While it was a radical expression of xenophobia, Know-Nothingism reflects the same basic ideological identification of the American nation and the Anglo-Saxon "race" that characterized the ideology of empire builders like Bancroft and Parkman, as explored in earlier chapters. Although there have been dozens of studies of nativism since it was written, Ray Allen Billington's *The Protestant Crusade, 1800–1860* (1938) still stands out. Underlying Billington's study, and the studies of his students, is this crucial distinction: "The hatred with which the average Englishman of the early seventeenth century looked upon Popery was due largely to the anti-national character of that religion, for Catholicism was feared not only as an antagonistic theology, but also as a force through which the English government itself was to be over thrown."[6] To suggest that Catholicism is intrinsically "anti-national" reflects the nativists' tribal conceptualization of "nation." To recall terms used earlier, "tribal nationalism" reflects a reactionary fear for the nation's stability, a fear it offsets by constructing a backward-looking primordial national mythology based in preliterate occupation and commonality. In contrast, "civic" forms of nationalism cultivate a creative, forward-looking engagement with the fact of the nation's inevitable diversity by basing membership on loyalty to agreed-upon laws and principles. By this logic, Catholicism—or any other sect or denomination—posed no threat to definitions of nations or nationalism based on shared loyalty to common civil rights and compacts, so long as the First Amendment kept it, and any other faith, from becoming a state religion, a protection that had not existed in Europe.

Catholicism, however, was viewed as a threat by tribal nationalists based not just on the vagaries of liturgy or even popery but also on its potential to displace loyalty to nation with loyalty to faith. Tribal nationalism, that is, fetishized the nation, and writers like Hall insightfully observed that, in the hands of nativists like Beecher, it had thus become a graven image, a sign of Calvinism's corruption through its entanglement with imperialism. This effort revealed innumerable anxieties and paradoxes at stake in the antebellum nation's flirtation with empire. As a set of a former colonies, as a postcolonial nation, and as a prospective empire, the United States in the early nineteenth century, like England one hundred years earlier, was anxious to secure and transmit—both internally and externally—a stable and knowable national identity through which its citizens could imagine themselves in opposition to the Others they meant to conquer or otherwise dominate. To match this outward-looking singularity, a narrative based in an inward-looking myopia regarding the nation's "cohesion" was required. For example, politically, anti-Catholicism transposed the hierarchy of the Catholic ecclesiastical structure from the private sphere of belief onto the public sphere of the citizen's engagement with politics and economics. Catholics, that is, because they acceded to the doctrine of papal infallibility, were the spiritual equivalents of peasants; in contrast, Protestants, by depending on individual reason and faith, were the equivalents of citizens. Religious passivity, the nativists argued, could not be detached from political obedience, and so Catholics could never truly be citizens.

Such illogic and deliberate historical blindness, given the republican rebellions by Catholics in France in 1789 and Ireland in 1798, served as a distraction: most Catholics were objectionable to nativists not because they were Catholics but because they were non-Anglo. Religious diversity entailed ethnic diversity and even more profoundly challenged any primordial American mythology. This paradox was reputed to reveal that the so-called republican experiment was exhibiting another sign of fraying at the edges. By the 1830s, the purity of the nation's "republican" identity had been challenged: northern white women and free African Americans, for example, were protesting the political system as proslavery and thus hypocritical, its claim to "republic" status specious and hollow so long as they were excluded. Various religious and philosophical dissidents simply jumped ship, expressing their dissatisfaction by experimenting with alternative communities, such as the Mormons or the transcendentalists.[7] In addition, immigrants from central and southern Europe and locally born white Americans were noticing the space between the public image of the United States as a land of opportunity and the realities of land speculation, industrial exploitation, and Anglo-owned monopolies in housing, employment, and political influence—and the economic depressions of 1837 and 1844 only made things worse. In short, a scapegoat was needed. The most available candidates were the very people who had contributed least to the troubled status quo: immigrants. Implicitly, the nativists sought a more narrow definition of the nation's culture and citizenship, one that protected the "purity" of the American experiment in republican self-governance—blaming the victim for tainting the results. In reference to the nativists' fear of European "despots," Jon Gjerde writes, "In the minds of many Americans, they ultimately intended to use these benighted peasants as political minions to destroy the American republican experiment. Americans insisted that a republic was the most beautiful and progressive form of government, but they also knew it was the most fragile."[8] Against these "threats," nativists revived the millennial themes of Puritan rhetoric that identified the United States as the end product of history, the final act signaling the return of Christ.

The nativists' millennial identification of race with nation, and nation with race, and each with Protestantism, diminished all three.[9] Nativism forced its less fanatical but still patriotic scholarly proponents to abandon the rationalist basis of Enlightenment-era historiography and instead compelled them to craft unified narratives of national cohesion from materials in which such unity was simply not present. Seeking legitimacy for their claim on the nation's present, they crafted colonial pasts in which the monolithic nation developed from an ongoing process of purification, perpetually purging inferior or flawed peoples and ideas. George Bancroft's story of the ambitious individual Anglo freeholder trumping the lazy French group-minded habitant represents the typical historiographic disregard for the truth. Anglo farmers were always supported by centralized systems of governmental support, military protection, and internal improvements. In contrast to the individualist myth, all of these depended on cooperative and collective efforts at the national level.[10]

Yet, from Bancroft through Frederick Jackson Turner, the myth of the individual Anglo yeoman informed nationalistic acts of agrarian self-identification and celebration. Not only does this misrepresent the past: it also imposes an impossible burden on the present. When Anglo-Americans in the 1840s heard German, French, patois and slave dialects, Spanish, and other languages in their midst, they considered their communities diminished from the ideal of Anglo purity mythologized by romantic historians.[11] Their paradoxical violence was intended to be corrective, each arson a justifiable act of self-defense. That those languages were all heard as much in 1740 as 1840 is not the point. By omitting the nation's racial, religious, economic, and gender-based diversity from its history, romantic historians subjectively narrated and imposed on their readers a singular version of national experience and identity that simply did not exist, as I discuss in the first section of this chapter.[12] The result was Beecher, bigotry, and, of course, torch-wielding mobs destroying the homes of mendicant Catholic nuns.

The similarly paradoxical link between this form of inward nationalist consolidation and outward imperialist enterprises is transparent. The Mexican-American War was partially justified along religious lines: Mexico was Catholic and thus not truly the republic it claimed to be. Disregarding that it was also abolitionist, the millennial mission to cleanse humanity through "republican" rebirth could tolerate no such leftover and corrupt European or feudal institutions, or so went the propaganda. "For some Protestants," writes historian Paul Foos, "the [Catholic] church was the master spirit of the racial miscegenation, political corruption, and social backwardness of Mexico."[13] Not only, then, was Mexico conquerable, but, from a moral perspective, *not* conquering it was immoral. On the other hand, abolitionists from Henry David Thoreau to Senator

Thomas Corwin recognized the inherently antirepublican nature of the American adventure in Texas in specific and of Manifest Destiny in general.[14] William Jay's *A Review of the Causes and Consequences of the Mexican War* (1849) lays out contemporary objections in great detail.[15] The dual attacks on Catholics in Monterrey and Charlestown are thus components of the same reactionary bigotry and close-mindedness. Nativism at home and the imperial war on the frontier reveal simply two manifestations of the same wellspring of anti-Catholic prejudice that betrays not only the "spiritual deficiencies" of Protestantism but also the moral and political deficiencies of antebellum (as opposed to Revolutionary) "republicanism."

As each theater of anti-Catholic violence was debated in the day's print culture, the resulting intranational conflicts were based in radically opposed readings and narratives of the colonial past. For most historians, American history began, in a meaningful way, with the arrival of "whites"—the Pilgrims—yet no one could deny that the first whites in most of what would become the territorial United States were French and Catholic. In their discussions of the role of colonial Catholics, writers imagined and wrote about the colonial French in different ways, revealing sets of opposing historical narratives that might be viewed as the microcosmic examples of more general fissures in the Republic as it strove either to suppress or to embrace the diversification of the antebellum era. George Bancroft and other historians enabled the nativist equation of race and nation along Anglo-Saxon lines by portraying the French and Indian War as the ultimate triumph of progressive Protestantism over regressive Catholicism.

The trouble was, even nativist national historians such as Bancroft, Richard Hildreth, Samuel Eliot, and William Prescott—and dozens of others—could not deny the fact of Catholic exploration and "discovery" throughout the American West. Furthermore, Beecher and other Protestant preachers—at a time when the pulpit wielded tremendous social and cultural power—could not deny the success of the Jesuit missionaries in the West in the seventeenth and eighteenth centuries in comparison with their own denominational forefathers. Worse yet, many of the explorers and discoverers were priests. The challenge was to find a way to include these "papists" in their nationalist narrative in ways that supported "republican" values, even as they meant to remove Catholicism from the national landscape. A number of issues swirled around the contest between their oversimplified representations of both Protestantism and Catholicism: the tension between group-based ethnic identity and individual-based American citizenship, the First Amendment's separation of public and private spheres, and the mounting tensions between the Anglo-American power structure and the increasingly non-Anglo population—between homogeneity and heterogeneity in terms of demographics, religion, and values. All of these would be more at the forefront following the Civil War, with the 1880s and 1890s witnessing the worst nativist insurgencies, this time coinciding with the Spanish-American War, another effort to conquer brown-skinned Catholics that forced an even more stringent normalization of "American" as white skinned, male, and Protestant.

In the 1830s and 1840s, however, the men who constituted old New England–based Calvinist power structure that had intimidated the North since the Revolution were losing control of the nation they had always considered "theirs." Ironically, other groups were taking seriously the civic values of democracy and liberty that the New Englanders had always mouthed but, apparently, rarely meant. How the colonial French—with the Irish, the first non-Anglo ethnic group encountered by post-Revolutionary Anglo-Americans—were written into or out of the nation's history, how they were rejected, accepted, assimilated, and, most important, absorbed, served as a template for how "native-born" Americans would understand or control their relationship with the increasing population of non-Anglo white immigrants throughout the rest of the century and beyond. I have chosen this subject, then, for my final chapter. In both the romantic historians' discussions of Jesuits and the conflict between Beecher and Hall, we can see rehearsals for later conflicts over the public function of national history. Each exposed for the first time the fundamental conflict between inclusion and exclusion that characterizes so many of the nation's public controversies.

First I discuss how, in the nativist histories, a proto-melting-pot concept of assimilation and incorporation developed, making the French missionaries and explorers less alien to American readers, de-Catholicizing and homogenizing them in an effort at retroactive historiographic Americanization. This involved a dissociation of the French Catholics of the colonial era from the immigrant Catholics of the mid-nineteenth century and the assignment of latent yet traditionally Protestant virtues to the former. Following that, I address Beecher's and Hall's confrontation in greater detail. In the conflict between the New Englander and the westerner, between Calvinism and other forms of Protestantism, we ultimately see the nation at once initiating and doubting its transition from peripheral former colony to emergent global power, engaging the complexities of blending imperial ambition and republican restraint.

The treatment of the French reveals paradoxes that still characterize debates over diversity and inclusion in the United States. On one level, the "outsiders" are threatened with erasure through absorption, their distinctive cultural traits, customs, and languages lost in the smothering promises of benevolent sameness and political inclusion. On another, if they resist assimilation, they are vulnerable to the old hatreds and exclusions.

> The shapeless knight errantry of the thirteenth and fourteenth centuries, rich as it was in romance and adventure, is not to be compared, in any valuable characteristic, to the noiseless self-devotion of the men who first explored the Western country. The courage of the knight was a part of his savage nature; his confidence was in the strength of his own right arm. . . . And from that chaotic scene of rapine, raid, and murder, we can turn with plea-

sure to contemplate the truer, nobler chivalry—the chivalry of love and peace whose weapons were the kindness of their hearts, the purity of their motives, and the self-denial of their lives.

So begins J. L. McConnel's description of the French explorer-priests in his *Western Characters or Types of Border Life in the Western States* (1853). His chapter on the priests immediately follows one on the Indians, whose ending betrays his nativism: "The extinction of the Indian race is decreed by a law of Providence which we cannot gainsay." He adds in a footnote: "The principle stated in the text will apply with equal force to the negro-race; and those who will look the facts firmly in the face, cannot avoid seeing, that the ultimate solution of the problem of American slavery, can be nothing but the *sword*." The Indians simply "emigrated in the wrong direction," from Asia to America rather than to Europe, as it turns out, and the African is simply a "barbarian." The American nation will and must be cleansed by the eradication of each.[16]

As opposed to these groups, McConnel admires the French, but only when they stop acting like Frenchmen. Presaging the Dawes Act's aspiration to assimilate Indian culture but not Indians—the motto of the Haskell Indian School, famously, was "Kill the Indian but not the Man"—McConnel's veneer of benevolence toward the French belies a covert nativist agenda.[17] To begin, meaningful history in the American West starts only when the explorer-priests appear. McConnel spends extensive time on Père Marquette especially. The chapter has a constant refrain, however, in which McConnel reinforces the always italicized virtues of kindness, purity, and self-denial of the heroic explorer-priests: "*sincerity, courage, and self-denial*," he emphasizes repeatedly almost as a chorus. These virtues he sets at odds with the traits of nineteenth-century French Catholics: "Enthusiasm is a characteristic of the French nation; a trait in some individuals elevated to sublime self-devotion, and in others degraded to mere excitability. The vivacity, gesticulation, and grimace, which characterize most of them, are the external signs of this nature; the calm heroism of the seventeenth century, and the insane devotion of the nineteenth were alike its fruits." On account of this contemporary instability, for McConnel, the French as a "race" themselves cannot transform missionary heroism into permanent settlement or, more important, "civilization": "Had either the French or the Spanish possessed the stubborn qualities which hold, as they had the useful which discover, the aspect of the continent would, at this day, have been far different." McConnel's further comment on French settlement reveals his thinking even more radically: "They left no permanent impress on the country; the most acute moral or political vision cannot now detect a trace of their influence, in the aspect of the lands they penetrated; and, so far from hastening the settlement of the Great Valley, it is more likely that their disastrous efforts rather retarded it—by deterring others from the undertaking. Their history reads like a romance; and their characters would better grace the pages of fiction, than the annals of civilization."[18] McConnel's final intertextual distinction intriguingly removes all forms of fiction from the meaningful historical record of civilization's progress. Note as well that fiction is not counterpoised with history—the usual Calvinist accusation—but with "civilization." Fiction's function is transgressive, useful only for inculcating values that lack functional or purposeful moral progress, and the only history that matters is that of "civilization," by which he clearly means Anglo Protestants. At best, the French become the stuff of legend and therefore irrelevant to the study of the superior Anglo civilization that could "hold" where the Catholics could not. At the same time, as de facto fictional characters, they provide an exotic narrative, lending romance to frontier history.

Typical of this group of popular historians, McConnel includes the priests in his pre-Revolutionary narrative and announces that he has excluded the coureurs de bois because he "aims only to notice those who either aided to produce, or indicated, the characteristics of the society in which they lived."[19] By celebrating how the explorer-priests "indicated" in some pre-Turnerian fashion the coming virtues of Anglo-American republicanism, McConnel rescues the priests—and banishes the coureurs de bois—because Marquette and the others brought to the region principles that foreshadow the ideals of republican virtue: kindness, sincerity, and selflessness. McConnel never dwells on their Catholicism; in fact, their faith is simply a means of harnessing the innate French immaturity—"enthusiasm"—to constructive ends. While McConnel's *Western Characters* is fairly obscure—and rightfully so—his treatment of the explorer-priests typifies standard historiographic method among nativist historians.

Timothy Flint's *A Condensed Geography and History of the Western States, or the Mississippi Valley* (1828) likewise employs a politics of de-Catholicizing through the incorporation and assimilation of the explorer-priests. Flint's nativism is far more subtle and, unlike McConnel's, his view on race far more liberal, reflecting the monogenism that opposed scientific racism's polygenetic narrative: "The more our species are studied, the more clearly it is found, that the human heart is everywhere the same."[20] Yet even though Flint consistently suggests a more inclusive agenda, it is still one that limits the cultural, moral, or behavioral options for non-Anglo European: assimilate or be erased. In one chapter— "Religious Character"—Flint, a former Calvinist missionary from New England, simply lists the Catholics as one more Christian denomination represented in the Valley.

He opens, however, with a long paragraph that establishes an individualized Protestant norm: "It is the settled political maxim of the West, that religion is a concern entirely between the conscience and God, and ought to be left solely to His guardianship and care." He notes as well that Protestant ministers and Catholic "eleves" alike "pursue the interests of their several denominations in their own way, and generally in profound peace."[21] Writing before the rise of organized nativism in the 1830s, Flint nonetheless reflects an emphasis on de-Catholicizing frontier Catholics (and deethnicizing non-Anglos) by assuming doctrinal and liturgical parallels with Protestants and coating over the whole with a facade of ecumenical cooperation and interdenominational companionship. Western Catholics, for Flint, never exercised or aspired to the hegemonic ambition as feared by the nativists. They never challenged or removed other Christian sects because they supposedly simply had become de facto Protestants.

When Flint turns to the explorer-priests, the assimilationist method can be seen in its early stages: the French were fit to explore the region but not settle it. For Flint, the Catholic imagination is too immature, and so when they "discover" the Mississippi, he comments: "Of course, we would rather attribute the wonderful accounts of the height of the Illinois bluffs, the descent of the falls at St. Anthony, the rapidity of the current of the Missouri, and the terrible monsters painted on the Grand Tower, together with their exaggerations of the fruits, flowers, birds, beasts, and every thing they saw, which we meet with in the accounts of the first French explorers on the Mississippi, to the influence of an imagination naturally and highly kindled, than to any intention to deceive."[22] While the French properly view the Mississippi Valley as a place rich in natural resources and physical beauty, their imaginations are "naturally and highly kindled" by the flawed and childish habit inculcated by their irrational faith, so their blindness to more practical, exploitable resources may be forgiven. The ethnic stereotype observed so often—the French are "jovial," convivial," "enthusiastic," and such—is used here to suggest an intrinsic childishness. Subsequently, unlike the Anglos, they would attempt to fit themselves into existing topographical and demographic structures rather than adjusting the environment to their needs and desires, as the Anglo model for colonization dictated. Flint links this to Catholicism through the passivity of its adherents—Catholics do nothing to bring on the millennium because they accept the world as it is.

For instance, Flint's ecumenical ideal lasts only as long as he writes about the Mississippi Valley as a synthetic whole. As his later chapters delve into each state's history, he reverts to nativist stereotyping, localizing the Catholic threat, compartmentalizing it to make its erasure easier. For example, more like McConnel, he is careful to distinguish seventeenth- and nineteenth-century versions of Catholicism. In a later chapter on Missouri, Flint contradicts his earlier assumption of intersectarian peace: "Their veneration for their priests is unlimited; and the latter dare rely upon a credulity, which in other catholic nations has long since passed away. For instance, they had, not many years since, processions to pray the Mississippi down, when it threatened a desolating inundation, and to banish the locusts by the intercession of the saints. So firmly are they fixed in their religious opinions, that they are apt to regard protestant efforts to convert them, not only as arrogant only, but impious."[23] While Flint seems tolerant of Catholicism as a creed, he finds it prone to the antirepublican characteristics later Know-Nothings would exploit more viciously and violently. By relying on superstition rather than reason, Catholicism is ultimately a leftover feudal and premodern system of belief and so an anachronism in the progressive republic environment of the new nation. Flint's infantilization of Catholic belief mirrors the processes of absorption central to melting-pot ideology. The foreign element is accepted, assimilated, and, after a while (a few hundred pages in the case of *A Condensed Geography*), quietly ridiculed and cast aside. Tolerance, he proves, is not the same as inclusion, and Catholicism as a source of cultural difference is written out of Flint's effort at regional history writing.

In his more popular *Recollections of the Last Ten Years* (1826), a memoir of his years as a Calvinist missionary, one incident epitomizes Flint's view of the Catholic French. In Missouri, Flint parts company with a young female acolyte while crossing a river and takes the opportunity to reiterate his religious instructions: "The ferryman was a flippant and unfeeling Frenchman, who understood not a word of our conversation, but marking her tears, concluded I was scolding her. He had a saucy frankness of taking every one to account, and when I returned, he began to chide me for scolding such a beautiful girl. '*Vous etre ministre Protestant,*' said he, '*c'est une religion tres seche, tres dure. Nous autres Catholiques n'avons coeurs faites comme ca.*' As he understood it, I had been giving her stern lessons, and harsh counsels, which had been the cause of her tears."[24] The failure to understand here has to do with more than language. The Frenchman has the spirit of democracy—"taking everyone to account"—and is clearly not "unfeeling" if he perceives the woman's fear. To Flint, the Frenchman is too immature to understand the context of his comments, too "unfeeling" to comprehend and practice the rigid responsibilities of patriarchal Protestant authority. The voyageur's accusation that Protestantism is "very dry and very hard" goes unnoted by Flint, as does the Frenchman's claim that "we Catholics, on the other hand, do not have hearts that are made like that." Flint, good Calvinist, values the mind over the heart, and for favoring the heart—emotion and compassion—Flint writes off the Frenchman as a nuisance.

While Flint in general admires the processes of civil and social democratization of Western society, at the same time, he rejects the simultaneous democratization of morality and spirituality and means to impose Calvinist order to eliminate the latter. The French are welcome, then, insofar as they acknowledge the Yankee standard and aspire to it. This fundamental contradiction is at the heart of assimilation's ultimate failure: there is still a national norm outsiders must emulate but not redirect. Flint rhetorically expels the Frenchman from meaning because he dared criticize Flint and Flint's Calvinist transfer of ecclesiastic primacy to social authority.

Finally, the early volumes of George Bancroft's *History of the United States* are cited in virtually every American history textbook, encyclopedia, and narrative on the West published after 1843, especially in books like McConnel's. Bancroft's subtly nativist absorption of the French explorers and Jesuits at once focused the work of earlier writers like Flint and influenced younger historians like McConnel. Early in volume 2, one paragraph in particular establishes the crucial parallels between Calvinists and Jesuits in colonial North America: "Religious enthusiasm colonized New England; religious enthusiasm took possession of the wilderness on the upper lakes and explored the Mississippi. Puritanism gave New England its worship and its schools; the Roman church and the Jesuit priests raised for Canada its altars, its hospitals, its seminaries. The influence of Calvin can be traced in every New England village; in Canada, not a cape was turned, nor a mission founded, nor a river entered, nor a mission begun, but a Jesuit led the way."[25] Furthermore, the Jesuits, Bancroft writes, were favored over the Franciscans on account of their egalitarian individualism: the former "were, by rules, never to become Prelates, and could gain power and distinction only by their sway over mind"—the Jesuits are democrats (like "us") and the Franciscans aristocrats (like "them"), and, like Protestants, the Jesuits base their faith in rational self-examination. Bancroft then spends considerable time discussing the heroic explorations of Allouez, Tonti, Joliet, and Marquette. Furthermore, Hennepin, a French associate of Marquette's who sold out to the British, is pilloried for his disloyalty. The explorer-priests demonstrate the same mixture of righteousness and compassion Bancroft values in Anglo heroes, celebrating their individual character traits while ignoring their Catholicism.

Next, Bancroft transposes Puritan typological techniques to incorporate the French priests just as his Puritan forefathers transcribed Old Testament Hebrews into their own millennial vision.[26] Of Marquette, he writes: "Like a patriarch he dwelt beneath a tent; and of the land through which he walked, he was the master. How often was the pillow of stones like that where Jacob felt the presence of God! How often did the ancient oak, of which the centuries were untold, seem like the tree of Mamre, beneath which Abraham broke bread with the Angels!"[27] Puritan typology was used in the seventeenth century to read Protestant models of thought and identity into Hebrew texts—foreshadowings of Calvinist ascendance through the observation of instructive parallels between New England Puritans and the Israelite tribes, each "Chosen Peoples." But for the Puritans, the patriarchs are *just* types and so more prehistory than history: it did not mean they were tolerant of Jews in their communities. The Puritan millennium, however, was contingent upon the conversion of the Jews, and, following the same typological reasoning, the republican millennium required the assimilation of the French and other non-Anglo ethnic groups. As such, the typological parallel Bancroft crafts between the French explorer-priests and the Hebrew patriarchs has a similarly double-edged paradox: while the priests were included in the American narrative, actual nineteenth-century Catholics were excluded by the same logic, unwelcome in Bancroft's Boston.

In fact, the title of the chapter describing the start of the French and Indian War establishes the millennial issues at stake in the conflict: "The Catholic Powers of the Middle Age against the New Protestant Powers." A subsequent paragraph leads Bancroft's readers right up to the vision of a republican millennium more concisely articulated by Lincoln at Gettysburg: "The contest raged in both hemispheres. The American question was: Shall the continued colonization of North America be made under the auspices of English Protestantism and popular liberty, or of the legitimacy of France in its connection with Roman Catholic Christianity? . . . Considered in its unity, as interesting mankind, the question was: Shall the reformation, developed to the fulness [*sic*] of free inquiry, succeed in its protest against the middle age?"[28] The difference between Bancroft and Lincoln ("a new nation, conceived in liberty, and dedicated to the proposition that all men are created equal"), however, is in Lincoln's repudiation of an explicitly antirepublican economic and social system: slavery. Bancroft depicts Catholicism as just as equally countermillennial as Lincoln would slavery, assigning it a place in the prehistorical age of ignorance, an impediment to the necessary epoch of "free inquiry" preceding the end of history.

Bancroft's cosmopolitan millennialism pushes nativism toward the romantic arena of "higher laws" in the Emersonian or, more precise, Hegelian sense. Protestantism's victory over Catholicism allows the creation of the American nation, the next step in the teleological progress of humanity, and most likely the final one, since Puritan-derived Americans reckon themselves inheritors of the Hebrew covenant. Bancroft's nativism is thus entangled in a more seemingly benevolent vision of American exceptionalism. By this logic, Catholicism is not defeated by Protestantism; rather, history destined its eradication just as it had feudalism's—its political analogue—by republicanism. Catholicism is then defeated by the progressive forces at the heart of a dialectical unfolding of history: it is an anachronism, like the priest described by Flint praying for the waters to recede, and has no place in any nation whose destiny is manifest.

_____ Every modern empire has undergone a period of internal consolidation prior to its undertaking the imperial absorption of other lands and peoples. Most notable is England, which transformed itself into the United Kingdom by absorbing Cornwall, Wales, Scotland, and various amounts of Ireland before venturing into America, Asia, and Africa. Usually, there was a cultural component to these acts of consolidation, literary or artistic reinterpretations of a common history, language, and identity for the members of the "imagined community" of the nation.[29] More often than not, these reinterpretations codify narratives of purification, purging the peoples or beliefs that would smudge or diminish the community members' identity when they encountered Others in the colonies.

As the United States mostly shifted from Enlightenment-era civic nationalism to a more romantic tribal nationalism as part of its larger transition to empire, the political legacy of the Revolutionary coalition was no longer viewed as strong enough to craft the type of cohesion desired by cultural nationalists: tribal nationalism and racial nativism are mutually constitutive. While such racial nationalists sought legitimacy by meeting a European standard of cultural coherence, most nativist historians—fellow travelers with the more radical Know-Nothings—asserted that membership in the tribe could be attained (so long as the candidate is "white" and male) simply by doing to oneself what the historians did to the nation's history: purging difference and diversity. Progressive Era sociologists such as Jane Addams would popularize an antebellum term: to Americanize. Addams and others shifted the paradigm of Bancroft from the past to the present: European immigrants could be included in the American nation if they discarded their language, religion, economics, and history to adopt those of the United States—if they immersed themselves in the melting pot.

To be Americanized, however, was nearly impossible for adults.[30] Thus Addams shifted her focus to educating the children so that they never knew any other way of life, a pedagogy mimicked in the simultaneously constructed Indian schools. In both Addams's settlement houses and Dawes's Indian schools, indoctrination went beyond simply political and economic reeducation—the markers of a civic nation—to address language, religion, and history, the criteria of primordialist cohesion. The invasive acculturation intrinsic to Americanization resembles tribal initiation, one that demands sacrifice—the old people and the old ways. Immigrants unwilling to make these sacrifices often returned to Europe; those who stayed had to buy in wholeheartedly: there was little discussion of blending political unity and cultural diversity in either 1848 or 1898, years when the United States conducted its two most overtly imperialist wars, conflicts whose timing not surprisingly coincided with nativist movements. All these processes were reflected in the rhetorical appropriation of the colonial French to establish the choices facing non-Anglo immigrants: become Americanized or become invisible.

Fifty years before Jane Addams, Lyman Beecher knew that the key to Americanization—to neutralizing the peasant/immigrant's supposed threat to republican values—was the education of children. The opening thirty pages of Beecher's *Plea for the West* in fact offer and champion a program of publicly funded education that reflects a useful transition from the utilitarian model of Benjamin Rush toward the more liberal ideas of Horace Mann or even Thomas Dewey—from memorization and toward acculturation. This section of Beecher's sermon has been available to readers almost continuously since it was delivered and subsequently reprinted in a variety of collections of "American eloquence" and such. Since 1970, for example, Conrad Cherry has reproduced Beecher's opening sequences in *God's New Israel: Religious Interpretations of American Destiny*.[31] In the opening section as well, Beecher admirably calls for public education in ways that echo Thomas Jefferson's "Bill for Establishing Religious Freedom." In that document, Jefferson writes that "truth is great and will prevail if left to herself, that she is proper antagonist to error, and has nothing to fear from the conflict, unless by human interposition disarmed of her natural weapons, free argument and debate, errors ceasing to be dangerous when it is permitted freely to contradict them."[32] Beecher begins in a similar place but ends far from Jefferson's secularism:

> But before I proceed, to prevent misapprehension, I would say I have no fear of the Catholics, considered simply as a religious denomination, and unallied to the church and state establishments of the European governments hostile to republican institutions. Let the Catholics mingle with us as Americans, and come with their children under the full action of our common schools and republican institutions and the various powers of assimilation, and we are prepared cheerfully to abide the consequences. If in those circumstances the protestant religion cannot stand before the Catholic, let it go down, and we will sound no alarm, and ask no aid, and make no complaint.[33]

In Beecher's convoluted logic, a few fallacies stand out. First, Beecher poses this as a winner-take-all competition. The possibility of coexistence is omitted from his construction of Catholicism's and Protestantism's combat for America. Second, Marie Lenore Fell's study *The Foundations of Nativism in American Textbooks, 1783–*

1860 (1941) lays out in detail the anti-Catholic biases in the public school curricula Beecher promoted as a level playing field for the battles of the sects, biases that hang over Beecher's diction.[34] Beecher's constant use of "our" betrays a human interposition in public school textbooks that would make the competition he imagines not only false in its construction but also specious in its execution. Jefferson's formula depends upon the absence of "human interposition" in the form of institutional biases, but Beecher's propagation of biased institutions and materials cannot be ignored.

Furthermore, Beecher lays out clearly the central conflicts he views as threatening the Republic's ability to sustain itself: "The great experiment is now making and from its extent and rapid filling up is making in the West, whether the perpetuity of our republican institutions can be reconciled with universal suffrage." Beecher's fears, though not well founded, at this point compel him only to ask for money and teachers to be sent from New England to the West. Next, he rightly identifies the lack of familiarity with republican institutions among immigrants from eastern, southern, and central Europe: "This danger from the uneducated mind is augmenting daily by the rapid influx of foreign emigrants, unacquainted with our institutions, unaccustomed to self-government, inaccessible to education, and easily accessible to prepossession, and inveterate credulity, and intrigue, and easily embodied and wielded by sinister design."[35] While the first half of this sentence lays out Beecher's observation of a potential problem, the second betrays his malevolent nativist paranoia. He mostly fears Catholics voting, by the order of the pope, in a "consolidated mass"—rather than on the basis of individual initiative—and so playing the American political parties off each other, positioning themselves as the balance-shifting kingmakers until they can establish their own majority. Such a "design" speaks to the danger of "faction" observed in Federalist 10 as one of the deepest threat to a republic.[36] Beecher's ethnocentrism, however, compels him to equate a religious congregation with a political faction.

Those passages represent Beecher at his most benign. In fact, his opening statement rings with what would seem to be a straightforward updating of John Winthrop's "City on a Hill" doctrine: "It was the opinion of [Jonathan] Edwards that the millennium would commence in America. When I first encountered this opinion, I thought it chimerical; but all providential developments since, and all the existing signs of the times, lend corroboration to it. . . . There is not a nation upon earth which, in fifty years, can by all possible reformation place itself in circumstances so favorable as our own for the free unembarrassed application of physical effort and pecuniary and moral power to evangelize the world." As he traces this progress, he mentions, almost casually, that Calvinism "laid the foundations of the republican institutions of our nation, and felled the forests, and fought the colonial battles with the Canadian Indians and the French Catholics."[37] In fact, Beecher's *Plea for the West* efficiently demonstrates the proximity of benign exceptionalism to its malicious consequences. The final one hundred pages of the sermon are an unending diatribe against the political incompatibility of Catholicism and republicanism. To his credit, Beecher never trots out the violence of the Inquisition, the supposed sexual proclivities of priests and nuns, or the conspiracy theories concerning the Masons, as did most nativists and Know-Nothing propagandists, such as Samuel Morse, Rebecca Reed, Maria Monk, or George Lippard, to name only a few anti-Catholic fiction writers.

Nonetheless, Beecher's statements reflect the same hatred and bigotry. He misrepresents Catholicism as antithetical to intellectual inquiry, contrary to individual moral conscience, and, on the whole, the opposite of the most basic characteristics of citizenship. For example, one sequence bears out his biases:

If they associated with republicans, the power of caste would wear away. If they mingled in our schools, the republican atmosphere would impregnate their minds. If they scattered, unassociated, the attrition of circumstances would wear off their predilections and aversions. If they could read the Bible, and might and did, their darkened intellect would brighten, and their bowed down mind would rise. If they dared to think for themselves, the contrast of protestant independence with their thralldom, would awaken the desire of equal privileges, and put an end to an arbitrary clerical dominion over superstitious minds.

In other words, a Catholic is always already an irrational peasant and never a thinking citizen. For Beecher, Catholics are by definition willingly unfree and thus ultimately nonassimilable in the millennial American nation, despite his claims to the contrary. Moreover, he mixes into his discussion of the refusal of Catholics to separate church and state some very ugly racial allusions: "For since the irruption of the northern barbarians, the world has never witnessed such a rush of dark-minded population from one country to another. . . . It is not the northern hive, but the whole hive which is swarming out upon our cities. . . . Clouds like the locusts of Egypt are rising from the hills and plains of Europe."[38] By implication, these non-northern European barbarians might as well be from Egypt. As in so many other sources examined in this book, behavior or beliefs at odds with self-defined Anglo-Saxon norms become grounds for rhetorically stripping the outsider of his or her whiteness: for Beecher, Catholics are not really white and thus excludable and removable. Small wonder Beecher's audience burned down a nunnery: he identified Catholicism as far more than just "an insulated system of religious error."[39] In his hands, the pope and Metternich become the rhetorical equivalent of the Cold War's Stalin and Khrushchev or the War on Terror's Osama bin Laden and Saddam Hussein: the unmediated Other set on the destruction of "our" way of life.

Carefully slipped into the message, however—for both Beecher and his like-minded descendants, say, Joseph McCarthy or Pat Robertson—is that, in opposition to the external threat, they assume, promote, and impose as unassailable fact a very contentious and

inaccurate premise: that there is a single "American way of life"—
the way of the WASP. Such reactionary monoculturalism pervades
Beecher's *Plea*: "We have surmounted past difficulties by means of a
comparative homogeneity of character, opinion, and interests, the
result of our colonial training and revolutionary struggle and while
the ship was navigated by those who aided in her construction and
launching."[40] In other words, immigrants whose parents were not
part of the colonial, Revolutionary, or constitutional eras need either
to attach themselves to the "comparative homogeneity" of the nation
or to accept the leadership of the native-born. Beecher, of course,
never perceives the irony of his request: while he diminishes papal
infallibility, he elevates New England's.

James Hall's first response to Beecher was based
not on the sermon itself but rather on a report of it from a Lowell,
Massachusetts, newspaper that found its way to Cincinnati. Beecher's sermon had been delivered throughout New England in the
summer of 1834, a boilerplate for fund-raising. Hall's essay, "The
March of Intellect," in the December 1834 issue of the journal he
edited, the *Western Monthly Magazine*, suggests that the reporter in
Lowell had either missed or wanted to ignore the second half of the
sermon.[41] Thus Hall responds only to Beecher's identification of the
West as primitive and backward, not to his anti-Catholicism. Even
in this partial foray into combating the forces of cultural imperialism, nonetheless, Hall seems aware of the global and racial aspects of
Beecher's intentions.

Writing in the Swiftian satiric mode typical of his youth in Philadelphia, Hall points out that, in the West, "the Bible is circulated
pretty generally among the people and the prospect of converting
the whole population to Christianity is quite as fair as in Burma or
Ceylon, and almost as good as in England, France, or Italy" and
"now canals and turnpikes, after the fashion of white people, inter-
sect the country in various directions." Hall internalizes Beecher's
assumption that the West is a colonial setting settled by a less-than-

white population ("after the fashion") and inverts Beecher's observations for the sake of satire before turning more serious: "But when, from high authority, we find the opinion expressed, that our country must be civilized in the manner in which the same result is proposed to be produced in Africa—by the introduction of a race superior to ourselves, and in possession of a more elevated moral code—we think the novelty of the enterprise . . . demands that we should give it publicity." Hall's identification not only of Beecher's imperialism but also of its global implications demonstrates a striking awareness of the implications of propaganda in the imposition of external, imperial order in a colonial setting. He ends by noting that westerners will soon be "served like the Cherokees" if Beecher turns Cincinnati into a western suburb of Boston.[42] Like Swift's parodic criticism of the British Empire's occupation of his homeland, Hall's response is based in a simple request that the East keep its constitutional promises of liberality and balance and the nation preserve the premise of local self-determination.

For being so irreverent, though, Hall was pilloried in the western Presbyterian press for mocking a minister. Yet Beecher and Hall had long been associates in the Semi-Colon Club, a group of expatriate easterners in Cincinnati. Hall, however, was also a member of the Buck-Eye Club, a more locally minded group started by Dr. Daniel Drake.[43] When responding to Beecher, Hall had thought himself among friends, just as Alexander Pope had a century earlier in London's more civic-minded public sphere. But Hall misjudged the vituperative and paranoid nature of nativist rhetoric: the tribal nation of the 1830s required an uncritical respect for authority, an intellectual passivity absent from the civic nation of the 1790s. Hall was raised in Philadelphia, where friends often publicly combated over public issues without a fear of losing their friendship. The Franklinian public sphere valued quality of argumentation over the politics of personality, and Hall's brothers and uncles had sparred in the same print-based arenas as Benjamin Rush, Francis Hopkinson, Charles Brockden Brown, Joseph Dennie, William Dunlap, Samuel

Stanhope Smith, and many others. In that sphere, satire and sarcasm were standard rhetorical techniques, and Hall responded to Beecher within that context.[44]

When Beecher published *A Plea for the West* in Cincinnati in April 1835, he added a few ad hominem attacks on Hall, revealing the extent to which eighteenth-century style had been eclipsed by the more emotional irrationalism of the romantic public sphere. Using what is known today as "oppositional research," in an extended footnote, he cites Hall's 1830 call for eastern immigration to the West without noting Hall's open invitation of all people of all creeds and regions.[45] In another note, Beecher—or, just as likely, one of his acolytes, David Brainerd or Theodore Weld—quoted a published note Hall had written as treasurer of the Illinois Sabbath School in 1831 to a Massachusetts charity thanking it for the donation of some prayer books. In it, Hall is gracious and encourages Calvinist missionary work in Illinois without promoting it as a dire need to meet the challenge of Catholic dominion. Yet on the basis of these few loose ends, Beecher means to paint Hall as either a closeted ally or a hypocrite on all issues relating to Catholicism.[46] However, in neither circumstance had Hall painted the West as barbarous or Catholics as "designing" papists. Instead, he is shown to be simply receptive to any faith that might come west. In contrast, both rhetorically and historically, like Bancroft, Beecher and his crew simply manipulate the evidence to tell the story they want to tell and overlook any contradiction, no matter that they misrepresent their sources. For example, their research omitted reference to Hall's attack on anti-Catholicism in the May 2, 1829, issue of the *Illinois Intelligencer*, material Hall would revise and include in "The Catholic Question."[47]

In the April 1835 issue of the *Western Monthly Magazine*, Hall reviewed *A Plea*, exercising a restraint his biographers link to the advice of Benjamin Drake and James Handasyd Perkins, fellow authors and editors in Cincinnati.[48] It must also be noted that, in the same issue, Hall contributed a positive review of Beecher's collected

Sermons on Skepticism, demonstrating, again, an intellectual receptivity based in his Philadelphia roots: his argument with Beecher is impersonal, even as Beecher made personal attacks. Hall begins his review of *A Plea* by recapping his experience since publishing "The March of Intellect." He recounts Beecher's hackneyed boosting of the West as a land of opportunity (as if "this very original idea has not advanced more than about fifty-two times a year throughout the last twenty years").[49] Then, he suggests Beecher is ignorant of the West, his mistakes simply oversights based in ignorance. Yet he reiterates that Beecher's comments are "pernicious" because "they drew a broad line of distinction between the East and the West, assigning a degree of moral purity and elevation to the one, and of darkness and degradation to the other, not justified by the actual condition of either." Specifically, Hall remarks: "We supposed the error of the writer to lie, in the mistaken vanity of advancing dogmas, in relation to a country whose threshold he had barely passed, whose laws and institutions he seemed not to have examined, and with whose population he could have had but slender acquaintance." Claiming that Beecher had kept himself "to the company of New England people" during his stay in Cincinnati, Hall depicts Beecher as the stereotypical colonial official: coming to the colony, assuming the inferiority of the locals, and mixing with them as little as possible. Next, he discusses Beecher's misrepresentation of his own earlier writings, identifying it as "certainly the most palpable *non sequitur*, ever uttered by the President of a college, and we should be tempted to doubt the value of the education which taught such logic."[50]

Having cleared the ad hominem decks, Hall spends the remainder of the review, and his subsequent essay, "The Catholic Question," in the June *Western Monthly Magazine*, addressing Beecher's anti-Catholicism. Hall bases his discussion in a revisionist regional history that reimagines the French, and not the Puritans, as the meaningful founding fathers of the West. Earlier in this book, Hall's sympathetic treatment of habitants, Indians, and Métis has been addressed, so his invocation of the French in his final public effort to resist the "Universal Yankee Nation" is not surprising. Starting in his review of *A Plea*, he sets the stage for reconsidering the separate French history of the Ohio and Mississippi valleys: "They were the first settlers of all that is now Louisiana, Mississippi, and Missouri. They first introduced education into our valley, and their schools and colleges were, for a series of years, the only nurseries of learning west of the mountains. They have not proven less patriotic than any other denomination. At the college at Bardstown, hundreds of young natives [whites and Métis] of the west have been educated and, among them, the sons of some of our most distinguished men." Beecher had singled out the Bardstown seminary as the center of papist "designs" for dominating the West because it had received more than $50,000 in contributions from European Catholics. Wisely, Hall does not counter the worst of Beecher's paranoid fantasies, instead focusing more precisely on documented historical precedent. Citing the antidespotic revolutions conducted by Catholics in Ireland and France, he comments, "The last place we should look for royalists, would be among our catholic population, a large portion of whom are poor, and inclined to the most radical school of democracy." Last, Hall quotes a passage exposing Beecher's aversion to evidence, a sign of his irrational extremism. He recalls Beecher's challenge—"Let the Catholics mingle with us as Americans, and come with their children under the full action of our common schools and republican institutions, and the various powers of assimilation, and we are prepared cheerfully to abide the consequences"—and then paraphrases: " 'let the catholics cease to be catholics, and we will be satisfied, but not till then'; to the world it addresses a specious proposition, rounded off with apparent candor, but which, when, touched, proves to be mere sound. The Catholics do already nearly all that Dr. Beecher asks of them in that sentence." In contrast, Hall imagines "a country of generous feeling, and liberal opinion, [in which] intolerance cannot long stalk abroad unrebuked."[51] Hall's invocation of an ideas-based public sphere challenges Beecher's corruption of it by the bigoted illogic and exclusionary arrogance of nativism, and he rejects Beecher's combative and theoretical binarism with a simple assumption of a functional de facto pluralism.

While reviewing *A Plea*, Hall addressed only the western focus of Beecher's ideas. In "The Catholic Question," Hall focuses on nativism as a national phenomenon and continues his demand for national diversity with a more extensive invocation of the French model. Before doing so, he defines his terms in a Jeffersonian definition of civic nationalism:

> We profess to guaranty [*sic*] to every inhabitant of our country, certain rights, in the enjoyment of which he shall not be molested, except through the instrumentality of a process of law which is clearly indicated. . . . But it is idle to talk of these inestimable rights, as having any efficacious existence, if the various checks and sanctions, thrown around them by our constitution and laws, may be evaded, and lawless majority, with a high hand, ravish them by force from a few individuals who may be effectually outlawed by a perverted public opinion, produced by calumny and clamor.

Sounding quite like Jefferson in his letters to Madison concerning the need for a bill of rights to protect the most important rights from the caprice of public opinion, Hall primarily bases membership in the nation on loyalty to its laws, a qualification he privileges above the circumstances of birth or belief. Hall's revival of eighteenth-century liberalism stands against the irrationality of the unmediated market-based antebellum print culture easily won over by the profitability of nativist hate mongering, castigating the editors and publishers who profit from salacious and false anti-Catholic propaganda: "Thus the vulgar prejudice against this sect of Christians is perpetuated, by holding them up as the enemies of religion and education. . . . There are unhappily persons enough in this world, who have sufficient wisdom—speaking after the manner of men—to know that wherever there is delusion, there is money to be made: and there is no hallucination which has furnished a richer harvest than the one now under discussion."[52] Hall identifies greed as a driving force behind anti-Catholicism rather than genuine doctrinal difference. Nonetheless, by conflating greed, prejudice, and coercive rhetoric, Hall offers a scathing critique of public discourse in Jacksonian America. In his earlier writings, he had addressed each of these, but only in "The Catholic Question" does he move toward a more comprehensive critique of their place at the center of the nation's treatment of all groups not fitting the national norm of the WASP male.

To find the sources of the nation's slippage from its Revolutionary and classical republican ideals, Hall next outlines a revisionist national historiography, one not dominated by the Puritans or the hubris of their millennial ambitions. Like an eighteenth-century Deist such as Franklin, Hall is interested in religion only as it affects people's public behavior. As to sectarian disagreements, he writes: "To combat error is a duty incumbent on every man whose sphere of action is such as to give him sway over the minds of others; but it is not allowable to oppose even error, by artifice or injustice, by violating private right, or disturbing the public peace." From there, he finds in the inclusive and tolerant French both a "model of" the potential for American heterogeneity and diversity and a "model for" himself and others to follow as they imagine themselves and their nation. Like all the other historians of his era, Hall begins with the conquest era: "At a period nearly contemporaneous with the settlement of the British colonies in America, the French began to settle Canada and Louisiana; and if we compare the early colonists, we find decidedly more toleration and benevolence on the part of the French Catholics than on that of the English puritans. In the treatment of the Indian tribes, the French were, with few exceptions in lower Louisiana [i.e., the Natchez Massacre of 1727], just, kind, and considerate, while the English colonists, all but the followers of Penn, were decidedly reckless, cruel, and unjust." Hall's admiration of Penn—again a link to Philadelphia and Quakerism—is consistent throughout his career and here serves as a precedent for an alternative American multiracialism. Through this section, then, Hall is careful to detach religious and national identities: the English were cruel to the Indians not because they were Puritan but because they had the "natural ruggedness" of their nation. Penn and the Quakers, however, are then held up as proof that such destructive tendencies, though "natural" and essential to the national type of British innate identity, can be resisted and overcome. Nonetheless, Hall concludes this section by noting the contrast in each sect's relative compassion in a way that further derides the profit-based nature of the nativist press: "It shows that the catholic appetite for cruelty is not so keen as is usually imagined, and that they exercised, of choice, an expensive benevolence, at a period when Protestants, similarly situated, were blood-thirsty and rapacious."[53]

Hall proceeds to the Revolutionary era by noting the heterogeneity of populations that contributed to its success: English Puritans, Dutch Protestants, Pennsylvania Quakers, Maryland Catholics, Virginia Episcopalians, and so on. To Hall, these distinctions had nothing to do with Revolutionary brotherhood. All, that is, built and steered the metaphorical ship Beecher found only Protestant New Englanders fit to captain. As to the role of religion, Hall writes:

> If the love of monarchy was a component principle of the catholic faith, it was not developed in our country when a fair opportunity was offered for its exercise; and that in the glorious struggle for liberty—for civil and religious emancipation when our fathers arrayed themselves in defense of the sacred principles involving the whole broad ground of contest between liberty and despotism, the catholic and the protestant stood side by side on the battle-field, and in the council, and pledged to their common country, with equal devotedness, their lives, their fortunes, and their sacred honor. Nor should it be forgotten, that in a conflict thus peculiarly marked, a catholic king was our ally, when the most powerful of protestant governments was our enemy.[54]

Hall reduces the Revolution to its purest essence, the "sacred principles" of liberty and freedom, and insists that, sixty years later, Americans remember that their Founding Fathers were Protestant and Catholic, northern and southern, English and French (and others). Had he sought to remove the Puritans from the roster of the Founders, Hall would have mirrored Beecher's exclusionary practices. Instead he models his historical narrative on their model of inclusion and heterogeneity. Methodologically, that is, he borrows from the virtues of his subjects to craft a narrative whose own message reflects their values: he relies upon humor, common sense, and inclusion to define his authorial voice, the same characteristics so common in his stories about the French in the Mississippi Valley.

Hall closes "The Catholic Question" with a diatribe against the local Cincinnati editors who had condemned him—a literary man—for intervening in church affairs. What can be gleaned from this exchange is that the conflict is not really about Catholicism or Protestantism. Hall sees at the core a more insidious and counterrepublican pattern: a public sphere governed by greed and prejudice that, in the end, will violate and destroy the very principles of its construction: "Little did Luther and Calvin, and other great lights of the Reformation imagine, that in the year 1835, a protestant minister would be standing up for the infallibility of the clergy, and rebuking laymen for looking too curiously into the affairs of the church!"[55] Hall fears the demise of the free exchange of ideas necessary in a democracy in the atmosphere of coercion and collusion created by the anti-Catholics and the nativists.

Unfortunately, Hall all too accurately foresaw the end of his own career as a man of letters as a result of his challenging Beecher. For the decade before 1835, Hall had been strikingly prolific as an editor, historian, pamphleteer, and fiction writer. However, he shared with Beecher a publisher, Truman and Smith, and the publishing house effactually ended the *Western Monthly Magazine* at Beecher's behest, the minister exercising a leverage based on greater sales in the evangelical community than Hall's in the literary one. After 1835,

Hall wrote only three short stories, published in 1846 as add-ons in a "Greatest Hits" short story collection, *The Wilderness and the War-Path*, that otherwise just republished stories written between 1828 through 1835. Hall's persistent presence in this study requires a little further examination of the relation of his admiration of the French to his career as an advocate of causes that reflect a similarly receptive and inclusive perspective.

As a fiction writer, by narrating the anticommercial values of the habitants, for example, Hall encouraged his readers to imagine a nation less obsessed with profit and production and more interested in their neighbors and the reasonable values of the Enlightenment. In his stories, the priests of the French villages were always presented sympathetically: nondogmatic, laid back, and generally nonintrusive. His habitants and voyageurs are Catholic, but being so does not disqualify them from the virtues of critical thought, religious toleration, and self-representation. At the same time, unlike Flint or McConnel, he does not absorb the French: his habitants and their priests integrate these values with a distinctive lack of ambition, disinterest in conquest, and locality in politics—they are still French.

Hall endeavored only one major authorial project after 1836, co-authorship with Thomas McKenney—author of the controversial Treaty of Fond du Lac as discussed in chapter 4—of the three-volume *History of the Indian Tribes of North America* (1836–44). The collection reflects both Hall's lasting admiration for the French and Quaker models and his hope to extend their vision of a nation not based on racial exclusion and violence. Hall's most important contribution is an extended essay that concludes the third volume. Based on a series of articles Hall had published in 1831 in the *Illinois Monthly Magazine*, the essay's opening section extends the revisionist historical narrative initiated in "The Catholic Question." Most significant, he persists in connecting American expansionism to British imperialist acts: "The track of carnage, and the maledictions of the heathen, which have marked the discoveries of the European in every corner of the globe are but too familiar to the reader of history." Furthermore, while he opens with an ethnocentric bias— "The North American Indians, when discovered by the Europeans, were a race of savages who had made no advance whatever toward civilization"—he later concedes that Aztec laws "were superior to those of Greece and Rome, and their magistrates more just," and he later praises "Iroquois republicanism."[56] Given his consistent critiques of Anglo "civilization," his working definition of "civilization" might be reconsidered as strictly materialist in nature: the Indians lacked houses, buildings, or complicated machinery. In any case, although Hall displays the biases of his times, he never lets these impede his inclusion of Indians in his version of the United States as a civic nation. One crucial set of syllogisms lays out Hall's inclusive model of national membership, one clearly rooted in his attachment to French patterns of cultural contact: "If they [Indians] are our equals, we should admit them to an equality of rights; if they are properly subject to the operation of our laws, we should break down the barrier which separates them from us, bring them at once into the bosom of the republic, and extend to them the benefits, immunities, and privileges that we enjoy ourselves." Answering in the affirmative, Hall extensively outlines the necessities of Indian citizenship and the inclusion of their territories as states. Moreover, he was aware that such a model would have to be voluntary and not compulsory, at the risk of repeating the errors of the Puritans in both the seventeenth and nineteenth centuries. So, he continues: "If it be objected that they are independent nations, and that we cannot in good faith destroy their national character, as we should do by imposing our laws and civilization upon them against their will; it will be necessary, before we advance any further in our argument, to examine whether the fact be so, that these tribes are independent, and to ascertain the sort of national existence which they have held."[57] While Hall finds few examples of genuine Indian nations not yet put into a state of dependence by white greed and interference by 1844, he insists that they are so because of Anglo conquest and colonization, not on account of any innate or essential racial failing. As such, their "independence," he fears, is no longer viable through no fault of their own. In the end, Hall is to be credited with asking a question that whites the world around either rarely conceived or dared to ask, even if he provided no comprehensive solution. To the posthumous edition of Benjamin Drake's *Life and Adventures of Black Hawk* (1848), Hall appended an apocryphal essay of Drake's, "The Colonization of the Indians," that likewise argues for statehood for Indian territories and for direct representation in the government in the postremoval era as a partial and practical means of making the best of a bad situation. John Marshall thought he had ended this discussion by appending "domestic" and "dependent" to any Indian nation. Hall and Drake—as well as other critics of imperial nationalism such as Herman Melville—reopened it by reclaiming a civic version of nation to oppose the exclusivity of Marshall's binary-based romantic definition of the nation and patriarchal vision of racial difference.

On the whole, Hall's critique of Anglo-American Indian policy might be read as a condemnation of imperial nationhood more generally and its insistence upon the racialization and regularization of citizenship. Throughout, Hall contributed to a revisionist national story by invoking the colonial French in two ways: as Catholic non-Anglos, they modeled multiethnicity within "white" America; second, and more important, as allies of the Indians, they modeled a diverse nation. For Hall, the French founding myth was a way of challenging nativism's equation of race and nation and shifting conversations about race and religion toward more inclusive models, ones based in French Kaskaskia as well as Puritan Boston.

Hall's voice, and voices like his, were largely lost as the next twenty years witnessed the rise of anti-Catholicism sentiments more virulent than Beecher's. Even in the 1830s, tracts like Samuel F. B. Morse's "A Foreign Conspiracy against the Liberties of the United States" (1834) explicitly urged a cleansing of Catholicism from the millennial nation and deployed every racial, ethnic, and religious rhetorical strategy to do so.[58] Yet despite such differing views, liberal westerners like Hall and Drake and conservative easterners like Beecher and Bancroft were all against slavery, and they largely tabled sectarian conflicts after 1855 or so to concentrate on sectional ones, a transition Franchot views as part of the secularization of American public life. The emergent Republican Party was the result of the coming together of Illinois and Ohio free-soil advocates with New England liberals. The Union army was both Protestant and Catholic, and the two groups' mutual fears were put aside, for the moment.

After the Civil War, however, the Catholics continued to come— from Germany, Poland, Italy, and throughout eastern and central Europe—and all the old hatreds came back. But that's another story, and the old stories and memories of the French frontier played little or no role in postbellum exchanges. Nonetheless, the exchange between Beecher and Hall rehearsed the core issues of debates concerning American diversity and identity even down to the present. The lines of conflict that emerged from this period—nativism versus heterogeneity—still define the axes along which Americans discuss race and ethnicity. Yet our current aspiration for an open-ended conversation is what Hall, from Franklin's Philadelphia, would have wanted: a public discourse moving forward armed with a national historiography that encompassed both French and English, both Catholic and Protestant, both Indian and white versions of the American past.

Such Were the Place,
and the Kind of People

Xavier belonged to alert morning on the glittering
rapids of unknown rivers. Neil saw him coming out
of Montreal on a spring morning, with a squadron of
canoes bound away for the pine-darkened fort at the
mouth of the Kaministikwia. Xavier Pic. He would
be a pink-cheeked and ribald roisterer with a short
and curly golden beard.

 Sinclair Lewis, *Kingsblood Royal* (1947)

A s Michael Chevalier observed in the passage
that opens this book, any nation made by
the French in North America most likely
would have stayed peripheral, and happily so, or at
least that's how the antebellum Anglo dissidents
seem to have imagined. They used the French
frontier to remind their readers that their participation in the imperial nation was a choice, not a
destiny. Their implication was that perhaps staying off the world stage and privileging the pursuit
of happiness over the acquisition of property might
have been a truer means of honoring the principles
of the Revolution than conquering Mexico, expanding slavery, and creating wealth through corporate endeavors.

 In the antebellum decades, the nation was at
a crossroads: stay marginal or ascend the world
stage. After all, Admiral Perry opened Japan for

American trade before April 1861. The debate between people who imagined the United States as a peripheral nation and those who imagined it as a world power reveals a diversity of the shapes and forms of nationalism imagined and pursued in the early nineteenth century. Those who remembered the colonial French in a positive way were not antinationalist or anticapitalist. Rather, they offered a narrative of restraint instead of ambition, diversity instead of singularity, and satisfaction instead of avarice. For them, trade, nation, and race were concerns, but they were secondary, subordinated to older notions of republican virtue and commonplace sensibility. By stressing the diverse and paradoxical nature of the colonial era, they endeavored a transformation of their readers; by reminding them of the anti-imperial features in their nation's past, they worked to check the imperial impulses that characterized so much of antebellum public culture. The past few decades have witnessed a resurgence in scholarly and historical focus on the French frontier. Most of the sources I have turned to for historical confirmation or correction of the representations of the French in antebellum texts—positive and negative—have been published since 1990. Most recently, John Mack Faragher's 2005 book on the Acadians, Colin Calloway's 2003 book on the pre-1800 Missouri Valley, and Shirley Christian's 2004 book on the Chouteau dynasty—all commercially marketed tomes—reflect a growing curiosity about the racial, political, economic, and ethnic complexity of the frontier, a complexity omitted from most Cold War–era textbooks, the transcripts of the Turnerians.[1]

However, a number of twentieth-century writers foresaw the cultural work that might still be done by the memory of the French, among them Sinclair Lewis, whose antisegregation novel featured a foray into the French frontier: "This pioneering Frenchman had been one of the builders, the primitive warrior-kings, of the new provinces of the Americans and the British: Minnesota and Wisconsin, Ontario and Manitoba. But, Neil improvised, Xavier's assistance to the Anglican vhiskyguzzlers must have been involuntary. He must still have borne in his heart the Lilies of the Sun, not the beef-red banner of the British nor the candy-striped bunting of the Yanks."[2] When a wartime knee injury keeps him from golfing, Lewis's Neil Kingsblood—in *Kingsblood Royal* (1947)—pursues his genealogy. A typical Lewis character—white, materialistic, and ignorant—Neil is shaken to his Anglo-Saxon roots to discover a French ancestor. Yet around Xavier Pic Neil builds a fantasy straight out of Bancroft or Cooper: the dashing and daring man of nature, the "warrior-king" free of the feminizing influences of middle-class encumbrances. Neil's coureur de bois fantasy stays within his whiteness, stirring in a harmless individuality—the Frenchman as the vanishing frontiersman, the French as the first step in the inevitable white conquest of the West—a continuation of the narrative of Parkman or Irving.

But more like Hall, Reynolds, Kinzie, Brackenridge, or Longfellow, however, Lewis had another, less romantic purpose in mind. Next, Neil learns that Xavier's "squaw" was "Chippewa." Yet, as I have noted, in the imperial historical memory Indian and "Celtic" genes were trumped by Anglo-Saxon genes: both the French and the "Chippewa" had long ago vanished as meaningful threats to the dominance of men like Neil. However, Neil still intended to keep his Métis lineage off the local cocktail circuit. The novel then turns on the knowledge that Xavier was, in fact, "a full-blooded Negro" in the terms of the Minnesota Historical Society librarian contacted by Neil to find the ancestors of a "fellow veteran." In 1947, "negroes" were very much viewed as threats to the dominance of men like Neil. The librarian relates this only after making sure the veteran is not a "*Croix de Feu* racialist."[3] Later, Neil finds Xavier's strikingly literate letters in which he asks a sympathetic Anglo-American Indian agent that his children be legally designated as Indians. Furthermore, in *Kingsblood Royal*'s prequel, *The God-Seeker* (1949), the French aid Xavier's labors as a conductor in the Underground Railroad. The Anglos who supplant the French are the bringers of racism, violence, and avarice. To Xavier, they bring blackness and all that it entailed. In his revisionist history of Minnesota, Lewis suggested that neither the nation nor the state started with the Anglo-American's conquest of the vanishing red man but rather with a categorically separate interracial interculturalism.

In these novels, Lewis imagines a pre-Anglo white population that was not obsessed with conquest, exploitation, and removal. Around it he crafts an alternative narrative for defining post–World War II Anglo-America's obsession with racial difference: the pre-Anglo French frontier as a symbolic alternative to the dominant historiography of the raced, classed, and manifestly destined nation, a narrative that led in 1947 to the new responsibility of being a global superpower while maintaining Jim Crow domestically. Yet by reminding his American readers of the diversity of their past, specifically America's French past, Lewis offers a devastating commentary on the definitions—legal, genetic, and cultural—of whiteness on the eve of the civil rights era.

By intertwining Xavier's French identity with his "blackness," Lewis did what so many writers of the antebellum era had done. He reminds us that the most interesting bits of the American past have been hidden, often on purpose, because they contradicted the foundational myths and histories of a triumphal nationalist historiography: an Afro-Frenchman with Caribbean roots married to an Ojibwa in early nineteenth-century Minnesota certainly complicated things.[4] For Lewis, Xavier and his fellow coureurs de bois of all racial shades represented a deliberately obscured chapter in American history, and by unveiling them, he comments on his own historical moment. More recent writers have also found in the French frontier other vehicles for addressing the state of race and gender relations, even into the current era. To be more precise, Lewis's invocation of the French and Métis pasts has been carried on by later Minnesotans.

Louise Erdrich's Nanapush testifies in *Tracks* (1986): "And as for government promises, the wind is steadier. I am a holdout, like the Pillagers, although I told the Captain and the Agent what I thought of the papers in good English. I could have written my name, and much more too, in script. I had a Jesuit education in the halls of Saint John before I ran back to the woods and forgot all my prayers."[5] Perhaps Erdrich's greatest character is Nanapush, an Ojibwa trickster she often uses as a narrator. In this passage, Nanapush explains his values: a combination of French and Ojibwa ideals. Whether Nanapush's Ojibwa tricksterism or his Jesuit contrarianism led him "back to the woods" matters less than Erdrich's use of him to critique "American" presences in the north woods. She uses him to reflect on everything from her caricatures of assimilated Indians to her staged conversations about faith and gender between Nanapush and his longtime partner and nemesis, the cross-dressed Catholic Father Damien. Erdrich's use of the French frontier insists that the French impact on American culture did not vanish like so much vapor after 1763, as Anglo nationalist historians tried so hard to prove. Fellow "crossblood" writer Gerald Vizenor likewise simply assumes a number of genetic contributions to the blood of most of his characters as well.[6]

What matters more is that their characters are "holdouts," people who resist assimilation, acculturation, or annihilation. In a less local way, we might still find great value in remembering the French frontier: in its paradigm of inclusion and absence of territorial hunger, our memory of it might be a useful way of historicizing American diversity even now. It reminds us of the type of nationalism postcolonial theorist Simon During endorsed: "Nationalism has different effects and meanings in a peripheral nation than in a world power."[7]

————————— This has been a book about the culture wars. We usually think of the culture wars as being the recent struggle between tradition and innovation within contemporary print and electronic media, between right and left. Fresh as these struggles appear, "culture wars" have defined the self-fashioning of America as both empire and antiempire from its origins. Those of the late twentieth century, when the pitched battles over "political correctness" swarmed out of the ivory tower and into mainstream public discourse, represent only the most recent manifestation of these struggles. During that era, as the Cold War was ending and the nation faced a future as the lone superpower, tense discussions about what that new role would mean matched competing narratives of history to justify the competing explanations of the present and plans for the future. For example, the tempests over the revisionist historiography of Patricia Nelson Limerick's *The Legacy of Conquest* (1986) led to profound changes in how Americans think about the West: from the triumph of the white man played by John Wayne or Matt Dillon to the tragic narrative of the death of the American Dream in Clint Eastwood's later, darker westerns such as *The Unforgiven*. The cowboy—like the French in the texts I have examined—in these post-Limerick texts is a still a symbol, but now a very ambiguous and contested one, through which issues of race, class, nation, gender, violence, and identity are debated and contrasted.

In this book, the crucial fissures in American culture at stake in debates over race, class, nation, and gender—the culture wars of the early nineteenth century—were revealed in the varying and contrasting representations of the French colonials that Anglo-Americans found everywhere once they crossed the Appalachians. The mere presence of the French troubles such concepts as virgin land, yeoman farmers, and vanishing Indians. Like the memory of the cowboy in the twentieth and twenty-first centuries, the rich ambiguity of the French legacy in the nineteenth similarly allowed Americans to engage the deeper ideological and moral issues at stake in their actions. The resisting or dissenting writers challenged this process by insisting upon French and, subsequently, Indian, mixed-race, and Catholic presences in American culture from the start. Their point is that our occasionally forgotten values of inclusion and diversity are our French inheritance, a legacy they set at odds with the British legacy of exclusion and ambition.

Let me finish by revisiting *Recollections of Persons and Places in the West* (1834), in which Henry Marie Brackenridge recalled his time among the French in St. Genevieve, Missouri. His father had sent him there to learn French, but young Henry learned more than the language. He mentions how the French incorporated African foodways, "intermingled" with their Kickapoo neighbors, practiced open-field agriculture, and served the fur trade's racially indeterminate denizens. By recalling this, Brackenridge hoped his compatriots would likewise recall the many cultures and languages that contributed to his upbringing: "Such were the place, and the kind of people, where, and among whom I was to pass some of the most important years of my life, and which would naturally extend a lasting influence over me."[8]

Notes

Introduction

1 Chevalier, *Society, Manners, and Politics*, 281.

2 Ibid., 280.

3 Most history writing about the American West elides all white populations into a single "European" or "white" identity. On the conservative side, following Frederick Jackson Turner, see Fussell, *Frontier*, or Smith, *Virgin Land*. Drinnon, *Facing West*, and Dippie, *Vanishing American*, use the same conflation for different reasons.

4 For documentary histories of the actual historical presence of the French, see Alvord, *Mississippi Valley in British Politics*; Winsor, *Mississippi Basin*; McDermott, *Frenchmen and French Ways*; Eccles, *French in North America*; Balesi, *Time of the French*; Christian, *Before Lewis and Clark*; Greer, *People of New France*; and Ekberg, *French Roots*.

5 See Taylor, *American Colonies*; Hinderaker, *Elusive Empires*; White, *Middle Ground*; McConnell, *Country Between*; Cayton, *Frontier Indiana*; Calloway, *New Worlds for All* and *One Vast Winter Count*; Dunaway, *First American Frontier*; and Merrell, *Into the American Woods*. Hinderaker and Mancall, *At the Edge of Empire*, synthesize most of the available materials. Mancall and Merrell, *American Encounters*, bring together the past twenty-five years of scholarship on the subject.

6 See Choquette, *Frenchmen into Peasants*; Sayre, *Les Sauvages Américains*; Perkins, *Border Life*; and Murphy, "To Live among Us" and *Gathering of Rivers*.

7 Sayre, *Les Sauvages Américains*, 3.

8 Tocqueville, "Two Weeks in the Wilderness," 916.

9 For discussions of the concept of the "vanishing" Indian, see Pearce, *Savagism and Civilization*; Slotkin, *Regeneration through Violence*; Dippie, *Vanishing American*; Berkhofer, *White Man's Indian*; and Drinnon, *Facing West*. Richter, *Facing East from Indian Country*, has also influenced my thinking on this subject.

10 Harrison, quoted in Edmunds, " 'Unacquainted with the Laws,' " 187.

11 Beecher, *Plea for the West*, 247.

12 See histories of "whiteness," such as Roediger, *Wages of Whiteness*; Crane, *Race, Citizenship, and Law*; Dain, *Hideous Monster of the Mind*;

Brown, "Native Americans"; Hannaford, *Race*; Malcomson, *One Drop of Blood*; and Fredrickson, *Racism*. See as well Ignatiev, *How the Irish Became White*. Throughout, Horsman, *Race and Manifest Destiny*, has influenced my thinking.

13 By "imperialism" here, I mean it in both its territorial and metaphorical dimensions. For similar usages, see Rowe, *Literary Culture and U.S. Imperialism*; Greenberg, *Manifest Manhood*; and Streeby, *American Sensations*. My use of the international concepts of "empire," "colony," and translation are also drawn from Cheyfitz, *Poetics of Imperialism*, and his articles, "Literally White, Figuratively Red" and "Savage Law." More immediately, Gould in *Persistence of Empire* studies concepts of "empire" during the period in question.

14 See Aron, "Pigs and Hunters," and Faragher, " 'More Motley than Mackinaw.' " See also White, *Middle Ground*; McConnell, *Country Between*; and Merrell, *Into the American Woods*.

15 See Cherry, *God's New Isreal*, and Hatch, *Democratization of American Christianity*. In 1838, "The Catholic Question" was reprinted by the Catholic Board of Cincinnati. It was next reprinted in *First West*, edited by Watts and Rachels in 2002.

16 Especially with regard to the issue of masculinity in the antebellum United States, see Douglas, *Feminization of American Culture*; Greenberg, *Manifest Manhood*; and Nelson, *National Manhood*. Other sources sensitive to the paradoxes of antebellum culture include Wiebe, *Opening of American Society*; Blumin, *Emergence of the Middle Class*; and Moore, *Religious Outsiders and the Making of Americans*.

17 During, "Literature—Nationalism's Other?," 138, 139.

18 Pocock, *Machiavellian Moment*, 531, 541. As early as 1905 (in *Studies in Colonial Nationalism*), Richard Jebb defined American expansionism as "Roman Imperialism."

19 See Kennedy, *Orders from France*, and Spurlin, *French Enlightenment in America*. See as well Jones, *America and French Culture*.

20 See Byrd, *Challenges of Roger Williams*, and Myles, "Dissent and the Frontier of Translation."

21 Ashcroft, *Post-Colonial Transformation*, 21.

22 Brackenridge, *Views of Louisiana*. His only existing biography is Keller, *Nation's Advocate*.

23 The best discussion of the presence of the French in Lewis and Clark can be found in Slaughter, *Exploring Lewis and Clark*.

Chapter One

1 Hildreth, *History of the United States*, is discussed in Vitzhum, *American Compromise*, and Levin, *History as Romantic Art*.

2 See Dain, *Hideous Monster of the Mind*; Hannaford, *Race*; Brown, "Native Americans"; Malcomson, *One Drop of Blood*; Horsman, *Race and Manifest Destiny*; and Fredrickson, *Racism*. See as well Young, *Colonial Desire*. As to the relation of race to the rights of citizenship, see Crane, *Race, Citizenship, and Law*.

3 Hildreth, *Pioneer History*, 21.

4 For discussions of the Treaty of Aix-la-Chapelle, especially as a prelude to the French and Indian War, see Anderson, *Crucible of War*, and Ekberg, *François Valle and His World*. See as well Way, "Cutting Edge of Culture."

5 Hildreth, *Pioneer History*, 23.

6 Ibid., 19–20.

7 Upon its receipt at the American Antiquarian Society, DeWitt Clinton, citing Caleb Atwater's communiqué to the society, described it in "A Description of a Leaden Plate."

8 On the role of craniology and phrenology in the construction of scientific racism in the early nineteenth century, see Dain, *Hideous Monster of the Mind*; Horsman, *Race and Manifest Destiny*; Hanneford, *Race*; Nelson, *National Manhood*; and Fredrickson, *Racism*.

9 Bancroft, *History of the United States*, 2:563.

10 Ibid., 321–32, 403–7.

11 On nineteenth-century middleclass American readership, see Brodhead, *Cultures of Letters*. Burstein, *Sentimental Democracy*, has also influenced my thinking on this subject.

12 Ashcroft, *Post-Colonial Transformation*, 32. For the best discussion of romantic nationalism's influence on American historiography, see Levin, *History as Romantic Art*, and Vitzhum, *American Compromise*. See as well Wertheimer, *Imagined Empires*; Ross, "Romancing the Nation-State"; and Brennen, "National Longing for Form." Carr, in *Inventing the American Primitive*, most cogently links tribal nationalism to romantic history writing.

13 Warner, "What's Colonial about Colonial America?," 58.

14 Cushman, "Reasons and Considerations," 92.

15 Williams, "Selections from *A Key into the Language of America*," 259.

16 Marshall, Majority Opinion, *Johnson and Graham's Lessee v. William McIntosh.*

17 Aside from Cheyfitz's articles, see Wilkinson, *American Indians*; Washburn, *Red Man's Land/White Man's Law*; Burnham, "Periphery Within"; Jacobs, *Dispossessing the American Indian*; and Scheckel, *Insistence of the Indian*. Prucha, in *Great Father*, studies the religious signification of such language.

18 See in particular Aron, *How the West was Lost*; Merrell, *Into the American Woods*; and Hinderaker, *Elusive Empires*, for more on this subject.

19 Marshall, Majority Opinion in *McIntosh*, 36–37.

20 See Jennings, *Invasion of America*, 60. See also Axtell, *Invasion Within*.

21 On the role and practice of seigneurship, see Ekberg, *French Roots*; Balesi, *Time of the French*; and Choquette, "Center and Periphery in French North America." All recognize the very informal nature of these arrangements once the French nobility understood the lack of mineral wealth in Upper Louisiana.

22 See White, *Middle Ground*, and also Cayton, " 'Noble Actors.' " See as well Shoemaker, *Strange Likeness*.

23 Cayton, *Frontier Indiana*, chap. 2 in particular.

24 Knox, "Message to Congress," 13.

25 Eliot, *Manual of United States History*, 143.

26 Smith, *Nationalism and Modernism*, 212. Waldstreicher has also discussed this transition in *In the Midst of Perpetual Fetes*.

27 See Young, *Colonial Desire*; Ignatiev, *How the Irish Became White*; Spurr, *Rhetoric of Empire*; and Axtell, "White Indians of North America."

28 Flint, *Condensed Geography and History*, 1:293–94.

29 See Ekberg, *French Roots*; Balesi, *Time of the French*; McDermott, *Frenchmen and French Ways*; and Choquette, *Frenchmen into Peasants*.

30 Parkman, *Conspiracy of Pontiac*, 163.

31 Crèvecoeur, *Letters from an American Farmer*, 78.

32 Fink's story first appeared as a short story—"The Last of the Boatmen" by Morgan Neville—in *Western Souvenir*, edited by Hall. See Oglesby, "The Western Boatman."

33 See as well Justus, *Fetching the Old Southwest*.

34 Warburton, *Conquest of Canada*, I: 65.

35 Crèvecoeur, *Letters from an American Farmer*, 70.

36 Ibid., 330.

37 Tocqueville, "Two Weeks in the Wilderness," 916–17.

38 Hildreth, *History of the United States*, 1:72.

39 Flint, *Condensed Geography and History*, 1:259–60.

40 Drake, *Life and Adventures of Black Hawk*, 269, 272.

41 On the literary scene in antebellum Cincinnati, see Glazer, *Cincinnati in 1840*; Venable, *Beginnings of Literary Culture*; and Watts, *American Colony*.

42 Drake, *Physician to the West*, 359, 363.

43 Ford, *History of Illinois*; Dillon, *History of Indiana*; Atwater, *History of the State of Ohio*; and Lanman, *History of Michigan*.

44 On how regional diversity could be absorbed by romantic national narratives, see Smith, *Nationalism and Modernism*, 17–18. See as well Anderson, *Imagined Communities*.

45 Smith, *History of Wisconsin*, 11–12.

46 Patterson, *History of the Backwoods*, 37

47 Sheldon, *Early History of Michigan*, 54.

48 Reynolds, *Pioneer History of Illinois*, 55. On his visit to Black Hawk, see Black Hawk, *Autobiography*, 102–4.

49 Cutler, *Explanation of the Map*, 14.

50 See Smith, *Virgin Land*; Kolodny, *Lay of the Land*; and Slotkin, *Fatal Environment*.

51 Reynolds, *Pioneer History of Illinois*, 55.

52 Ibid., 144.

53 Ford, *History of Illinois*, 106.

54 Smith, *History of Wisconsin*, 112–13.

55 Cramer's *Navigator* is cited or mentioned in dozens of travel accounts, histories, geographies, and journals. I am using the 11th (and final) edition of 1814.

56 Ibid., 235.

57 Ibid., 236.

58 Atwater, *History of the State of Ohio*, 139.

Chapter Two

1 Ekberg, *French Roots*, 252.

2 On open-field agricultural practices, see Eccles, *French in North America*; Choquette, *Frenchmen into Peasants*; and McDermott, *Frenchmen and French Ways*.

3 Stoddard is quoted in Ekberg, *French Roots*, 254.

4   Griffiths, "Myth of Authenticity," 75.

5   See Pocock, *Machiavellian Moment*, sec. 3, and Nelson, *National Manhood*, 29–60. As to how this affected frontier and land policy, see Hallock, *From the Fallen Tree*, and Linklater, *Measuring America*.

6   See Fliegelman, *Declaring Independence*, 43.

7   Dillon, *History of Indiana*, 124–45. Dillon reprints in its entirety the slave code put in place in Vincennes prior to the French and Indian War.

8   See Christian, *Before Lewis and Clark*.

9   On class stratification in the antebellum era, see Blumin, *Emergence of the Middle Class*. In the West in specific, see Mahoney, *Provincial Lives*, and Gray, *Yankee West*,

10 Both stories can be found in *Selected Writings of Washington Irving*, 767–86 and 1058–88, respectively.

11 Tocqueville, *Democracy in America*, 216, 218–19, 219.

12 Of this particular context, Doyle writes in *"North of America"*: "The stereotype is reminiscent of the typical nineteenth-century American image of the Negro or the Latin America, those 'lesser breeds' who, according to prevalent conceptions of nationality and race were unfitted to the grand enterprise of taming the frontier, and were relegated to the status of hewers of wood and drawers of water" (25). Scholarly discussions of the representations of mixed-race African Americans in nineteenth-century American literature are numerous; see Lemire, *"Miscegenation"*; Jackson, *Barriers between Us*; Edwards, *Gothic Passages*; and Weierman, *One Nation, One Blood*. In a few texts, however, they are discussed in the context of Hispanophone Americans as well. See Rosenthal, *Race-Mixture*, and Goldman, *Continental Divides*, in particular. More generally, see Castronovo, *Fathering the Nation*, and Shoemaker, *Strange Likeness*.

13 Cutler, *Topographical Description*, 26.

14 See James, *Ohio Company*.

15 Turner, "Ohio Valley," 91–113.

16 Spurr, *Rhetoric of Empire*, 129, 132.

17 Imlay, *The Emigrants*, 204–5.

18 Clark, *Conquest of the Illinois*, 79.

19 Here and in subsequent chapters, I have used the following for biographical information on Schoolcraft: Bremer, *Indian Agent and Wilderness Scholar*; Brazer, *Harps upon the Willows*; and Osborn and Osborn, *Schoolcraft—Longfellow—Hiawatha*. See as well Schoolcraft, *Personal Memoirs*, and Mumford, "Mixed-Race Identity."

20 Schoolcraft, *Narrative Journal of Travels*, 68.

21 Biddle, *History of the Expedition*, 1:8–39. Because I am interested in the immediate early nineteenth-century contexts of the expedition's presentation to and effect on the American reading public, I am using the Biddle edition, following Dana Nelson and Greenfield.

22 Schoolcraft, *Narrative Journal of Travels*, 369, 64, 75.

23 See Choquette, *Frenchmen into Peasants*; Ekberg, *French Roots*; and McDermott, *Frenchmen and French Ways*. For the transition to Anglo-style agriculture, see Faragher, *Sugar Creek*. See as well Linklater, *Measuring America*, and Stilgoe, *Common Landscape*.

24 Schoolcraft, *Personal Memoirs*, 126.

25 Flint, *Condensed Geography and History*, 2:105, 106, 107. On Jefferson and western agriculture, see Smith, *Virgin Land*; Hallock, *From the Fallen Tree*; Gray, *Yankee West*; Stilgoe, *Common Landscape*; and Van Every, *Ark of Empire*, for discussions of the concept of "yeomanry" in the context of the frontier. On the role of the government in helping Anglo "yeomen" farmers, see Larson, *Internal Improvements*.

26 Spurr, *Rhetoric of Empire*, 76.

27 Parkman, *Conspiracy of Pontiac*, 75, 76.

28 Ibid., 214.

29 Eccles, *French in North America*, 80.

30 Croghan quoted in White, *Middle Ground*, 316.

31 Birkbeck, *Notes on a Journey*, 119.

32 Gjerde, *Minds of the West*, 31–50, discusses experimental agricultural settlements in the West.

33 Smith, *Nationalism and Modernism*, 37.

34 Cayton and Onuf, *Midwest and the Nation*, 118.

35 Larson, *Internal Improvements*, 5.

36 Gray, *Yankee West*, 78.

37 Tocqueville, *Democracy in America*, 214.

38 Fuller, "Summer on the Lakes," 175.

39 See Keller, *Nation's Advocate*. I have also used Brackenridge's *Recollections*.

40 Ward, *Andrew Jackson*, remains a fascinating discussion of this subject. Burstein, in *Passions of Andrew Jackson*, also studies Jackson and race.

41 I discuss his writing about the Whiskey Rebellion in *American Colony*, 36–37.

42 Brackenridge, *Views of Louisiana*, 146.

43 Ibid., 134, 135, 137, 139.

44 Ibid., 139, 145.

45 Both here and in subsequent chapters, for biographical information on Hall, I have relied on Venable, *Beginnings of Literary Culture*. The best sources, however, remain his biographies: Flanagan, *James Hall*, and Randell, *James Hall*.

46 Ford, *History of Illinois*, 125.

47 "The Indian Hater" first appeared in Hall's *Western Souvenir* (1828) and was republished repeatedly. "The Pioneer" appeared only in *Tales of the Border*. Most of Hall's stories initially appeared serially in journals he edited. I am using the more polished versions he published in collections, all of which had wider circulation than his journals. His interest in the French is expanded in "Notes on Illinois."

48 Hall, "Legend of Carondolet," in *Legends of the West*, 115, 116, 117.

49 Ibid., 130.

50 Hall, "French Village," in *Tales of the Border*, 105, 106, 125.

51 Hall, "Michel de Coucy," in *Legends of the West*.

52 See Buell, introduction to *Selected Poems of Henry Wadsworth Longfellow*, xvi.

53 See Faragher, *Great and Noble Scheme*, for the definitive history of the Acadian displacement.

54 Longfellow, "Evangeline," in *Selected Poems of Henry Wadsworth Longfellow*, 69.

Chapter Three

1 Parkman, *Oregon Trail*, 234.

2 Jacobs, *Francis Parkman*, 20. Doughty, *Francis Parkman*, reflects similar conclusions.

3 Chapman and Hendler, introduction to *Sentimental Men*, vii.

4 Throughout this chapter, my discussion of masculinity is informed by Nelson, *National Manhood*; Douglas, *Feminization of American Culture*; Greenberg, *Manifest Manhood*; and Castronovo, *Fathering the Nation*. Leverenz, *Manhood and the American Renaissance*, and Slaughter, *Exploring Lewis and Clark*, have also been consulted.

5 Birkbeck, *Notes on a Journey*, 108.

6 See Smith, *Virgin Land*, and Lewis, *American Adam*. See as well Slotkin, *Regeneration through Violence*, for more on this myth.

7 Deloria, *Playing Indian*, and Herman, "Romance on the Middle Ground," discuss this theme.

8 On class stratification in this period, see Mahoney, *Provincial Lives*; Blumin, *Emergence of the Middle Class*; Leverenz, *Manhood and the American Renaissance*; and Hendler, *Public Sentiments*. On its relation to class, see Roediger, *Wages of Whiteness*.

9 Parkman, *Oregon Trail*, 106.

10 The scholarly research on the fur trade, as it pertains to class and gender, is extensive. I have been most influenced both in this and in the subsequent chapters by Gilman, *Where Two Worlds Meet*; Balesi, *Time of the French*; Brown, *Strangers in the Blood*; Bumsted, "Cultural Landscape of Early Canada"; Sleeper-Smith, *Indian Women and French Men;* Calloway, *One Vast Winter Count*; Eccles, *French in North America*; Ekberg, *French Roots*; Christian, *Before Lewis and Clark;* Murphy, *Gathering of Rivers*; and Thorne, *Many Hands of My Relations*.

11 Nelson, *National Manhood*, 176–203.

12 Ibid., ix.

13 Parkman, *Oregon Trail*, 462–63.

14 Ibid., 225.

15 Ibid., 170, 177, 188.

16 Warren, *History*. I use the modern spelling "Ojibwa," although "Ojibwe" is also in use. Warren's "Ojibway" is not currently in use; each, however, reflects the word the French and the tribe themselves used in their encounters. "Chippewa" is an Anglo mishearing. Along the same lines, I use "Odawa" (formerly "Ottawa") and "Potawotamie" ("Pottawottomi"). See Bellfy, *Indians and Other Misnomers*.

17 See Christian, *Before Lewis and Clark*.

18 Biographical information on Warren is based Williams, "Memoir of William W. Warren." See as well Konkle, *Writing Indian Nations*, and Kugel, *To Be the Main Leaders of Our People*. Buffalohead's introduction to Warren's book is also useful.

19 Warren, *History*, 135.

20 Ibid., 385–86.

21 Ibid., 27.

22 Ibid., 133.

23 Fanon's *Black Skins, White Masks* represents the classic articulation of this theme.

24 Parkman, *Oregon Trail*, 385.

25 Ibid., 260, 351.

26 Ibid., 463.

27 Ibid., 49–50.

28 See Ziff, *Return Passages*, on antebellum travel writing. On the use of the "western motif" in travel accounts written by privileged eastern males, see Miner, "Western Travelers"; Flanagan, "Western Sportsmen Travelers"; and McDermott, "Up the Wide Missouri."

29 See McConnell, introduction to Parkman's *Conspiracy of Pontiac*, xi. On Parkman's tendency toward conflation of the Sioux and the Iroquois, see Slotkin, *Fatal Environment*; Doughty, *Francis Parkman*; and Jacobs, *Francis Parkman*, as well as Fussell, *Frontier*; Sayre, *Les Sauvages Américains*; and Carr, *Inventing the American Primitive*.

30 See Nelson, *National Manhood*, 85–88. See note 21 of chapter 2 in Nelson's book.

31 Jefferson in Biddle, introduction to *History of the Expedition*, xliv.

32 For Jefferson's ideas about the expedition more generally, see Slaughter, *Exploring Lewis and Clark*; Kessler, *Making of Sacajawea*; Nelson, *National Manhood*, 61–101; Greenfield, "Problem of the Discoverer's Authority"; and Nelson, *Interpreters with Lewis and Clark*.

33 Biddle, *History of the Expedition*, 1:38–39, 235.

34 Ibid., 1:368, 408; 2:27, 255.

35 Irving, *Tour of the Prairies*, 421, 422. I have used the Modern Library edition because the edition of *Tour* reproduced in the authoritative Twayne edition includes radical changes Irving made after initial publication. Because I am more interested in the book's immediate context, I have used the best modern reproduction of the 1836 edition. My reading here is informed by Anteyles, *Tales of Adventurous Enterprise*.

36 Parkman, *Oregon Trail*, 118.

37 Ibid., 174, 171, 182.

38 Ibid., 355.

39 Biddle, *History of the Expedition*, 1:242.

40 Ibid., 157.

41 See Dain, *Hideous Monster of the Mind*; Hannaford, *Race*; Horsman, *Race and Manifest Destiny*; and especially Lemire, *"Miscegenation"*; Kinney, *Amalgamation*; and Jackson, *Barriers between Us*.

42 Irving, *Tour of the Prairies*, 415, 419, 459, 472.

43 Parkman, *Oregon Trail*, 48, 438.

44 Ibid., 461.

45 See Rubin-Dorsky, *Adrift in the Old World*, for a discussion of Irving and sexuality.

46 Jacobs, *Francis Parkman*, 146.

47 Castronovo, *Fathering the Nation*, 40.

Chapter Four

1 Motley, *American Abraham*, 1.

2 See the introductions to both Nelson, *National Manhood*, and Castronovo, *Fathering the Nation*, on the rise of "fatherhood" as a subject within the field of men's studies.

3 See Fliegelman, *Prodigals and Pilgrims*, and Rogin, *Fathers and Children*, for two distinct readings of patriarchal authority in the early Republic. In *Great Father*, Prucha discusses the metaphorical extension of patriarchy to Indians.

4 See Levin, *Abigail Adams*. More generally, see Schlosser, *Fair Sex*.

5 Adams and Adams, *Book of Abigail and John*, 57.

6 In his majority opinion in *Cherokee Nation*, Marshall used "domestic dependent nations" to describe the wardship of Indian tribes under the United States. See Wilkinson, *American Indians*, 13–31.

7 Adams and Adams, *Book of Abigail and John*, 57.

8 See in particular Haltunnen, *Confidence Men and Painted Women*. See as well Hendler, *Public Sentiments*, and Brodhead, *Cultures of Letters*. On the scientific definition of the female gender, see Nelson, *National Manhood*, 135–60.

9 See Gjerde, *Minds of the West*; Mahoney, *Provincial Lives*; Fussell, *Frontier*; and Gray, *Yankee West*.

10 Brown, *Edgar Huntly*, 5.

11 Cooper, *Prairie*, 9. My reading of Cooper is informed by Motley, *American Abraham*, and Scheckel, *Insistence of the Indian*.

12 Maddox, *Removals*, 96.

13 Cooper, *Last of the Mohicans*, 103.

14 Cooper, *Prairie*, 10.

15 Brackenridge, *Views of Louisiana*, 118.

16 Handley, *Marriage, Violence, and the Nation*, 5.

17 See Bremer, *Indian Agent and Wilderness Scholar*; Brazer, *Harps upon the Willows*; and Osborn and Osborn, *Schoolcraft—Longfellow—Hiawatha*. On Johnston family history, see Brazer, *Harps upon the Willows*. For Jane in particular, see Mumford, "Mixed-Race Identity" and "Metis and the Vote in 19th-Century America," and Schoolcraft, "Notes for a Memoir of Mrs. Henry Rowe Schoolcraft" and "Memoir of John Johnston." Johnston's own "Autobiographical Letters" have been consulted as well.

18 Flint, *Recollections*, 158–59, 128.

19 Schoolcraft, *Journal of a Tour*, 49–50.

20 Schoolcraft, *Narrative Journal of Travels*, 338.

21 Brazer, *Harps upon the Willows*, 158, 179.

22 McKenney, *Sketches of a Tour*, 151–52.

23 Henry Rowe Schoolcraft, "On the Unchangeable Character of the Indian Mind," in Schoolcraft and Schoolcraft, *Literary Voyager*, 13–14.

24 Jane Johnston Schoolcraft ("Rosa"), "Invocation," in Schoolcraft and Schoolcraft, *Literary Voyager*, 143.

25 Bellin, *Demon of the Continent*, 132–52.

26 Bremer, *Indian Agent and Wilderness Scholar*, 216.

27 Schoolcraft, *Black Gauntlet*, 540–41.

28 Schoolcraft, *Personal Memoirs*, 117, 522.

29 James, *Account of an Expedition*, 1:248.

30 See Brown, *Strangers in the Blood*; Lurie, *Wisconsin Indians*; Van Kirk, *Many Tender Ties*; Thorne, *Many Hands of My Relations*; Calloway, *One Vast Winter Count*; Murphy, *Gathering of Rivers*; Devens, *Countering Colonization*; Choquette, *Frenchmen into Peasants*; and Sleeper-Smith, *Indian Women and French Men*. For opposing views, mostly limited to Canadian territory, see Anderson, *Chain Her by One Foot*, and Foster, *Captors' Narrative*. In general, the current historiography of the fur trade focuses on its gender relations. For a prefeminist reading, see O'Meara, *Daughters of the Country*.

31 Sleeper-Smith, *Indian Women and French Men*, 43.

32 Franchot, *Roads to Rome*, 194.

33 For a critique of "the Middle Ground," see Herman, "Romance on the Middle Ground."

34 On the treatment of Anglo women during this era, see, among others, Kerber, *Women of the Republic*; Isenberg, *Sex and Citizenship in Antebellum America*; and Baym, *American Women of Letters and the Nineteenth-Century Sciences*.

35 Kinzie, *Wau-Bun*, 252, 254.

36 Baym, introduction to *Wau-Bun*, x.

37 White, *Middle Ground*, 423.

38 Kinzie, *Wau-Bun*, 4.

39 Black Hawk, *Autobiography*, 61–67.

40 Kinzie, *Wau-Bun*, 250, emphasis in original.

41 Ibid., 124–29.

42 Ibid., 10–11.

43 Ibid., 90–91, emphasis in original.

44 Forsyth is quoted in Kinzie, *Wau-Bun*, 266.

45 Devens, *Countering Colonization*, 37.

46 See Vitzhum, *American Compromise*; Wertheimer, *Imagined Empires*; and Levin, *History as Romantic Art*, for comments on the androcentrism of most American historiography.

47 Devens, *Countering Colonization*, 118, 119.

48 See Tanner's *Narrative*, especially Loomis's introduction to the 1956 edition.

49 Bryant, "Prairies," in *Poetical Works*, lines 1–4. For more discussion of Anglo writers' use of "Prairie," see Thacker's *Great Prairie Fact and Literary Imagination*.

50 Aside from the above-cited books on the fur trade more generally, my comments on the Métis as a historical presence are drawn from Dickason, "From 'One Nation' in the Northwest"; Peterson, "Many Roads to Red River"; White, *Middle Ground*; Perdue, *"Mixed Blood" Indians*; and Edmunds, " 'Unacquainted with the Laws.' " For discussions of this issue in postcolonial settings, see Young, *Colonial Desire*, and Allen, *Blood Narrative*.

51 Erkkila, *Mixed Bloods and Other Crosses*, and Lemire, *"Miscegenation,"* speak to this issue in the context of antebellum culture more generally,

52 Whitman, "Half-Breed." See especially Scheick, *Half-Blood*; Weierman, *One Nation, One Blood*; Rosenthal, *Race-Mixture*; and Brown, *Injun Joe's Ghost*.

53 See Rosenthal, *Race-Mixture*, chap. 3 in particular.

54 Snelling's novella "Bois Brule" is in *Tales of the Northwest*.

55 Loomis, introduction to Tanner's *Narrative*, 1–16. Edwin James transcribed and edited the illiterate Tanner's account. Subsequent biographical information on Tanner and his children can be found as well in Schoolcraft, *Personal Memoirs*, and Widder, *Battle for the Soul*. See Bellin, *Demon of the Continent*, 142–46.

56 See Kugel, *To Be the Main Leaders of Our People*.

57 See Cooper, *Prairie*, 5–6. Natty makes similar statements in most of the Leatherstocking series. His un-"crossed" whiteness seems very important both to him and to Cooper.

58 For biographical information on Le Clair, see Jackson, introduction to *Life of Ma-Ka-Tai-Me-She-Kia-Kiak*. Sayre's "Abridging Two Worlds" introduces Gloria Anzaldua's concept of "mestizo/a consciousness" to the definition of Métis, a transposition I find somewhat difficult on account of both Indian tribal differences and European ethnic ones.

59 Szasz, *Between Indian and White Worlds*, 6. On the polarization of race in early America, see Shoemaker, *Strange Likeness*.

60 Edmunds, "'Unacquainted with the Laws,'" 189, 191.

61 For discussion of the Treaty of Fond du Lac, see Viola, introduction to McKenney, *Sketches of a Tour*; Warren, *History*; White, *Middle Ground*; Jacobs, *Dispossessing the American Indian*; and Kinietz, *Indians of the Western Great Lakes*, for background information. Schmitz, *White Robe's Dilemma*, has also influenced my thinking on this subject. See as well Malcomson, *One Drop of Blood*, and Prucha, *Great Father*.

62 McKenney, *Sketches of a Tour*, 398.

63 Ibid., 404.

64 McKenney's letter to Cass is quoted on p. xiv in Viola, introduction to McKenney's *Sketches of a Tour*.

65 On "crossblood" writing, see Watts, *American Colony*, 81–98. Vizenor's "Shadows at La Pointe" features the Métis reaction to the Treaty of Fond du Lac, for example.

66 Henry quoted in Warren, *History*, 214.

67 Warren, *History*, 214–16.

68 Ibid., 284.

69 Ibid., 290.

70 Ibid., 298, 299–300.

71 On Tenskatawa and Tecumseh more generally, see Sugden, *Tecumseh*; Dowd, *War under Heaven* and *Spirited Resistance*; and Tanner, " Glaize in 1792."

72 Warren, *History*, 326.

73 For biographical information on Richardson, see Beasley, *Canadian Don Quixote*, and Hurley, *Borders of Nightmare*.

74 Richardson, *Hardscrabble* and *Wau-Nan-Gee*. Beasley in particular notes Richardson's use of Kinzie's pamphlet in both these novels and in his *Major Richardson's The War of 1812*.

75 Richardson, "Trip to Walpole Island and Port Sarnia," 113, 125.

76 Irving, *Tour of the Prairies*, 423.

77 Catlin, *North American Indians*, 123. On Catlin and Irving in general, see Dippie, *Catlin and His Contemporaries*.

78 In *Four Souls* (2004), Erdrich likewise has a Métis character nurse an enemy back to health before exacting her revenge.

79 Robb, *Kaam*, 22.

80 Biographical information on Robb is available in the introduction to Oelschlaeger, *Old Southwest Humor*, 19–23.

81 See Drinnon, *Facing West*; Slotkin, *Regeneration through Violence*; and Fussell, *Frontier*, for negative readings of Hall's "The Indian Hater," especially as it is refracted through Melville, *Confidence Man*, chaps. 22–26. Each reading, however, suggests that none had read "The Pioneer."

82 Drake, *Life and Adventures of Black Hawk*. See Watts, *American Colony*, 100–112.

83 See Hall, "Obituary of John Moredock" and "Indian Hating." Randall, *James Hall*, covers the theme extensively. See Orians, "Indian Hater in Early American Fiction," and Quirk, "Pragmatic Defense of Source Study." "The Indian Hater" was republished in *Legends of the West*, 247–62.

84 For a similar reading of "The Pioneer," see Simeone, *Democracy and Slavery*, 158–64. "The Pioneer" was published in *Tales of the Border*, 13–102.

Chapter Five

1 Hall, "Catholic Question," 377.

2 Franchot, *Roads to Rome*, xx, xxii.

3 Biographical information on Beecher is in *Autobiography of Lyman Beecher*; Henry, *Unvanquished Puritan*; and Fraser, *Pedagogue for God's Kingdom*.

4 Beecher's letter to Harriet is quoted in Randall's *James Hall*, 244.

5 Hall documented these occurrences in "March of Intellect." See Randall, *James Hall*. Beecher's speech and its aftereffects are also discussed in Franchot, *Roads to Rome*. On my reading of the culture of Catholicism in the United States more generally, see Giles, *American Catholic Arts and Fictions*.

6 Billington, *Protestant Crusade*, 2. On nativism in general, I have relied on the following: Dohen, *Nationalism and American Catholicism*; Fell, *Foundations of Nativism*; Knobel, *"America for Americans"*; and Moore, *Religious Outsiders and the Making of Americans*.

7 See Schlosser, *Fair Sex*; Wiebe, *Opening of American Society*; and Gjerde, *Minds of the West*, for discussions of the instability and experimental nature of the 1840s.

8 Gjerde, *Minds of the West*, 43.

9 Throughout this chapter, Bloch, *Visionary Republic*, and Hatch, *Democratization of American Christianity*, have influenced my thinking.

10 See Larson, *Internal Improvements*, 37.

11 See Baron, *Grammar and Good Taste*, and Simpson, *Politics of American English*, on the diversity of languages in colonial America.

12 See Levin, *History as Romantic Art*; Ross, "Romancing the Nation-State"; and Vitzhum, *American Compromise*.

13 Foos, *Short, Offhand Killing Affair*, 128.

14 Thoreau's "Resistance to Civil Government" and Corwin's "Against the Mexican War," 78.

15 Jay, *Review of the Causes and Consequences of the Mexican War*.

16 McConnel, *Western Characters*, 62–63.

17 Prucha's *Churches and the Indian Schools* has informed my comments on this subject. See as well Kugel, *To Be the Main Leaders of Our People*; Berkhofer, *White Man's Indian*; and Dippie, *Vanishing American*.

18 McConnel, *Western Characters*, 70, 60, 106–7.

19 Ibid., 107.

20 Flint, *Condensed Geography and History*, 1:179.

21 Ibid., 2:216, 217.

22 Ibid., 1:251.

23 Ibid., 2:108.

24 Flint, *Recollections*, 189; translation by the author.

25 Bancroft, *History of the United States*, 2:138. On the writings of the Jesuit explorers themselves, see Sayre's *Les Sauvages Américains*.

26 On Bancroft, aside from previously cited sources, see McWilliams, *American Epic*. Two biographies have been consulted as well: Nye, *George Bancroft*, and Handlin, *George Bancroft*. On typology, see Bercovitch, *Puritan Origins of the American Mind*.

27 Bancroft, *History of the United States*, 2:153.

28 Ibid., 470, 473

29 See Anderson, *Imagined Communities*; Waldstreicher, *In the Midst of Perpetual Fetes*; and Smith, *Nationalism and Modernism*. Brennen, "National Longing for Form," has also influenced my thinking. Carr, *Inventing the American Primitive*, 58–100, develops the idea of tribal and romantic nationalism more succinctly.

30 Addams, *Twenty Years at Hull House*.

31 Cherry, *God's New Israel*. The first edition was published in 1970.

32 Jefferson, "Bill for Establishing Religious Freedom," 83.

33 Beecher, *Plea for the West*, 60.

34 Fell, *Foundations of Nativism*, cf. 41–63.

35 Beecher, *Plea for the West*, 40, 49.

36 Hamilton, Madison, and Jay, "Federalist 10," in *Federalist Papers*.

37 Beecher, *Plea for the West*, 9–10, 80.

38 Ibid., 119–20, 68–69.

39 Ibid., 140.

40 Ibid., 122.

41 For biographical information on Hall, see Randall, *James Hall*, and Flanagan, *James Hall*. Other sources have been cited previously.

42 Hall, "March of Intellect," 655, 656, 659, 660.

43 On Cincinnati at this time, see Glazer, *Cincinnati in 1840*; Venable, *Beginnings of Literary Culture*; Watts, *American Colony*; and Aaron, *Cincinnati*.

44 Looby, *Voicing America*, and Shields, *Civil Tongues and Polite Letters*, among many others, document the early Republic's culture of letters, especially Philadelphia's.

45 Beecher, *Plea for the West*, 18–19.

46 Ibid., 20–21.

47 Cited in Randall, *James Hall*, 236.

48 On the Drakes and Perkins, see Venable, *Beginnings of Literary Culture*.

49 Hall, "Review of *A Plea for the West*," 320. On boosterism, see Cayton and Onuf, *Midwest and the Nation*, 43–53.

50 Hall, "Review of *A Plea for the West*," 321, 323.

51 Ibid., 324, 325, 326.

52 Hall, "Catholic Question," 376, 381.

53 Ibid., 382, 383.

54 Ibid., 384.

55 Ibid., 388.

56 Hall, "North American Indians," 3:111, 102, 131. See Drinnon, *Facing West*, for a critical treatment of it. Large sections of Hall's essay were first published as "On the Intercourse of the American People with the Indians" in 1831.

57 Hall, "North American Indians," 3:220–21.

58 See Billington, *Protestant Crusade*, and Knobel, *"America for the Americans,"* on later nineteenth-century form and manifestations of nativist thought.

Conclusion

1 See Faragher, *Great and Noble Scheme*; Calloway, *One Vast Winter Count*; and Christian, *Before Lewis and Clark*. Following Limerick, *Leg-*

acy of Conquest, in 1986 and White, *Middle Ground*, in 1991, the historiography of the diversity of the frontier has been persistent.

2 Lewis, *Kingsblood Royal*, 54–55.

3 Ibid., 57, 60.

4 See Watts, "*Kingsblood Royal, The Godseeker*, and the Racial History of the Midwest." See Sleeper-Smith, *Indian Women and French Men*, and White, *Middle Ground*, in general.

5 Erdrich, *Tracks*, 33.

6 Vizenor, *Crossbloods*. This collection reflects Vizenor's call for a reintroduction of Métis values to Indian activism.

7 During, "Literature—Nationalism's Other?," 139.

8 Brackenridge, *Recollections*, 26.

Bibliography

Primary Sources

Adams, Abigail, and John Adams. *The Book of Abigail and John: Selected Letters of the Adams Family.* Edited by L. H. Butterfield et al. Cambridge, Mass.: Harvard University Press, 1975.

Addams, Jane. *Twenty Years at Hull House, with Autobiographical Notes.* Edited by James Hurt. 1903. Reprint, Urbana: University of Illinois Press, 1992.

Atwater, Caleb. *A History of the State of Ohio, Natural and Civil.* 2nd ed. Cincinnati, Ohio: Giezer and Shepherd, 1832.

Bancroft, George. *History of the United States of America from the Discovery of the American Continent.* 10 vols. Boston: Little, Brown, 1834–75.

Beecher, Lyman. *The Autobiography of Lyman Beecher.* Edited by Barbara M. Cross. 2 vols. 1864. Reprint, Cambridge, Mass.: Harvard University Press, Belknap Press, 1961.

———. *A Plea for the West.* Cincinnati, Ohio: Truman and Smith, 1835.

Biddle, Nicholas, ed. *History of the Expedition under the Command of Captains Lewis and Clarke to the Sources of the Missouri, Thence across the Rocky Mountains, and down the Columbia to the Pacific Ocean, Performed during the Years 1804-5-6 by the Order of the Government of the United States.* 3 vols. Philadelphia, Pa.: Biddle, 1814.

Birkbeck, Morris. *Notes on a Journey in America from the Coast of Virginia to the Territory of Illinois.* 4th ed. London: Ridgeway, 1818.

Black Hawk. *An Autobiography.* Edited by Donald Jackson. Reprint of *Life of Ma-Ka-Tai-Me-She-Kia-Kiak or Black Hawk*, 1833. Urbana: University of Illinois Press, 1964.

Brackenridge, Henry Marie. *Recollections of Persons and Places in the West.* Philadelphia, Pa.: Kay, 1834.

———. *Views of Louisiana, Together with a Journal of a Voyage up the Missouri River, in 1811.* Pittsburgh, Pa.: Cramer, 1814.

Brown, Charles Brockden. *Edgar Huntly; or, Memoirs of a Sleep-Walker.* 1799. Reprint, New York: Penguin, 1998.

Bryant, William Cullen. *Poetical Works.* Edited by Park Godwin. 2 vols. New York: Russell and Russell, 1883.

Catlin, George. *North American Indians.* 1866. Reprint, New York: Penguin, 1996.

Chateaubriand, François René de. *Travels in America and Italy.* London: H. Colbourne, 1828.

Chevalier, Michael. *Society, Manners, and Politics in the United States Being a Series of Letters on North America.* Translated from the 3rd Paris edition by T. G. Bradford. Boston: Tuttle, 1839.

Clark, George Rogers. *The Conquest of the Illinois.* Edited by Milo Milton Quaife. 1788. Reprint, Chicago: Donnelly, 1920.

Clinton, DeWitt. "A Description of a Leaden Plate, or Medal, Found near the Mouth of the Muskingum, in the State of Ohio." *Archaeologia Americana: Transactions and Collections of the American Antiquarian Society* 2 (1836): 535–42.

Cooper, James Fenimore. *Last of the Mohicans; A Narrative of 1757.* 1826. Reprint, New York: Dutton, 1951.

———. *The Pioneers, or, The Sources of the Susquehanna.* 1823. Reprint, New York: Signet, 1964.

——— *The Prairie.* 1827. Reprint, New York: Penguin, 1987.

Corwin, Thomas. "Against the Mexican War." In *Life and Speeches of Thomas Corwin: Orator, Lawyer, and Statesman,* edited by Josiah Marrow. Cincinnati: W. H. Anderson, 1896.

Cramer, Zadok. *The Navigator; Containing Directions for Navigating the Monongahela, Allegheny, Ohio, and Mississippi Rivers.* 11th ed. Pittsburgh, Pa.: Cramer, 1814.

Crèvecoeur, Hector St. John de. *Letters from an American Farmer and Sketches of 18th-Century America.* Edited by Albert E. Stone. 1927. Reprint, New York: Penguin, 1981.

Cushman, Robert. "Reasons and Considerations Touching the Lawfulness of Removing out of England into the Parts of America." In *Mourt's Relation. A Journal of the Pilgrims at Plymouth,* edited by Dwight B. Heath, 88–96. 1626. Reprint, Plymouth, Mass.: Applewood Books, 1963.

Cutler, Jervis. *A Topographical Description of the State of Ohio, Indiana Territory, and Louisiana.* 1812. Reprint, New York: AMS Press, 1971.

Cutler, Manasseh. *An Explanation of the Map of Federal Lands.* 1787. Reprint, New York: Readex Imprints, 1966.

Dillon, John B. *A History of Indiana from Its Earliest Exploration by Europeans to the Close of Territorial Government in 1816.* Indianapolis, Ind.: Bingham and Doughy, 1859.

Drake, Benjamin. *Life and Adventures of Black Hawk with Sketches of Keokuk and the Black Hawk War.* 7th ed. Cincinnati, Ohio: Truman and Smith: 1849.

Drake, Daniel. *Physician to the West: Selected Writings of Daniel Drake on Society and Science.* Edited by Henry D. Shapiro and Zane L. Miller. Lexington: University of Kentucky Press, 1970.

Eliot, Samuel. *Manual of United States History from 1492 to 1850.* Boston: Hickling, 1858.

Erdrich, Louise. *Four Souls.* New York: HarperCollins, 2004.

——. *Tracks.* New York: Random House, 1986.

Flint, Timothy. *A Condensed Geography and History of the Western States, or The Mississippi Valley.* 2 vols. Cincinnati, Ohio: Flint, 1828.

——. *Recollections of the Last Ten Years Passed in Occasional Residences and Journeyings in the Valley of the Mississippi.* Boston: Cummings, 1826.

Ford, Thomas. *A History of Illinois from Its Commencement as a State in 1818 to 1847.* Chicago: Griggs, 1859.

Fuller, Margaret. "A Summer on the Lakes, during 1843." In *The Portable Margaret Fuller,* edited by Mary Kelley, 69–227. New York: Penguin, 1994.

Hall, James. "The Catholic Question." *Western Monthly Magazine* 3 (June 1835): 375–90.

——. "Indian Hating." *Western Monthly Magazine* 1 (September 1833): 403–8.

——. *Legends of the West.* Philadelphia, Pa.: Hall, 1832.

——. "The March of Intellect." *Western Monthly Magazine* 2 (December 1834): 655–60.

——. "The North American Indians." In *The Indian Tribes of North America with Biographical Sketches and Anecdotes of the Principal Chiefs,* edited by James Hall and Thomas McKenney, 3:83–346. 3 vols. 1836–44. Reprint, Edinburgh: Grant, 1934.

——. "Notes on Illinois: The French Settlements." *Illinois Monthly Magazine* 2 (August 1832): 488–99.

——. "Obituary of John Moredock." *Illinois Intelligencer,* November 7, 1829.

——. "Review of *A Plea for the West* by Lyman Beecher." *Western Monthly Magazine* 3 (May 1835): 320–27.

——. *Tales of the Border.* Cincinnati, Ohio: Truman, 1835.

——, ed. *The Western Souvenir, a Christmas and New Year's Gift for 1829.* Cincinnati, Ohio: Guilford, 1828.

——. *The Wilderness and the War-Path.* New York: Wiley, 1849.

Hamilton, Alexander, James Madison, and John Jay. *The Federalist Papers.* Edited by Clinton Rossiter. New York: Mentor, 1961.

Hildreth, Richard. *The History of the United States of America from the Discovery of the Continent to the Organization of Government under the Federal Constitution, 1497–1789.* 8 vols. New York: Harper and Brothers, 1849.

Hildreth, Samuel P. *Pioneer History: Being an Account of the First Examinations of the Ohio Valley, and the Early Settlement of the Northwest Territory.* Cincinnati, Ohio: Derby, 1848.

Imlay, Gilbert. *The Emigrants, &c. Or the History of an Expatriated Family, Being a Delineation of English Manners, Drawn from Real Characters, Written in America.* Edited by W. M. Verhoeven and Amanda Gilroy. 1793. Reprint, New York: Penguin, 1998.

Irving, Washington. *Selected Writings of Washington Irving.* Edited by William P. Kelly. 1836. Reprint, New York: Modern Library, 1984.

———. *A Tour of the Prairies.* In *Selected Writings of Washington Irving,* edited by William P. Kelly, 409–590. 1836. Reprint, New York: Modern Library, 1984.

James, Edwin. *Account of an Expedition from Pittsburgh to the Rocky Mountains.* 2 vols. 1823. Reprint, Ann Arbor, Mich.: University Microfilms, 1966.

Jay, William. *A Review of the Causes and Consequences of the Mexican War.* Boston: B. B. Bussey, 1849.

Jefferson, Thomas. "A Bill for Establishing Religious Freedom in Virginia (1779)." In *Paine and Jefferson on Liberty,* edited by Lloyd S. Kramer, 81–83. New York: Continuum, 1997.

Johnston, John, Esq. "Autobiographical Letters. Introductory Remarks by Henry R. Schoolcraft, 1844." *Michigan Pioneer and Historical Collections* 32 (1903): 328–45.

Kinzie, Juliette M. *Wau-Bun: The "Early Day" in the North-West.* 1855. Reprint, Urbana: University of Illinois Press, 1992.

Knox, Henry. "Message to Congress." In *Documents of United States Indian Policy,* edited by Francis Paul Prucha, 12–14. Lincoln: University of Nebraska Press, 1975.

Lanman, James H. *History of Michigan from Its Earliest Colonization to the Present Time.* New York: Harper and Brothers, 1852.

Lewis, Sinclair, *Kingsblood Royal.* New York: Random House, 1947.

Longfellow, Henry Wadsworth. *Selected Poems of Henry Wadsworth Longfellow.* Edited by Lawrence Buell. New York: Penguin, 1988.

Marshall, John. Majority Opinion, *Cherokee Nation v. Georgia* (1832). In *Documents in United States Indian Policy*, edited by Francis Paul Prucha, 58–60. 2nd ed. Lincoln: University of Nebraska Press, 1990.

———. Majority Opinion, *Johnson and Graham's Lessee v. William McIntosh*. 21 *U.S. Reports* 240–60 (1823).

McConnel, J. L. *Western Characters or Types of Border Life in the Western States*. New York: Redfield, 1853.

McKenney, Thomas. *Sketches of a Tour of the Lakes, of the Character and Customs of the Chippeway Indians and of Incidents Connected with the Treaty of Fond du Lac*. 1828. Reprint, Barre, Mass.: Imprint Society, 1972.

Melville, Herman. *The Confidence Man: His Masquerade*. 1856. Reprint, New York: Signet, 1954.

Neville, Morgan. "The Last of the Boatmen." In *Half-Horse Half Alligator: The Growth of the Mike Fink Legend*, edited by Walter Blair and Franklin J. Meine, 43–55. Chicago: University of Chicago Press, 1956.

Oelschlaeger, Fritz, ed. *Old Southwest Humor from the St. Louis Reveille, 1844-1850*. Columbus: University of Missouri Press, 1990.

Parkman, Francis. *The Conspiracy of Pontiac and the Indian War after the Conquest of Canada*. 2 vols. 1851. Reprint, Lincoln: University of Nebraska Press, 1994.

———. *France and England in North America*. 7 vols. Boston: Little, Brown, 1897–1902.

———. *The Oregon Trail*. Edited by David Levin. 1849. Reprint, New York: Penguin, 1982.

Patterson, A. W. *History of the Backwoods, or The Region of the Ohio Authentic, from the Earliest Accounts*. Pittsburgh, Pa.: By the author, 1843.

Reynolds, John. *The Pioneer History of Illinois Containing the Discovery in 1673 and the History of the Country to the Year 1818, When the State Government Was Organized*. Belleville, Ill.: Randall, 1852.

Richardson, Major John. *Hardscrabble; or The Fall of Chicago: A Tale of Indian Warfare*. New York: DeWitt, 1851.

———. "A Trip to Walpole Island and Port Sarnia in the Year of 1848." In *Major John Richardson's Short Stories*, edited by David Beasley, 113–31. Penicton, B.C.: Theytus, 1985.

———. *Wau-Nan-Gee: The Massacre at Chicago*. New York: DeWitt, 1852.

Robb, John S. *Kaam; or, Daylight: The Arapahoe Half-Breed*. Boston: Star Spangled Banner Press, 1847.

Schoolcraft, Henry Rowe. *Algic Researches: Comprising Inquiries Respecting the Mental Characteristics of the North American Indians.* 1st ser. Indian Tales and Legends. New York: Harper, 1839.

———. *Journal of a Tour into the Interior of Missouri and Arkansaw, from Potosi, or Mine a Burton, in Missouri Territory, in a South-West Direction, toward the Rocky Mountains: Performed in the Years 1818 and 1819.* London: Phillips and Co., 1821.

———. "Memoir of John Johnston." *Michigan Pioneer and Historical Collection* 36 (1908): 53–94.

———. *Narrative Journal of Travels from Detroit Northwest through the Great Chain of American Lakes to the Sources of the Mississippi River in the Year 1820.* Albany, N.Y.: Hosford, 1823.

———. "Notes for a Memoir of Mrs. Henry Rowe Schoolcraft." *Michigan Pioneer and Historical Collection* 36 (1908): 95–100.

———. *Personal Memoirs of a Residence of Thirty Years with the Indian Tribes on the American Frontiers.* Philadelphia, Pa.: Lippincott, 1854.

Schoolcraft, Henry Rowe, and Jane Johnston Schoolcraft. *The Literary Voyager or Muzzeniegun.* Edited by Philip P. Mason. 1827. Reprint, East Lansing: Michigan State University Press, 1962.

Schoolcraft, Mrs. Henry Rowe [Mary Howard]. *The Black Gauntlet: A Tale of Plantation Life in South Carolina.* Philadelphia, Pa.: Lippincott, 1860.

Sheldon, Eliza M. *The Early History of Michigan. From the First Settlement to 1815.* New York: Barnes, 1856.

Smith, William R. *The History of Wisconsin, in Three Parts, Historical, Documentary, and Descriptive.* Madison, Wis.: Brown, 1854.

Snelling, William Joseph. *Tales of the Northwest.* Edited by John T. Flanagan. 1828. Reprint, Minneapolis: University of Minnesota Press, 1936.

Tanner, John. *A Narrative of the Adventures of John Tanner (U.S. Interpreter at the Sault Ste. Marie) during Thirty Years Residence among the Indians in the Interior of North America.* 1828. Reprint, Minneapolis, Minn.: Ross and Haines, 1956.

Thoreau, Henry David. "Resistance to Civil Government." In *Walden and Civil Disobedience*, edited by Sherman Paul. Boston: Houghton Mifflin, 1960.

Tocqueville, Alexis de. *Democracy in America.* Edited by Richard D. Heffner. 1835. Reprint, New York: Signet, 1956.

———. "Two Weeks in the Wilderness (1831)." In *Democracy in America and*

Two Essays on America, translated and edited by Gerald E. Bevan, 875–926. New York: Penguin, 2003.

Turner, Frederick Jackson. "The Ohio Valley." In *The Frontier in American History*. 1920. Reprint, Tucson: University of Arizona Press, 1997.

Warburton, George. *The Conquest of Canada*. 2 vols. New York: Harper and Brothers, 1850.

Warren, William Whipple. *History of the Ojibway People*. 1885. Reprint, St. Paul: Minnesota Historical Society, 1984.

Whitman, Walt. "The Half-Breed (1843)." In *The Early Poems and the Fiction*, edited by Thomas L. Brasher for *The Collected Writings of Walt Whitman*, 257–91. New York: New York University Press, 1963.

Williams, Roger. "Selections from *A Key into the Language of America*" (1636). In *Early American Writings*, edited by Carla Mulford, 257–61. New York: Oxford University Press, 2002.

Secondary Sources

Aaron, Daniel. *Cincinnati: Queen City of the West, 1819-1838*. Columbus: Ohio State University Press, 1992.

Allen, Chadwick. *Blood Narrative: Indigenous Identity in American Indian and Maori Literary and Activist Texts*. Durham, N.C.: Duke University Press, 2002.

Alvord, Clarence. *The Mississippi Valley in British Politics: A Study of the Trade, Land, Speculation, and Experiments with Imperialism Culminating with the American Revolution*. Cleveland, Ohio: Clark, 1917.

Anderson, Benedict. *Imagined Communities: Reflections on the Origin and Spread of Nationalism*. Rev. ed. New York: Verso, 1991.

Anderson, Fred. *Crucible of War: The Seven Years' War and the Fate of Empire in British North America, 1754-1766*. New York: Vintage, 2000.

Anderson, Karen L. *Chain Her by One Foot: The Subjugation of Women in Seventeenth-Century New France*. New York: Routledge, 1991.

Anteyles, Peter. *Tales of Adventurous Enterprise: Washington Irving and the Poetics of Western Expansion*. New York: Columbia University Press, 1990.

Aron, Stephen. *How the West Was Lost: The Transformation of Kentucky from Daniel Boone to Henry Clay*. Baltimore: Johns Hopkins University Press, 1996.

———. "Pigs and Hunters: 'Rights in the Woods' on the Trans-Appalachian

Frontier." In *Contact Points: American Frontiers from the Mohawk Valley to the Mississippi, 1750–1830*, edited by Andrew R. L. Cayton and Fredrika Teute, 175–204. Chapel Hill: University of North Carolina Press, 1998.

Ashcroft, Bill. *Post-Colonial Transformation*. London: Routledge, 2001.

Axtell, James. *The Invasion Within: The Contest of Cultures in Colonial North America*. New York: Oxford University Press, 1985.

———. "The White Indians of North America." In *American Encounters: Natives and Newcomers from European Contact to Indian Removal, 1500–1850*, edited by Peter C. Mancall and James H. Merrell, 324–50. New York: Routledge, 2000.

Balesi, Charles. *The Time of the French in the Heart of North America, 1677–1818*. Chicago: Alliance Français, 1992.

Baron, Dennis. *Grammar and Good Taste: Reforming the American Language*. New Haven: Conn.: Yale University Press, 1982.

Baym, Nina. *American Women of Letters and Nineteenth-Century Sciences: Styles of Affiliation*. New Brunswick, N.J.: Rutgers University Press, 2002.

———. Introduction to *Wau-Bun: The Early Day in the "North-West,"* by Juliette M. Kinzie, ix–xix. Urbana: University of Illinois Press, 1992.

Beasley, David R. *The Canadian Don Quixote: The Life and Works of Major John Richardson*. Erin, Ont.: Porcupine, 1977.

———. Introduction to *Major John Richardson's Short Stories*, edited by David R. Beasley, 6–19. Peniction, B.C.: Theytus, 1985.

Bellfy, Phil. *Indians and Other Misnomers: A Cross-Referenced Dictionary of the Peoples, Persons, and Places of Native North America*. Golden, Colo.: Fulcrum Press, 2001.

Bellin, Joshua David. *The Demon of the Continent: Indians and the Shaping of American Literature*. Philadelphia: University of Pennsylvania Press, 2001.

Bercovitch, Sacvan. *The Puritan Origins of the American Mind*. New Haven, Conn.: Yale University Press, 1975.

Berkhofer, Robert F., Jr. *The White Man's Indian: Images of the American Indian from Columbus to the Present*. New York: Vintage, 1979.

Billington, Ray Allen. *The Protestant Crusade, 1800–1860: A Study of the Origins of American Nativism*. New York: Macmillan, 1938.

Blair, Walter, and Franklin J. Meine, eds. *Half-Horse Half Alligator: The Growth of the Mike Fink Legend*. Chicago: University of Chicago Press, 1956.

Bloch, Ruth H. *Visionary Republic: Millennial Themes in American Thought, 1756-1800.* New York: Cambridge University Press, 1985.

Blumin. Stuart M. *The Emergence of the Middle Class: Social Experience in the American City, 1760-1900.* New York: Cambridge University Press, 1989.

Brazer, Marjorie Cahn. *Harps upon the Willows: The Johnston Family of the Old Northwest.* Ann Arbor, Mich.: Historical Society of Michigan, 1993.

Bremer, Richard G. *Indian Agent and Wilderness Scholar: The Life of Henry Rowe Schoolcraft.* Mt. Pleasant, Mich.: Clark Historical Library, 1987.

Brennen, Timothy. "The National Longing for Form." In *Nations and Narration,* edited by Homi Bhabha, 44–70. New York: Routledge, 1991.

Brodhead, Richard. *Cultures of Letters: Scenes of Reading and Writing in Nineteenth-Century America.* Chicago: University of Chicago Press, 1993.

Brown, Harry J. *Injun Joe's Ghost: The Indian Mixed Blood in American Writing.* Columbia: University of Missouri Press, 2004.

Brown, Jennifer S. H. *Strangers in the Blood: Fur Trade Company Families in Indian Country.* Vancouver: University of British Columbia Press, 1980.

Brown, Kathleen. "Native Americans and Early Modern Concepts of Race." In *Empire and Others: British Encounters with Indigenous Peoples, 1600-1850,* edited by Martin Daunton and Mark Halpern, 79–100. Philadelphia: University of Pennsylvania Press, 1999.

Buell, Lawrence. Introduction to *Selected Poems of Henry Wadsworth Longfellow,* edited by Lawrence Buell, x–xxi. New York: Penguin, 1988.

Buffalohead, W. Roger. Introduction to *History of the Ojibway People,* by William Warren, ix–xxvii. 1885. Reprint, St. Paul: Minnesota Historical Society Press, 1984.

Bumsted, J. M. "The Cultural Landscape of Early Canada." In *Strangers within the Realm: Cultural Margins of the First British Empire,* edited by Bernard Bailyn and Philip D. Morgan, 363–91. Chapel Hill: University of North Carolina Press, 1991.

Burnham, Michelle. "The Periphery Within: Internal Colonialism and the Rhetoric of US Nation-Building." In *Messy Beginnings: Postcoloniality and Early American Studies,* edited by Malini Johar Schueller and Edward Watts, 139–54. New Brunswick, N.J.: Rutgers University Press, 2003.

Burstein, Andrew. *The Passions of Andrew Jackson*. New York: Random House, 2003.

———. *Sentimental Democracy: The Evolution of America's Romantic Self-Image*. New York: Hill and Wang, 1999.

Byrd, James P. *The Challenges of Roger Williams: Religious Liberty, Violent Persecution, and the Bible*. Macon, Ga.: Mercer University Press, 2002.

Calloway, Colin G. *New Worlds for All: Indians, Europeans, and the Remaking of Early America*. Baltimore, Md.: Johns Hopkins University Press, 1997.

———. *One Vast Winter Count: The Native American West before Lewis and Clark*. Lincoln: University of Nebraska Press, 2003.

Carr, Helen. *Inventing the American Primitive: Politics, Gender, and Representation of Native American Literary Traditions, 1789-1936*. New York: New York University Press, 1996.

Castronovo, Russ. *Fathering the Nation: American Genealogies of Slavery and Freedom*. Berkeley: University of California Press, 1995.

Cayton, Andrew R. L. *Frontier Indiana*. Bloomington: Indiana University Press, 1999.

———. " 'Noble Actors' upon 'the Theatre of Honour': Power and Civility in the Treaty of Greenville." In *Contact Points: American Frontiers from the Mohawk Valley to the Mississippi, 1750-1830*, edited Andrew R. L. Cayton and Fredrika Teute, 234–69. Chapel Hill: University of North Carolina Press, 1998.

Cayton, Andrew R. L., and Peter Onuf. *The Midwest and the Nation: Rethinking the History of an American Region*. Bloomington: Indiana University Press, 1990.

Cayton, Andrew R. L., and Fredrika Teute, eds. *Contact Points: American Frontiers from the Mohawk Valley to the Mississippi, 1750-1830*. Chapel Hill: University of North Carolina Press, 1998.

Chapman, Mary, and Glenn Hendler. Introduction to *Sentimental Men: Masculinity and the Politics of Affect in American Culture*, edited by Mary Chapman and Glenn Hendler. Berkeley: University of California Press, 1999.

Cherry, Conrad, ed. *God's New Israel: Religious Interpretations of American Destiny*. Rev. and updated ed. Chapel Hill: University of North Carolina Press, 1998.

Cheyfitz, Eric. "Literally White, Figuratively Red: The Frontier of Translation in *The Pioneers*." In *James Fenimore Cooper: New Critical*

Essays, edited by Robert Clark, 55–95. Totowa, N.J.: Barnes and Noble, 1985.

———. *The Poetics of Imperialism: Translation and Colonization from The Tempest to Tarzan*. Expanded ed. Philadelphia: University of Pennsylvania Press, 1997.

———. "Savage Law: The Plot against the Indian in *Johnson and Graham's Lessee* v. M'Intosh and *The Pioneers*." In *Cultures of United States Imperialism*, edited by Amy Kaplan and Donald Pease, 109–28. Durham, N.C.: Duke University Press, 1993.

Choquette, Leslie. "Center and Periphery in French North America." In *Negotiated Empires: Centers and Peripheries in the Americas, 1500–1820*, edited by Christine Daniels and Michael V. Kennedy, 193–206. New York: Routledge, 2002.

———. *Frenchmen into Peasants: Modernity and Tradition in the Peopling of French Canada*. Cambridge, Mass.: Harvard University Press, 1997.

Christian, Shirley. *Before Lewis and Clark: The Story of the Chouteaus, the French Dynasty That Ruled America's Frontier*. New York: Farrar, Straus and Giroux, 2004.

Crane, Gregg B. *Race, Citizenship, and Law in American Literature*. New York: Cambridge University Press, 2002.

Crawford, John C. "What Is Michif?" In *The New Peoples: Being and Becoming Metis in North America*, edited by Jacqueline Peterson and Jennifer S. H. Brown, 231–42. Winnipeg: University of Manitoba Press, 1985.

Dain, Bruce. *A Hideous Monster of the Mind: American Race Theory in the Early Republic*. Cambridge, Mass.: Harvard University Press, 2002.

Deloria, Philip. *Playing Indian*. New Haven, Conn.: Yale University Press, 1998.

Devens, Carol. *Countering Colonization: Native American Women and the Great Lakes Missions, 1630–1900*. Berkeley: University of California Press, 1992.

Dickason, Olive Patricia. "From 'One Nation' in the Northwest: A Look at the Emergence of the *Metis*." In *The New Peoples: Being and Becoming Metis in North America*, edited by Jacqueline Peterson and Jennifer S. H. Brown, 19–36. Winnipeg: University of Manitoba Press, 1985.

Dippie, Brian W. *Catlin and His Contemporaries: The Politics of Patronage*. Lincoln: University of Nebraska Press, 1990.

———. *The Vanishing American: White Attitudes and U.S. Indian Policy*. Middleton, Conn.: Wesleyan University Press, 1982.

Dohen, Dorothy. *Nationalism and American Catholicism*. New York: Sheed and Ward, 1967.

Doughty, Howard. *Francis Parkman*. New York: Macmillan, 1962.

Douglas, Ann. *The Feminization of American Culture*. New York: Noonday, 1998.

Dowd, Gregory Evans. *A Spirited Resistance: The North American Indian Struggle for Unity, 1745-1815*. Baltimore, Md.: Johns Hopkins University Press, 1992.

——. *War under Heaven: Pontiac, the Indian Nations, and the British Empire*. Baltimore, Md.: Johns Hopkins University Press, 2002.

Doyle, James. *"North of America": Images of Canada in the Literature of the United States*. Toronto: ECW Press, 1982.

Drinnon, Richard. *Facing West: The Metaphysics of Indian-Hating and Empire Building*. New York: New American Library, 1980.

Dunaway, Wilma. *The First American Frontier: The Transition to Capitalism in Southern Appalachia, 1700-1860*. Chapel Hill: University of North Carolina Press, 1996.

During, Simon. "Literature—Nationalism's Other?" In *Nation and Narration*, edited by Homi K. Bhabha, 138–55. New York: Routledge, 1990.

Eccles, W. J. *The French in North America, 1500-1765*. Rev. ed. East Lansing: Michigan State University Press, 1998.

Edmunds, R. David. " 'Unacquainted with the Laws of the Civilized World': American Attitudes toward the Metis Communities in the Old Northwest." In *The New Peoples: Being and Becoming Metis in North America*, edited by Jacqueline Peterson and Jennifer S. H. Brown, 185–94. Winnipeg: University of Manitoba Press, 1985.

Edwards, Justin. *Gothic Passages: Racial Ambiguity and the American Gothic*. Iowa City: University of Iowa Press, 2003.

Ekberg, Carl J. *François Valle and His World: Upper Louisiana before Lewis and Clark*. Columbus: University of Missouri Press, 2002.

——. *French Roots in the Illinois Country: The Mississippi Frontier in Colonial Times*. Urbana: University of Illinois Press, 1998.

Erkkila, Betsy. *Mixed Bloods and Other Crosses: Rethinking American Literature from the Revolution to the Culture Wars*. Philadelphia: University of Pennsylvania Press, 2005.

Fanon, Frantz. *Black Skins, White Masks*. Translated by Charles Lam Markmann. New York: Grove, 1967.

Faragher, John Mack. *A Great and Noble Scheme: The Tragic Story of the*

Expulsion of the French Acadians from Their American Homeland. New York: Norton, 2005.

——. " 'More Motley Than Mackinaw': From Ethnic Mixing to Ethnic Cleansing on the Frontier of the Lower Missouri, 1783–1833." In *Contact Points: American Frontiers from the Mohawk Valley to the Mississippi, 1750-1830*, edited by Andrew R. L. Cayton and Fredrika Teute, 304–26. Chapel Hill: University of North Carolina Press, 1998.

——. *Sugar Creek: Life on the Illinois Prairie*. New Haven, Conn.: Yale University Press, 1986.

Fell, Sister Marie Lenore. *The Foundations of Nativism in American Textbooks, 1783-1860*. Washington, D.C.: Catholic University of America Press, 1941.

Flanagan, John T. *James Hall: Literary Pioneer of the Ohio Valley*. Minneapolis: University of Minnesota Press, 1941.

——. "Western Sportsmen Travelers in the New York *Spirit of the Times*." In *Travelers on the Western Frontier*, edited by John Francis McDermott, 168–86. Urbana: University of Illinois Press, 1970.

Fliegelman, Jay. *Declaring Independence: Jefferson, Natural Language, and the Culture of Performance*. Stanford, Calif.: Stanford University Press, 1993.

——. *Prodigals and Pilgrims: The American Revolution against Patriarchal Authority, 1750-1800*. New York: Cambridge University Press, 1982.

Foos, Paul. *A Short, Offhand Killing Affair: Soldiers and Social Conflict during the Mexican-American War*. Chapel Hill: University of North Carolina Press, 2002.

Foster, William Henry. *The Captors' Narrative: Catholic Women and Their Puritan Men on the Early American Frontier*. Ithaca, N.Y.: Cornell University Press, 2003.

Franchot, Jenny. *Roads to Rome: The Antebellum Protestant Encounter with Catholicism*. Berkeley: University of California Press, 1994.

Fraser, James W. *Pedagogue for God's Kingdom: Lyman Beecher and the Second Great Awakening*. New York: University Press of America, 1985.

Fredrickson, George. *Racism: A Short History*. Princeton, N.J.: Princeton University Press, 2002.

Fussell, Edwin. *Frontier: American Literature and the American West*. Princeton, N.J.: Princeton University Press, 1965.

Giles, Paul. *American Catholic Arts and Fictions: Culture, Ideology, Aesthetics*. New York: Cambridge University Press, 1992.

Gilman, Carolyn. *Where Two Worlds Meet: The Great Lakes Fur Trade.* St. Paul: Minnesota Historical Society, 1982.

Gjerde, Jon. *The Minds of the West: Patterns of Ethnocultural Evolution in the Rural Midwest, 1830–1917.* Chapel Hill: University of North Carolina Press, 1997.

Glazer, Walter Stix. *Cincinnati in 1840: The Social and Functional Organization of an Urban Community in the Pre-Civil War Period.* Columbus: Ohio State University Press, 1999.

Goldman, Anne. *Continental Divides: Revisioning American Literature.* New York: Palgrave, 2000.

Gould, Eliga H. *The Persistence of Empire: British Political Culture in the Age of the American Revolution.* Chapel Hill: University of North Carolina Press, 2000.

Gray, Susan E. *The Yankee West: Community Life on the Michigan Frontier.* Chapel Hill: University of North Carolina Press, 1996.

Greenburg, Amy S. *Manifest Manhood and the Antebellum American Empire.* New York: Cambridge University Press, 2005.

Greenfield, Bruce M. "The Problem of the Discoverer's Authority in Lewis and Clark's *History.*" In *Macropolitics of Nineteenth-Century Literature: Nationalism, Exoticism, Imperialism,* edited by Jonathan Arac and Harriet Ritvo, 12–36. Philadelphia: University of Pennsylvania Press, 1991.

Greer, Allan. *The People of New France.* Toronto: University of Toronto Press, 1997.

Griffiths, Gareth. "The Myth of Authenticity: Representation, Discourse, and Social Practice." In *De-Scribing Empire: Post-Colonialism and Textuality,* edited by Chris Tiffin and Alan Lawson, 70–85. New York: Routledge, 1994.

Hallock, Thomas. *From the Fallen Tree: Frontier Narratives, Environmental Politics, and the Roots of a National Pastoral, 1749–1826.* Chapel Hill: University of North Carolina Press, 2003.

Haltunnen, Karen. *Confidence Men and Painted Women: A Study of Middle-Class Culture in America, 1830–1870.* New Haven, Conn.: Yale University Press, 1982.

Handley, William R. *Marriage, Violence, and the Nation in the American Literary West.* New York: Cambridge University Press, 2002.

Handlin, Lilian. *George Bancroft: Intellectual as Democrat.* New York: Harper and Row, 1984.

Hannaford, Ivan. *Race: A History of an Idea in the West*. Baltimore, Md.: Johns Hopkins University Press, 1996.

Hatch, Nathan O. *The Democratization of American Christianity*. New Haven, Conn.: Yale University Press, 1989.

Hendler, Glenn. *Public Sentiments: Structures of Feeling in Nineteenth-Century American Literature*. Chapel Hill: University of North Carolina Press, 2001.

Henry, Stuart C. *Unvanquished Puritan: A Portrait of Lyman Beecher*. Grand Rapids, Mich.: Eerdmans, 1973.

Herman, Daniel J. "Romance on the Middle Ground." *Journal of the Early Republic* 19 (Summer 1999): 279–91.

Hinderaker, Eric. *Elusive Empires: Constructing Colonialism in the Ohio Valley, 1763–1800*. New York: Cambridge University Press, 1997.

Hinderaker, Eric, and Peter C. Mancall. *At the Edge of Empire: The Backcountry in British North America*. Baltimore, Md.: Johns Hopkins University Press, 2003.

Horsman, Reginald. *Race and Manifest Destiny: The Origins of American Racial Anglo-Saxonism*. Cambridge, Mass.: Harvard University Press, 1981.

Hurley, Michael. *The Borders of Nightmare: The Fiction of John Richardson*. Toronto: University of Toronto Press, 1992.

Ignatiev, Noel. *How the Irish Became White*. New York: Routledge, 1995.

Isenberg, Nancy. *Sex and Citizenship in Antebellum America*. Chapel Hill: University of North Carolina Press, 1998.

Jackson, Cassandra. *Barriers between Us: Interracial Sex in Nineteenth-Century American Literature*. Bloomington: Indiana University Press, 2004.

Jackson, Donald. Introduction to *The Life of Ma-Ka-Tai-Me-She-Kia-Kiak or Black Hawk*, edited by Donald Jackson, 1–31. Urbana: University of Illinois Press, 1955.

Jacobs, Wilbur R. *Dispossessing the American Indian: Indians and Whites on the Colonial Frontier*. New York: Scribner's, 1972.

———. *Francis Parkman, Historian as Hero: The Formative Years*. Austin: University of Texas Press, 1991.

James, Alfred P. *The Ohio Company: Its Inner History*. Pittsburgh, Pa.: University of Pittsburgh Press, 1959.

Jebb, Richard. *Studies in Colonial Nationalism*. New York: Arnold, 1905.

Jennings, Francis. *The Invasion of America: Indians, Colonialism, and the Cant of Conquest*. New York: Norton, 1975.

Jones, Howard Mumford. *America and French Culture, 1750–1848.* Chapel
  Hill: University of North Carolina Press, 1927.
Jones, Landon Y. *William Clark and the Shaping of the West.* New York: Hill
  and Wang, 2004.
Justus, James H. *Fetching the Old Southwest: Humorous Writing from
  Longstreet to Twain.* Springfield: University of Missouri Press, 2004.
Keller, William F. *The Nation's Advocate: Henry Marie Brackenridge and
  Young America.* Pittsburgh, Pa.: University of Pittsburgh Press, 1956.
Kennedy, Roger M. *Orders from France: The Americans and the French in a
  Revolutionary World, 1780–1820.* New York: Knopf, 1989.
Kerber, Linda K. *Women of the Republic: Intellect and Ideology in
  Revolutionary America.* Rev. ed. New York: Norton, 1986.
Kessler, Donna J. *The Making of Sacajawea: A Euro-American Legend.*
  Tuscaloosa: University of Alabama Press, 1996.
Kinietz, W. Vernon. *The Indians of the Western Great Lakes, 1615–1760.*
  Ann Arbor: University of Michigan Press, 1965.
Kinney, James. *Amalgamation! Race, Sex, and Rhetoric in the Nineteenth-
  Century American Novel.* Westport, Conn.: Greenwood Press, 1985.
Knobel, Dale T. *"America for the Americans": The Nativist Movement in the
  United States.* New York: Twayne, 1996.
Kolodny, Annette. *The Lay of the Land: Metaphor as Experience and History
  in American Life and Letters.* Chapel Hill: University of North Carolina
  Press, 1975.
Konkle, Maureen. *Writing Indian Nations: Native Intellectuals and the
  Politics of Historiography.* Chapel Hill: University of North Carolina
  Press, 2004.
Kugel, Rebecca. *To Be the Main Leaders of Our People: A History of
  Minnesota Ojibwe Politics, 1825–1898.* East Lansing: Michigan State
  University Press, 1998.
Larson, John Lauritz. *Internal Improvements: National Public Works and the
  Promise of Popular Government in the Early United States.* Chapel Hill:
  University of North Carolina Press, 2001.
Lemire, Elise Virginia. *"Miscegenation": Making Race in America.*
  Philadelphia: University of Pennsylvania Press, 2002.
Leverenz, David. *Manhood and the American Renaissance.* Ithaca, N.Y.:
  Cornell University Press, 1989.
Levin, David. *History as Romantic Art: Bancroft, Prescott, Motley, and
  Parkman.* New York: AMS Press, 1967.

Levin, Phyllis Lee. *Abigail Adams: A Biography.* New York: St. Martin's, 1987.

Lewis, R. W. B. *The American Adam: Innocence, Tragedy, and Tradition in the Nineteenth Century.* Chicago: University of Chicago Press, 1951.

Limerick, Patricia Nelson. *The Legacy of Conquest: The Unbroken Past of the American West.* New York: Norton, 1987.

Linklater, Andro. *Measuring America: How an Untamed Wilderness Shaped the United States and Fulfilled the Promise of Democracy.* New York: Walker, 2002.

Looby, Christopher. *Voicing America: Language, Literary Form, and the Origins of the United States.* Chicago: University of Chicago Press, 1996.

Loomis, Neil. Introduction to *A Narrative of the Captivity and Adventures of John Tanner during Thirty Years Residence among the Indians in the Interior of North America*, 1–16. Minneapolis, Minn.: Ross and Haines, 1956.

Lott, Eric. *Love and Theft: Blackface Minstrelsy and the American Working Class.* New York: Oxford University Press, 1993.

Lurie, Nancy Ostreich. *Wisconsin Indians.* Madison: Wisconsin Historical Society, 2002.

Maddox, Lucy. *Removals: Nineteenth-Century American Literature and the Politics of Indian Affairs.* New York: Oxford University Press, 1991.

Mahoney, Timothy. *Provincial Lives: Middle-Class Experience in the Antebellum Middle West.* New York: Cambridge University Press, 1999.

Malcomson, Scott L. *One Drop of Blood: The American Misadventure of Race.* New York: Farrar, 2000.

Mancall, Peter C., and James H. Merrell, eds. *American Encounters: Natives and Newcomers from European Contact to Indian Removal, 1500–1850.* New York: Routledge, 2000.

McConnell, Michael N. *A Country Between: The Upper Ohio Valley and Its Peoples, 1724–1774.* Lincoln: University of Nebraska Press, 1992.

———. Introduction to *The Conspiracy of Pontiac and the Indian War after the Conquest of Canada*, by Francis Parkman. 2 vols. 1851. Reprint, Lincoln: University of Nebraska Press, 1994.

McDermott, John Francis, ed. *Frenchmen and French Ways in the Mississippi Valley.* Urbana: University of Illinois Press, 1969.

———. "Up the Wide Missouri: Travelers and Their Diaries, 1794–1861." In *Travelers on the Western Frontier*, edited by John Francis McDermott, 3–78. Urbana: University of Illinois Press, 1970.

McWilliams, John P., Jr. *The American Epic: Transforming a Genre, 1770–1860*. New York: Cambridge University Press, 1989.

Merrell, James H. *Into the American Woods: Negotiators on the Pennsylvania Frontier*. New York: Norton, 1999.

Merritt, Jane T. *At the Crossroads: Indians and Empires on a Mid-Atlantic Frontier, 1700–1763*. Chapel Hill: University of North Carolina Press, 2003.

Miner, Donald D. "Western Travelers in Quest of the Indian." In *Travelers on the Western Frontier*, edited by John Francis McDermott, 267–89. Urbana: University of Illinois Press, 1970.

Moore, R. Laurence. *Religious Outsiders and the Making of Americans*. New York: Oxford University Press, 1986.

Motley, Warren. *The American Abraham: James Fenimore Cooper and the Frontier Patriarch*. New York: Cambridge University Press, 1987.

Mumford, Jeremy. "Metis and the Vote in 19th-Century America." *Journal of the West* 39 (Summer 2000): 38–45.

——. "Mixed-Race Identity in a Nineteenth-Century Family: The Schoolcrafts of Sault Ste. Marie, 1824–1827." *Michigan Historical Review* 25 (Spring 1999): 1–23.

Murphy, Lucy Eldersveld. *A Gathering of Rivers: Indians, Metis, and Mining in the Western Great Lakes, 1737–1832*. Lincoln: University of Nebraska Press, 2000.

——. "To Live among Us: Accommodation, Gender, and Conflict in the Western Great Lakes Region, 1760–1832." In *Contact Points: American Frontiers from the Mohawk Valley to the Mississippi, 1750–1830*, edited by Andrew R. L. Cayton and Fredrika Teute, 270–303. Chapel Hill: University of North Carolina Press, 1998.

Myles, Anne G. "Dissent and the Frontier of Translation: Roger Williams's *A Key into the Language of America*." In *Possible Pasts: Becoming Colonial in Early America*, edited by Robert Blair St. George, 88–108. Ithaca, N.Y.: Cornell University Press, 2000.

Nelson, Dana D. *National Manhood: Capitalist Citizenship and the Imagined Fraternity of White Men*. Durham, N.C.: Duke University Press, 1998.

Nelson, W. Dale. *Interpreters with Lewis and Clark: The Story of Sacajawea and Toussaint Charbonneau*. Denton: University of North Texas Press, 2003.

Nye, Russel Blaine. *George Bancroft: Brahmin Rebel*. New York: Knopf, 1945.

Oglesby, Richard E. "The Western Boatman: Half-Horse, Half Myth." In

Travelers on the Western Frontier, edited by John Francis McDermott, 252–66. Urbana: University of Illinois Press, 1970.

O'Meara, Walter. *Daughters of the Country: The Women of the Fur Traders and Mountain Men*. New York: Harcourt, 1968.

Orians, G. H. "The Indian Hater in Early American Fiction." *Journal of American History* 27, no. 1 (1933): 34–44.

Osborn, Chase S., and Stellanova Osborn. *Schoolcraft-Longfellow-Hiawatha*. Lancaster, Pa.: Cattell Press, 1942.

Pearce, Roy Harvey. *Savagism and Civilization: A Study of the Indian and the American Mind*. Baltimore, Md.: Johns Hopkins University Press, 1971.

Perdue, Theda. *"Mixed Blood" Indians: Racial Construction in the Early South*. Athens: University of Georgia Press, 2003.

Perkins, Elizabeth. *Border Life: Experience and Memory in the Revolutionary Ohio Valley*. Chapel Hill: University of North Carolina Press, 1998.

Peters, Bernard C. "John Johnston's 1822 Description of the Lake Superior Chippewa." *Michigan Historical Review* 20 (Summer 1994): 24–46.

Peterson, Jacqueline. "Many Roads to Red River: Metis Genesis in the Great Lakes Region, 1680–1815." In *The New Peoples: Being and Becoming Metis in North America*, edited by Jacqueline Peterson and Jennifer S. H. Brown, 37–72. Winnipeg: University of Manitoba Press, 1985.

Pocock, J. G. A. *The Machiavellian Moment: Florentine Political Thought and the Atlantic Republican Tradition*. Princeton, N.J.: Princeton University Press, 1975.

Prucha, Francis Paul. *The Churches and the Indian Schools, 1888–1912*. Lincoln: University of Nebraska Press, 1979.

———. *Great Father: United States Government Policy and the American Indians*. Lincoln: University of Nebraska Press, 1984.

Quirk, Tom. "A Pragmatic Defense of Source Study: Melville's 'Borrowings' from Judge James Hall." *Mosaic* 26 (Fall 1993): 21–35.

Randall, Randolph C. *James Hall: Spokesman of the New West*. Columbus: Ohio State University Press, 1964.

Richter, Daniel K. *Facing East from Indian Country: A Native History of Early America*. New York: Oxford University Press, 2001.

Roediger, David. *The Wages of Whiteness: Race and the Making of the American Working Class*. New York: Verso, 1991.

Rogin, Michael Paul. *Fathers and Children: Andrew Jackson and the Subjugation of the American Indian*. New York: Knopf, 1975.

Rosenthal, Debra. *Race-Mixture in Nineteenth-Century U.S. and Spanish-*

American Fictions. Chapel Hill: University of North Carolina Press, 2004.

Ross, Marlon B. "Romancing the Nation-State: The Poetics of Romantic Nationalism." In *Macropolitics of Nineteenth-Century Literature: Nationalism, Exoticism, Imperialism*, edited by Jonathan Arac and Harriet Ritvo, 56–87. Philadelphia: University of Pennsylvania Press, 1991.

Rowe, John Carlos. *Literary Culture and U.S. Imperialism: From the Revolution to World War Two*. New York: Oxford University Press, 2000.

Rubin-Dorsky, Jeffrey. *Adrift in the Old World: The Psychological Pilgrimage of Washington Irving*. Chicago: University of Chicago Press, 1988.

Salisbury, Neal. "The Indians' Old World: Native Americans and the Coming of Europeans." In *American Encounters: Natives and Newcomers from European Contact to Indian Removal, 1500-1850*, edited by Peter C. Mancall and James H. Merrell, 3–25. New York: Routledge, 2000.

Sayre, Gordon M. "Abridging Two Worlds: John Tanner as American Indian Autobiographer." *American Literary History* 11 (Fall 1999): 480–99.

———. *Les Sauvages Américains: Representations of Native Americans in French and English Colonial Literature*. Chapel Hill: University of North Carolina Press, 1997.

Scheckel, Susan. *The Insistence of the Indian: Race and Nationalism in Nineteenth-Century American Culture*. Princeton, N.J.: Princeton University Press, 1998.

Scheick, William J. *The Half-Blood: A Cultural Symbol in 19th-Century American Fiction*. Lexington: University of Kentucky Press, 1979.

Schlosser, Pauline. *The Fair Sex: White Women and Patriarchy in the Early American Republic*. New York: New York University Press, 2002.

Schmitz, Neil. *White Robe's Dilemma: Tribal History in American Literature*. Amherst: University of Massachusetts Press, 2001.

Shields, David S. *Civil Tongues and Polite Letters in British America*. Chapel Hill: University of North Carolina Press, 1997.

Shoemaker, Nancy. *A Strange Likeness: Becoming Red and White in Eighteenth-Century North America*. New York: Oxford University Press, 2004.

Simeone, James. *Democracy and Slavery in Frontier Illinois: The Bottomland Republic*. DeKalb: Northern Illinois University Press, 2000.

Simpson, David. *The Politics of American English, 1776–1860*. New York: Oxford University Press, 1986.

Slaughter, Thomas P. *Exploring Lewis and Clark: Reflections on Men and Wilderness*. New York: Vintage, 2003.

Sleeper-Smith, Susan. *Indian Women and French Men: Rethinking Cultural Encounter in the Western Great Lakes*. Amherst: University of Massachusetts Press, 2001.

Slotkin, Richard. *Fatal Environment: The Myth of the Frontier in the Age of Industrialization*. New York: Atheneum, 1985.

———. *Regeneration through Violence: The Mythology of the American Frontier, 1600–1860*. Norman: University of Oklahoma Press, 1973.

Smith, Anthony D. *Chosen Peoples*. New York: Oxford University Press, 2003.

———. *Nationalism and Modernism: A Critical Survey of Recent Theories of Nations and Nationalism*. New York: Routledge, 1998.

Smith, Henry Nash. *Virgin Land: The American West as Symbol and Myth*. Cambridge, Mass.: Harvard University Press, 1950.

Spurlin, Paul Merrell. *The French Enlightenment in America: Essays on the Times of the Founding Fathers*. Athens: University of Georgia Press, 1984.

Spurr, David. *The Rhetoric of Empire: Colonial Discourse in Journalism, Travel Writing and Imperial Administration*. Durham, N.C.: Duke University Press, 1993.

Stilgoe, John R. *Common Landscape in America, 1580–1845*. New Haven, Conn.: Yale University Press, 1982.

Streeby, Shelley. *American Sensations: Class, Empire, and the Production of American Culture*. Berkeley: University of California Press, 2002.

Sugden, John. *Tecumseh: A Life*. New York: Owl, 1997.

Szasz, Margaret Connell, ed. *Between Indian and White Worlds: The Cultural Broker*. Norman: University of Oklahoma Press, 1994.

Tanner, Helen Hornbeck. "The Glaize in 1792: A Composite Indian Community." In *American Encounters: Natives and Newcomers from European Contact to Indian Removal, 1500–1850*, edited by Peter C. Mancall and James H. Merrell, 404–25. New York: Routledge, 2000.

Taylor, Alan. *American Colonies: The Settling of North America*. New York: Penguin, 2002.

Thacker, Robert. *The Great Prairie Fact and Literary Imagination*. Albuquerque: University of New Mexico Press, 1989.

Thorne, Tanis C. *The Many Hands of My Relations: French and Indians on the Lower Missouri*. Columbia: University of Missouri Press, 1996.

Van Every, Dale. *Ark of Empire: The American Frontier, 1784-1803*. New York: Morrow, 1963.

Van Kirk, Sylvia. *Many Tender Ties: Women in Fur-Trade Society, 1670-1870*. Norman: University of Oklahoma Press, 1980.

Venable, W. H. *Beginnings of Literary Culture in the Ohio Valley: Historical and Biographical Sketches*. Cincinnati, Ohio: Clarke, 1891.

Viola, Herman J. Introduction to *Sketches of a Tour of the Lakes*, by Thomas McKenney, ix–xx. Barre, Mass.: Imprint Society, 1972.

Vitzhum, Richard C. *The American Compromise: Theme and Method in the Histories of Bancroft, Parkman, and Adams*. Norman: University of Oklahoma Press, 1974.

Vizenor, Gerald. *Crossbloods: Bone Courts, Bingo, and Other Reports*. Minneapolis: University of Minnesota Press, 1990.

——. "Shadows at La Pointe." In *Touchwood: A Collection of Ojibway Prose*, edited by Gerald Vizenor, 120–37. Minneapolis, Minn.: New Rivers Press, 1987.

Waldstreicher, David. *In the Midst of Perpetual Fetes: The Making of American Nationalism, 1776-1820*. Chapel Hill: University of North Carolina Press, 1997.

Ward, John William. *Andrew Jackson: Symbol for an Age*. New York: Oxford University Press, 1955.

Warner, Michael. "What's Colonial about Colonial America?" In *Possible Pasts: Becoming Colonial in Early America*, edited by Robert Blair St. George, 49–71. Ithaca, N.Y.: Cornell University Press, 2000.

Washburn, Wilcomb. *Red Man's Land/White Man's Law: A Study of the Past and Present Status of the American Indian*. New York: Scribner's, 1971.

Watts, Edward. *An American Colony: Regionalism and the Roots of Midwestern Culture*. Athens: Ohio University Press, 2002.

——. "*Kingsblood Royal, The Godseeker*, and the Racial History of the Midwest." In *Sinclair Lewis: New Essays in Criticism*, edited by James M. Hutchisson, 94–109. New York: Whitson, 1997.

Watts, Edward, and David Rachels, eds. *The First West: Writing from the American Frontier, 1776-1850*. New York: Oxford University Press, 2002.

Way, Peter. "The Cutting Edge of Culture: British Soldiers Encounter Native Americans in the French and Indian War." In *Empire and

Others: British Encounters with Indigenous Peoples, 1600–1850, edited by Martin Daunton and Mark Halpern, 123–48. Philadelphia: University of Pennsylvania Press, 1999.

Weierman, Karen Woods. *One Nation, One Blood: Interracial Marriage in American Fiction, Scandal, and Law, 1820–1870*. Amherst: University of Massachusetts Press, 2005.

Wertheimer, Eric. *Imagined Empires: Incas, Aztecs, and the New World of American Literature, 1771–1876*. New York: Cambridge University Press, 1999.

White, Richard. *The Middle Ground: Indians, Empires and Republics in the Great Lakes Region, 1650–1815*. New York: Cambridge University Press, 1991.

Widder, Keith R. *Battle for the Soul: Metis Children Encounter Evangelical Protestants at Mackinaw Mission, 1823–1837*. East Lansing: Michigan State University, 1999.

Wiebe, Robert H. *The Opening of American Society: From the Adoption of the Constitution to the Eve of Disunion*. New York: Vintage, 1984.

Wilkinson, Charles F. *American Indians, Time and the Law: Native Societies in a Modern Constitutional Democracy*. New Haven, Conn.: Yale University Press, 1987.

Williams, J. Fletcher. "Memoir of William W. Warren." In *History of the Ojibway People,* by William Warren, 9–22. St. Paul: Minnesota Historical Society Press, 1984.

Winsor, Justin. *The Mississippi Basin: The Struggle in America between England and France, 1697–1763*. Boston: Houghton Mifflin, 1895.

Young, Robert R. C. *Colonial Desire: Hybridity in Theory, Culture, and Race*. New York: Routledge, 1995.

Ziff, Larzer. *Return Passages: Great American Travel Writing, 1780–1910*. New Haven, Conn.: Yale University Press, 2000.

Index